WITTGENSTEIN'S *TRACTATUS*

Ludwig Wittgenstein's *Tractatus Logico-Philosophicus* is one of the most important books of the twentieth century. It influenced philosophers and artists alike and it continues to fascinate readers today. It offers rigorous arguments but clothes them in enigmatic pronouncements. Wittgenstein himself said that his book is "strictly philosophical and simultaneously literary, and yet there is no blathering in it." This introduction considers both the philosophical and the literary aspects of the *Tractatus* and shows how they are related. It also shows how the work fits into Wittgenstein's philosophical development and the tradition of analytic philosophy, arguing strongly for the vigor and significance of that tradition.

ALFRED NORDMANN is Professor of Philosophy at Technische Universität Darmstadt. He has translated and edited works by Wittgenstein, has published on the philosophy and science of Heinrich Hertz, and is president of the Lichtenberg Society.

D1610562

CAMBRIDGE INTRODUCTIONS TO KEY
PHILOSOPHICAL TEXTS

This new series offers introductory textbooks on what are considered to be the most important texts of Western philosophy. Each book guides the reader through the main themes and arguments of the work in question, while also paying attention to its historical context and its philosophical legacy. No philosophical background knowledge is assumed, and the books will be well suited to introductory university-level courses.

Titles published in the series:

WITTGENSTEIN'S
TRACTATUS

An Introduction

ALFRED NORDMANN

Technische Universität Darmstadt

CAMBRIDGE
UNIVERSITY PRESS

CAMBRIDGE UNIVERSITY PRESS
Cambridge, New York, Melbourne, Madrid, Cape Town, Singapore, São Paulo

Cambridge University Press
The Edinburgh Building, Cambridge CB2 2RU, UK

Published in the United States of America by Cambridge University Press, New York

www.cambridge.org
Information on this title: www.cambridge.org/9780521616386

© Alfred Nordmann 2005

First published 2005

Printed in the United Kingdom at the University Press, Cambridge

A catalogue record for this book is available from the British Library

ISBN-13 978-0-521-85086-5 hardback
ISBN 0-521-85086-x hardback
ISBN-13 978-0-521-61638-6 paperback
ISBN 0-521-61638-7 paperback

It requires no art to say something with brevity when, like Tacitus, one has something to say. If, however, one has nothing to say and still writes a book, giving the lie to truth itself and its *from nothing nothing can come*, now that's what I call an accomplishment.   *Georg Christoph Lichtenberg* (1775/76)

My difficulty is only an – enormous – difficulty of expression.
Ludwig Wittgenstein (March 8, 1915)

Contents

Preface

"An aspect of Wittgenstein's work which is certain to attract growing attention is its language." Georg Henrik von Wright wrote this in a biographical essay about his teacher in 1955. The essay has been reprinted numerous times since then, with the prediction carried forward apparently unfulfilled. Indeed, philosophical readers of the *Tractatus* used to bracket or dismiss the idiosyncracy of Wittgenstein's language. They found a statement in its preface which seemed to indicate that considerations of language, method, and style can only obscure his philosophical point: "What can be said at all can be said clearly."

Thanks are therefore due to Cora Diamond, James Conant, Matthew Ostrow, and others for drawing increased attention in recent years to Wittgenstein's method. In particular, they have established the need to take literally Wittgenstein's claim that his sentences are non-sensical. Though I disagree with them on nearly all of the particulars, they have prepared the way for my own attempt to take Wittgenstein literally in the context and tradition of analytic philosophy.

This book has been a long time in the making. Its beginnings can be traced to a seminar with Hide Ishiguro in the early 1980s. Accordingly, its intellectual debts reach equally far back. In ways entirely unbeknownst to them, Ernie Alleva, Lisa Leizman, and Veronica Vieland continue holding watch over my work – they are my philosophical conscience. For much needed encouragement at various stages of this work I wish to thank Georg Henrik von Wright, Garry Hagberg, Jim Klagge, and David Stern, also Bernd Buldt, Sabine Döring, Péter Forgásc, Manfred Frank, Gottfried Gabriel, Kathrin Kaiser, Richard Raatzsch, Tom Oberdan, Christiane Schildknecht, Joachim Schulte, Ilse Somavilla, and Jörg Zimmermann. For collegial and institutional support I thank the Pittsburgh Center for the Philosophy of Science, where a substantial draft was produced, but especially Davis Baird and all my other friends at the University of South Carolina. The debt I owe to my wife Angela cannot be put into words – I wish I could repay her in kind rather than in the questionable currency of a book.

Abbreviations of works by Wittgenstein

CL	*Cambridge Letters*
CV	*Culture and Value*
L30–32	*Wittgenstein's Lectures: Cambridge 1930–1932*
L32–35	*Wittgenstein's Lectures: Cambridge 1932–1935*
LCA	*Lectures and Conversations on Aesthetics, Psychology and Religious Belief*
LE	"Lecture on Ethics"
LFM	*Wittgenstein's Lectures on the Foundations of Mathematics Cambridge, 1939*
LO	*Letters to C. K. Ogden*
LvF	"Letters to Ludwig von Ficker"
LWPP	*Last Writings on the Philosophy of Psychology.*
MT	"Movements of Thought: Diaries 1930–1932, 1936/1937"
NB	*Notebooks 1914–1916*
OC	*On Certainty*
PG	*Philosophical Grammar*
PI	*Philosophical Investigations*
PO	*Philosophical Occasions*
PPO	*Public and Private Occasions*
PR	*Philosophical Remarks*
PT	*Prototractatus*
RFM	*Remarks on the Foundations of Mathematics*
SD	"Secret" Diaries 1914–1916 (*Geheime Tagebücher*)
TLP	*Tractatus Logico-Philosophicus*
WA2	*Philosophische Betrachtungen. Philosophische Bemerkungen*

WA4	*Bemerkungen zur Philosophie. Bemerkungen zur philosophischen Grammatik*
WA11	*The Big Typescript*
WVC	*Wittgenstein and the Vienna Circle*
Z	*Zettel*

Introduction: Wittgenstein's provocation

A DISTURBING CONCLUSION

This investigation is another in a long series of responses to the extraordinary provocation by a small book that was published in 1922. Many philosophers provoke admiration and respect, and when we find them difficult to understand our response is puzzlement and the desire to explore the depth of their thought. In striking contrast, readers of Ludwig Wittgenstein's *Tractatus Logico-Philosophicus* typically respond with "It can't be so," resisting its conclusion, seeking out where it might have gone wrong. While much is disputed about Wittgenstein's work, this uncomfortable and still provocative conclusion can be sketched with a few broad strokes.

In his book, the *Tractatus* for short, Wittgenstein distinguishes three uses of language or, more precisely, three types of sentences. Then he shows us what good these sentences are or whether they are any good at all. At the end of this investigation he leaves us with precious little and a rather restrictive view of what one can and cannot say. Moreover, this view flies in the face of what we thought we could say, brazenly contradicting how we like to think of ourselves.

The first of the three types of sentences is ordinary and familiar enough: "The blue car hit the red car from the right," "The sample of iron melted at 1,535 degrees Celsius," "Rita is not at home but George is." These kinds of sentences show language at its best. We use them to describe how things are, to represent the world as we find it, to identify what is the case and what is not. In principle at least, it is easy to determine whether such sentences are true or false: we simply compare them to reality and call them "true" if they correctly identify what really is or is not the case; we call them "false" if they do not agree with how things are. The sentences of science are like this insofar as science aims to provide a correct, perhaps complete representation of the physical and social world. Equally good are many of the sentences that we use to negotiate daily life by telling each other what happened, what to look out for, what is in the refrigerator, where to find that piece of paper.

Why does this first type of sentence show language at its best? It relies on an elegant and compelling symmetry between language and the world: at any given time something either is or is not the case in the world – no ambiguity here; and at any given time these descriptive sentences are either true or false with nothing in between. This symmetry allows us to define "being true or false" as "agreeing or disagreeing with what is the case." We now find that the meanings of these sentences are perfectly clear: They mean to assert or deny something about the world and we can itemize for each sentence just what needs to be the case for it to be true. Indeed, we can equate the sense of such a sentence with its so-called truth-conditions, that is, the conditions under which a sentence would be true or the situation that would make it true. Aside from the obvious fact that these sentences and their use *make* sense to us, they also *have* a very definite sense or meaning. When we use them, language is working very well, indeed: the sentences *do* something (they serve to determine what is and is not the case) and they communicate effectively (we can completely understand them and agree among one another about their meaning and their truth or falsity).

A single example suffices to introduce the second of Wittgenstein's three types of sentences: "A statement and its contrary cannot be true at the same time" or -(p & -p) in the logician's shorthand. This "law of noncontradiction" tells us that it cannot possibly be the case that Lewis Carroll wrote *Alice in Wonderland* and that he did not. Either he is the author or he is not, but for all his delight in paradox, he certainly did not simultaneously write and not write the book. Now, does the law of noncontradiction really *tell* us this? Did we need to be told? Are we surprised to find out? Will we conduct library research to discover whether he might be both author and nonauthor of *Alice in Wonderland*? The answer to these questions is no. It goes without saying that something contradictory cannot obtain, that everything (you name it) either is or is not the case. How many sentences like the law of noncontradiction are there – sentences that do not tell us anything but formalize only what is self-evident and should go without saying? There is no clear-cut answer to this question: the theorems and laws of logic should be included for sure, but what about all of mathematics (is mathematics a branch of logic?), and what about tautologies ("all bachelors are unmarried"), so-called analytic statements ("all matter occupies space"), axioms and rules in formal systems ("a bishop in chess travels in straight diagonal lines forward and backward on white or black fields only"), or definitions ("a mule is a sterile cross of donkey and horse")?

Regardless of how many sentences should be included with this second type, even for the narrowly logical ones, the question arises what they are good for. On the one hand, there is nothing wrong with them: we understand them well enough, they are perfectly grammatical and therefore not nonsensical. On the other hand, these sentences do not seem to do any of the work that is so admirably performed by sentences of the first type: they do not determine what is or what is not the case in the world, nor do they communicate any particular content, since we are already agreed upon them. Sentences of the first type had definite meaning or sense, but these are senseless: they have no truth-conditions, there is no situation in the world that would *render* them true or false, indeed, they cannot be true *or* false (tautologies, for example, *are already* true for all situations, and contradictions already false). Since sentences of the second type go without saying, Wittgenstein provides the following answer to the question what they are good for: "Logic must take care of itself" (*TLP* 5.473).[1]

Third and last are sentences like "Truth is the highest good," "Life has absolute value," "Unicorns live on the lost continent of Atlantis," "The beauty of this painting touches me," "My conscience tells me what is right," "He can feel your pain," "God exists," "Thou shalt not kill," "I love you," and many, many more. The one thing all these

---

[1] Wittgenstein's *Tractatus-Logico Philosophicus* consists of seven main propositions that are numbered 1 to 7. Wittgenstein explains in a footnote to proposition 1 that he uses an elaborate numbering system to "indicate the logical importance" of the propositions. According to this system, 5.473 comes after 5.472 and remarks upon 5.47, which remarks upon 5.4, which remarks upon main proposition 5. This book follows the custom of using the numbers to refer to and cite the remarks from the *Tractatus Logico-Philosophicus* (*TLP*).

different sentences have in common is that, according to Wittgenstein, they only pretend to be sentences but are not grammatical at all. They are nonsensical and in this respect quite like "All mimsy were the borogoves." We have arrived at Wittgenstein's startling conclusion: there are descriptive sentences including those of science and then there is logic, which must take care of itself, and that's it. The rest is silence. "Whereof one cannot speak, about that one must remain silent" concludes the *Tractatus* (*TLP* 7).

But why are the sentences of this third type no sentences at all? After all, while they may not constitute the lion's share of spoken language, such formulations occupy us when we think about ourselves and others, when we reflect upon our values, our relation to this world, and what may lie beyond it. How can Wittgenstein banish all such formulations from language, declare them nonsensical, and condemn us to silence about these most important matters?

Wittgenstein was quite aware of the magnitude of his conclusion: "We feel that even once all *possible* scientific questions are answered, our problems of life have still not been touched upon" (*TLP* 6.52).

Before addressing (in chapter 1) just what compelled him nevertheless to advance such an unpalatable verdict, I wish to consider how, in principle, one might object to Wittgenstein's conclusion. This will take me to the central question of this book.

STRATEGIES OF AVOIDANCE

There are three strategies for criticizing Wittgenstein's conclusions. The first two apply to any philosophical work, while the third aims at the *Tractatus* specifically.

The first of these strategies is the hardest to pursue and I will not do so in this book. It consists in a so-called immanent critique that takes Wittgenstein on his own terms and probes the soundness of his argument. It asks whether he somewhere committed a mistake that would invalidate his conclusion. This amounts to the difficult task of finding an inconsistency in his argument. While the immanent critics need to establish that it is quite impossible to reconcile some of Wittgenstein's statements, his defenders have a much easier task (it is not a fair fight): all they need to show is that his statements can *somehow* be reconciled with more or less ingenuity and with the help of any and all interpretive resources. But though it is least likely to succeed, immanent critique provides the most valuable line of attack because it can teach us the most about Wittgenstein's philosophical commitments.

The second critical strategy brings external considerations to bear: rather than demonstrate that the *Tractatus* is somehow flawed on its own terms, one might show that it fails to do justice to the phenomena of language and thought, that it fails to provide a complete picture, that it is seriously limited and takes far too much for granted. The one who pursued this strategy most vigorously and most successfully was Wittgenstein himself, especially in his *Philosophical Investigations* of 1953. This kind of external critique will add numerous qualifications to the *Tractatus*, pointing out the narrowness of its approach, determining the limits inherent in its focus on the descriptive language of science. And yet, all of this may leave untouched its core insight and disturbing conclusion. Yes, there is a lot more to be said about our uses of language, but does that in any way diminish the force of the original conclusion, namely that some sentences "work" pretty straightforwardly while many others deceive and confuse us by seeming to work like the straightforward ones? It is because of Wittgenstein's later recognition of the many uses of language that many have spoken of two Wittgensteins – the early and the late Wittgenstein, Wittgenstein I and Wittgenstein II – as if these were different persons, each the author of an important work with a lasting impact.[2] For example, Bertrand Russell declared a few years after the death of his former student: "During the period since 1914 three philosophies have successively dominated the British philosophical world: first that of Wittgenstein's *Tractatus*, second that of the Logical Positivists, and third that of Wittgenstein's *Philosophical Investigations*."[3]

Since these first two strategies may fail to directly engage and refute Wittgenstein's disturbing conclusion, a third strategy combines the others in a manner that is specifically aimed at the *Tractatus*. This strategy is as old as the book itself. It was first advanced in Russell's

[2] Compare, for example, Stegmüller 1970, pp. 394 and 423.   [3] Russell 1959, p. 216.

introduction to the *Tractatus*. After noting that Wittgenstein's conclusion "grows naturally out of his doctrine," Russell gives us good
reason to quickly dismiss it nonetheless: "What causes hesitation is
the fact that, after all, Mr Wittgenstein manages to say a good deal
about what cannot be said, thus suggesting to the skeptical reader
that possibly there may be some loophole through a hierarchy of
languages, or by some other exit."[4]

This is an immanent critique in that it discovers a tension within
the *Tractatus* itself; it is external in that it adopts an outside point
of view and points out how the work is systematically incomplete by
failing to adequately reflect its own use of language. Russell draws our
attention not to the aesthetic or stylistic peculiarities of Wittgenstein's
language. He simply asks how the pronouncements of the *Tractatus*
fit into Wittgenstein's threefold division of sentences. Statements like
"The world is all that is the case" or "A sentence is a picture of
reality" (*TLP* 1, 4.021) are unlike scientific descriptions of fact, nor
are they logical theorems like the law of noncontradiction. If all other
sentences are nonsensical then, surely, this must include the sentences
of the *Tractatus* itself. Indeed, Wittgenstein himself embraced this
implication: "My sentences elucidate through this: who understands
me recognizes them in the end as nonsensical" (*TLP* 6.54).

By biting this bullet, Wittgenstein claims consistency for his work.
But as we saw from Russell's introduction, Wittgenstein's willingness
to concede that his own sentences are nonsensical has encountered
incredulity from the very start. Where Russell tactfully noted "a certain sense of intellectual discomfort," others took their gloves off. A. J.
Ayer, for example, considered Wittgenstein's claim "a vain attempt to
have it both ways. No doubt some pieces of nonsense are more suggestive than others, but this does not give them any logical force. If
the verification principle really is nonsensical, it states nothing; and
if one holds that it states nothing, then one cannot also maintain that
what it states is true."[5]

Even less tactful than that, others considered Wittgenstein's
"attempt to have it both ways" profoundly disingenuous:

---

[4] See pages 22f. in the 1922 edition of the *Tractatus*.
[5] Ayer 1959, p. 15. For further expressions of this "intellectual discomfort" see Fann 1969,
pp. 34f.; Favrholdt 1964, pp. 139ff.; Garver and Lee 1994, pp. 201–204; also Hintikka and
Hintikka 1986, p. 216.

> For he talks nonsense, numerous statements makes,
> Forever his own vow of silence breaks:
> Ethics, aesthetics, talks of day and night,
> And calls things good or bad, and wrong or right.[6]

Such accusations make it easy to write off Wittgenstein's provocative conclusion: since he did not stick to it himself, he cannot very well have meant it. Or are we missing something?

I have now arrived at the central question of this book. It concerns Wittgenstein's language but also the language of philosophy, indeed, any attempt to communicate more than statements of empirical fact. To be sure, there is a serious problem here. Why would anyone set out to write nonsensically? No matter how one goes about answering this question, the *Tractatus* seems to be seriously flawed. For example, if Wittgenstein was intent to persuade his readers, his action (writing a persuasive book) would be running counter to his words (according to which he is only writing something nonsensical). In that case, he would be implicated in what is called a performative contradiction. However, if he was not intent to persuade his readers and instead produced empty words that he knew to be nonsensical, why did he bother at all and why should we pay attention to him? In this second case, we would call his efforts moot. And if we are to believe that he set out in good faith only to discover as he went along that his theory renders nonsensical the very statements that are necessary for its formulation, should we not consider this discovery an indictment of the theory? We might then call his attempt to persuade us self-defeating because his own theory deprived his proposed persuasions of their persuasive power. Or, to consider a fourth and last possibility, if the *Tractatus* actually persuaded us that there are very narrow limits to the sayable, would this not tempt us to take the very existence of this book as a welcome opportunity to escape from these limits through some loophole or some other exit? We might conclude, for example, that Wittgenstein somehow persuaded us and communicated matters without actually "saying" them. In this case, we would begin speculating about this mystically "other" means of communication and turn Wittgenstein's clear analysis into an obscure flight from reason.

[6] Julian Bell's "An Epistle on the Subject of the Ethical and Aesthetic Beliefs of Herr Ludwig Wittgenstein" first appeared in 1930; see Bell 1966, p. 70.

The *Tractatus* either involves a performative contradiction, or is moot, or self-defeating, or invites mystical speculation – none of these judgments is very flattering, and none of them compels us to accept its provocative conclusion. It therefore seems that by choosing to consider the *Tractatus* a meaningful philosophical document, we are already indicating that something must be wrong with it – at the very least, it cannot be (literally) true that (all) its propositions are nonsensical. And since for reasons of consistency Wittgenstein was forced to declare that his sentences are nonsensical, far more might be wrong with the *Tractatus*.

THE TASK AHEAD

Charitable readers of the *Tractatus* thus have their task cut out for them. Recognizing the magnitude of this task, Cora Diamond urges us to confront Wittgenstein's conclusion for what it is – a conclusion that leaves no loopholes, no exit. She warns us not to "chicken out." As I will show, however, Diamond has it both ways herself and in ingenious fashion may well be chickening out, too.[7] Still needed, therefore, is a defense of the following claim: *the* Tractatus *is written in a nonsensical language and it advances a persuasive argument.*

All attempts to provide this defense will encounter a curious phenomenon: though it aims to survey and classify all of language, the *Tractatus* does not reflect on the sentences in which it is written, save for a few cryptic remarks. The silence it prescribes extends to its own composition. This silence needs to be broken if one wants to save the *Tractatus* from the charge that it commits a performative contradiction or that Wittgenstein could not have meant what he wrote or that by referring to Wittgenstein's practice one can somehow escape his disturbing conclusion.

---

[7] Diamond 1991 suggests that the *Tractatus* was written in a "transitional language," one that makes sense only when one understands the argument. However, this idea of a "transitional language" only gives a name to Wittgenstein's attempt "to have it both ways." It does not help us to understand how its persuasive force can linger on even once the nonsensicality of the language is revealed. In a later essay, the idea of a transitional language gives way to that of a transitional state, namely the state of a reader who is neither "inside" nor "outside" of nonsensical writing but goes as far as one can with the idea that there is an "inside" (Diamond 2000, p. 157; cf. p. 169). Her approach is discussed more extensively at the end of chapter 2, see also chapter 4, note 58.

After reconstructing in chapter 2 the compelling argument for Wittgenstein's disturbing conclusion, chapter 3 will characterize Wittgenstein's manner of writing. Chapter 4 then establishes the complementarity between structure of argument and method of composition. It will show that an argument of the type that is employed by Wittgenstein requires the type of language in which the *Tractatus* is written, for which the *Tractatus* leaves room, and about which the *Tractatus* maintains an artful silence. This leads to the conclusion that the theory and practice of the *Tractatus* distinguishes not just three, but four uses of language, including the one in which it is written.

Paradoxically, perhaps, my proposal will incur suspicion because it sets out to meet the test of literal consistency with the *Tractatus*. It agrees with Wittgenstein that his statements must be considered nonsensical and that they can nevertheless advance his philosophical argument because they are not senseless. While Wittgenstein scholars have learned to accept that some sentences might be senseless but not nonsensical (the logical propositions described above), most will not find intelligible the inverse claim that other expressions are literally nonsensical and yet make sense, for example, in that they help us "see the world right" (*TLP* 6.54). In order to render this conception plausible, chapter 5 will gather evidence for Wittgenstein's lifelong exploration of this fourth kind of expression.

If this reconstruction succeeds, it will not just solve a peculiar problem in the interpretation of the *Tractatus*, but will shed light more generally on Wittgenstein's conception of philosophy as critical practice, a conception that unites his early and later work. This view also illuminates the tentative character of all philosophy, of all our probing when we attempt to understand each other in matters of value or feeling.

INTRODUCING THE *TRACTATUS*

By looking at the form and content of the *Tractatus*, this books seeks to engage the experience of a first encounter with the text. It is best read by those who are impressed, perhaps taken aback by Wittgenstein's verdict about the limits of language, and who are intrigued by his manner of writing even where they find it exasperating.

As we have seen, a book that claims to be written in a nonsensical language and yet to make sense, demands interpretation. In light of the many interpretations that have been advanced so far – some of the most interesting and most controversial coming in the last few years – one can find no shelter in supposedly innocent paraphrase or summary. Every statement about the *Tractatus* enters a contested field of claims and traditions. An introduction to the *Tractatus*, therefore, can do no better than to carry its interpretation on its sleeves. According to the very first sentence of its preface, the book cannot be understood by mere readers but requires those who think its thoughts for and by themselves. By laying my cards on the table and being as transparent as possible, I aim to expose to scrutiny some of the interpretive choices that are made by this self-thinking reader. The introduction to the work may thus give way to critical engagement – with a clear sense, I hope, of what is at stake in our understanding of the *Tractatus*.

Interpretive choices and critical engagement have so far produced three translations of the *Tractatus* and several editions of Wittgenstein's drafts, manuscripts, and typescripts.[8] Indeed, among the first choices by any interpreter of the book is how to define the source. Do we limit ourselves to the self-contained text in the book before us or do we include source documents (publication in the original language, notes, drafts, contemporary letters about the manuscript)? And do we include remarks by the later Wittgenstein only where he critically reflects upon his earlier work or also, more or less eclectically, where this may help elucidate some aspect of the *Tractatus*?

Different interpretations answer these questions differently. The following chapters rely heavily on textual evidence. Especially where novel claims are advanced in a field of numerous plausible interpretations, it may not be sufficient to establish consistency among Wittgenstein's remarks or to indicate interesting points of contact with the work of other philosophers. The appeal to textual evidence

[8] The works by Wittgenstein in the references itemize the three translations and two critical editions of the *Tractatus Logico-Philosophicus* (*TLP*), but see also on pp. 218f. Wittgenstein's *Prototractatus* (*PT*), the *Notebooks 1914–1916* (*NB*), and the *Geheimes Tagebuch* or so-called "Secret" Diaries (SD). Von Wright 1982 includes a chapter about the origin of the *Tractatus*, as does McGuinness 2002; see also Geschkowski 2001.

leads me to answer the questions about relevant sources both strictly and liberally. Strict literalness demands that we consider Wittgenstein's frequently idiosyncratic German formulations. Attention to these formulations, to figures of speech and characteristic movements of thought, quickly move the reader beyond the present to adjacent and more remote texts, drawing in at times remarks by the later Wittgenstein.

Questions of translation, justifications for the consideration of sources, and discussions of alternative interpretations can often be found in endnotes. While it should never be necessary to consult them, they provide glimpses of the lively and contentious character of Wittgenstein scholarship. And while it may be irritating to encounter English translations that differ from those in the printed editions, this highlights further that our questioning of the text must begin with the choice of words. Offering very literal translations can also serve to simplify matters. For example, guided by extant translations of the *Tractatus*, it may be necessary to define as follows what Wittgenstein means by "proposition": "A proposition is a sentence with its sense, but this should not imply that sentences are detachable from their sense."[9] Matters may become easier once we recognize that, in German, Wittgenstein does not distinguish between "sentence" and "proposition" but that he everywhere uses the colloquial term "*Satz* (sentence)." Accordingly, "sentence" is always used in the translation offered here.

THE SIGNIFICANCE OF PHILOSOPHY

Every statement about the *Tractatus* faces competing claims and traditions. The parties to the contest have sometimes been labeled "analytic" as opposed to "mystical" readers. Currently, "resolute" or "austere" readings of the *Tractatus* are contrasted with "irresolute" or "substantial" ones. I find these ways of labeling the different approaches misleading. Behind many "analytic" and all "resolute" readings of the *Tractatus* stands the conviction that Wittgenstein inherited a rather specific conception of philosophy from the logician-philosophers Gottlob Frege and Bertrand Russell. On some accounts,

[9] Carruthers 1989, p. 40.

Wittgenstein furthered their philosophical program in the *Tractatus* and abandoned it in his later work.[10] According to the "resolute" reading, the *Tractatus* aimed to undermine or dissolve this conception of philosophy. On this reading, the *Tractatus* shares with Wittgenstein's later philosophy that it helps us escape the "ensnarement of thought" by philosophy – in this case the philosophy of Frege and Russell.[11] Accordingly, the significance of the *Tractatus* depends entirely on how significant (and significantly seductive) one finds the views of Frege and Russell.

These "analytic" and "resolute" approaches are countered by those who argue that Wittgenstein acquired a much broader conception of philosophy well before he came across Frege and Russell. Growing up in *Wittgenstein's Vienna*, he was introduced to creative and radical developments in science, philosophy, literature, and cultural criticism. A century was coming to a close that had seen the formulation of new philosophical problems by Immanuel Kant and produced enormously varied responses to them. The philosophical scientists Heinrich Hertz and Ludwig Boltzmann, the literary philosophers Arthur Schopenhauer and Otto Weininger, the programmatic architect Adolf Loos, the author and critic Karl Kraus, and many others left their trace on Wittgenstein's intellectual development.[12] Most importantly, they shaped a conception of philosophy that was already seeking to escape the ensnarement of thought by philosophy, that self-critically examined the limits of language and philosophy, and that sought to undermine metaphysics.

The acknowledgment of Wittgenstein's intellectual background opens the door for the interpretation that is offered here: Wittgenstein was never interested in philosophy for its own sake and therefore had little incentive merely to liberate himself from the philosophical

---

[10] There is considerable variety among these "standard" interpretations of Wittgenstein. See, for example, Anscombe 1971, Black 1964, Hacker 1996, Pears 1987 or Stegmüller 1970.

[11] An excellent introduction of the resolute approach emerges from Williams 2004 together with the response by Conant and Diamond 2004. Rich presentations and discussions can be found in Crary and Read 2000 and in Kölbel and Weiss 2004. I take the expression "ensnarement of thought" from Ostrow 2002.

[12] This introduction to the *Tractatus* is short on intellectual biography, though it introduces its readers to many of the thinkers who influenced Wittgenstein. The allusion to *Wittgenstein's Vienna* points to Janik and Toulmin 1973. This book provides an excellent introduction to Wittgenstein's cultural and philosophical background. Equally compelling and readable is Ray Monk's biography of Wittgenstein (Monk 1990).

ambitions of Frege and Russell. Instead, he finds that philosophy, including the philosophical theories of Frege and Russell, gets in the way of what he is interested in, namely the very practical problems of self-expression and happiness. And since philosophy kept getting in the way while he unhappily struggled with these problems, Wittgenstein kept seeking to escape it also in his later work.

Starting with a chapter on critical philosophy, the following pages contend that this interpretation is decidedly not mystical as opposed to analytic – and is perhaps more resolutely antimetaphysical than the proposed resolute readings of the *Tractatus*.

CHAPTER I

Critical philosophy

"All philosophy is 'critique of language'" Wittgenstein wrote in the *Tractatus Logico-Philosophicus*, but also: "All the sentences of our ordinary language are indeed, just as they are, logically completely ordered" (*TLP* 4.0031, 5.5563). Taken together, these two remarks appear contradictory at first. The contradiction vanishes, however, when we come to understand that "critique" is something very different from criticism or the attempt to find fault. Instead, the notion of critique belongs to the tradition of critical philosophy, a tradition founded by Immanuel Kant. In this tradition, philosophical critique examines human language or reason to determine its implicit presuppositions, its capacities, its limits. From such a critique of language emerges Wittgenstein's verdict that the sentence "France lies to the south of England" is perfectly good, while "Murder is evil" is nonsense.

Before reconstructing the argument that led to Wittgenstein's conclusion, this chapter will consider its motivation, which is rooted in the critical tradition. We will see that the critique of language and reason is always also a critique of metaphysics. It claims a middle ground between dogmatism and skepticism. Dogmatism establishes and defends metaphysical doctrines in a manner that ultimately glosses over rather than answers the questions of philosophy. Skepticism abandons all hope that these questions can ever be answered. It therefore fails to offer a satisfactory explanation of how our ordinary lives can proceed as easily as they do and without being haunted by the unanswered questions.

I will consider three influential ancestors from the critical tradition and then Wittgenstein himself.[1] Despite their differences of background, style, and ambition, all four determine the limits of science from a scientific point of view, all four provide a critique of language, and all four pursue essentially the same strategy in answering the main question of theoretical philosophy.

What is that all-important question?

KANT AND THE LIMITS OF REASON

When Immanuel Kant (1724–1804) began work on *The Critique of Pure Reason*, he wrote to Marcus Herz about his discovery of a new question that in his long metaphysical studies he and others "had failed to pay attention to and that, in fact, contains the key to the whole secret of hitherto still obscure metaphysics." The question was: "What is the ground of the relation of that in us which we call representation to the object?"[2]

Nine years later Kant explained in his preface to the first edition of the *Critique of Pure Reason* how the problem arose in the first place and why it has become so important to critically investigate the relation of our representations to their objects. In the course of experience arises quite unavoidably the warranted conviction that our representations usually conform to the objects: when we describe what we see, we assume safely and naturally that our descriptions agree with some object out there, namely the object we saw. Upon this conviction our reason rises "ever higher, to more remote conditions" and begins to inquire into the grounds of our conviction. How is it possible, we may ask, that our descriptions agree with some object out there? The two are of very different stuff, after all. Our descriptions take the form

---

[1] According to David Pears, "the simplest general characterization" of Wittgenstein's philosophy is "that it is critical in the Kantian sense of that word" (1987, p. 3). Pears goes on to explore and qualify this characterization. Compare Stekeler 2004 and the chapter "Wittgenstein as a Kantian Philosopher" in Stenius 1960.

[2] Kant's letter to Marcus Herz of February 21, 1772 is quoted in Paul Guyer and Allen Wood's introduction to their edition of *The Critique of Pure Reason* (Kant 1997, pp. 47f.). The question reappears in the *Critique*: "What is truth? The nominal definition of truth, namely that it is the agreement of cognition with its object, is here granted and presupposed; but one demands to know what is the general and certain criterion of the truth of any cognition" (A58/B82). All passages quoted from the *Critique of Pure Reason* are cited in standard fashion by providing the page numbers of the first (A) and/or second (B) editions.

of thoughts or sentences and reside entirely inside our minds, while the objects are material things that exist independently in the external world, indifferent to how we think of them. Moreover, we are directly acquainted only with perceptions and sensations, with feelings and thoughts, not with the objects themselves. So, what makes us think that there can be agreement between entities as dissimilar as our representations (which we know very well) and the objects (of which we have no direct knowledge)?

It is the very success of human reason and the experience of making correct representations that gave rise to this question in the first place. But in order to answer it, reason would have to do the impossible and "surpass the bounds of all experience." It would have to step outside of human cognition and assume a divine perspective, one that would allow a direct comparison of our representations with their objects. The perplexing question thus arises quite naturally from our common experience and "[r]eason falls into this perplexity through no fault of its own." Yet it finds itself perplexed and in a peculiar predicament that is described by the opening sentences of the *Critique of Pure Reason*: "Human reason has the peculiar fate in one field of knowledge that it is burdened with questions which it cannot dismiss, since they are given to it as problems by the nature of reason itself, but which it also cannot answer, since they transcend the capacity of human reason."[3]

From this predicament arise interminable disagreements: "The battlefield of these endless controversies is called *metaphysics*" and the combatants on this battlefield are dogmatism and skepticism. Dogmatism catapults reason well beyond the bounds of experience. Indeed, it uses reason to construct a kind of divine perspective from which we can be reassured that our representations agree with the external world. The most prominent representatives of dogmatism were René Descartes, Gottfried Wilhelm Leibniz, and – for Kant – Christian Wolff. Descartes, for example, first attempts to prove the existence of God and then deduces from God's perfection that He would not deceive us but vouchsafes the agreement between representations and objects.

---

[3] All the quotes in this discussion of the predicament of human reason are from Kant 1997, A vii–xii.

While dogmatism thus develops metaphysical contrivances to force the inner and the outer world together, skepticism pries that union apart: "the skeptics, a kind of nomads who abhor all permanent cultivation of the soil, shattered civil unity from time to time. But since there were fortunately only a few of them, they could not prevent the dogmatists from continually attempting to rebuild, though never according to a plan unanimously accepted among themselves."[4]

While the many proposed answers of the dogmatists fell into anarchy for a lack of compelling arguments that might have produced agreement, the few skeptics declared the question to be unanswerable in the first place. And while the dogmatists readily ignored the bounds of experience and claimed outside them a superhuman vantage point for reason, the skeptics showed that for all its exertions, reason cannot transcend experience but remains forever stuck within. John Locke may be regarded as one of these skeptics in that he showed how we cannot from our sensory experience penetrate outward to real substances. But the main representative of skepticism was David Hume. He had argued that we always experience only the temporal succession of perceived events and that nothing in our perceptions allows us to conclude with certainty that there is causality in nature. Indeed, our representations of the world, built as they are around notions of substance and causality, may not agree with the objects at all.

Kant's colorful caricature of the battle between dogmatism and skepticism is further exaggerated by my presentation of his text. But despite the temptation to ridicule the interminable battle between dogmatism and skepticism, Kant insists that we cannot take a dismissive attitude toward philosophy because the question is too important:

[I]t is pointless to affect *indifference* with respect to such inquiries, to whose object human nature *cannot* be *indifferent* . . . reason should take on anew the most difficult of all its tasks, namely, that of self-knowledge, and to institute a court of justice, by which reason may secure its rightful claims while dismissing all its groundless pretensions, and this not by mere decrees but according to its own eternal and unchangeable laws; and this court is none other than the *critique of pure reason* itself.[5]

[4] Ibid., A ix.　　[5] Ibid., A x–xii.

Immanuel Kant thus opens the door for a third approach. Does reason have a rightful claim to objective knowledge of the outer world? To answer this question, reason must come to know itself: "Reason must subject itself to critique in all its undertakings."[6] Instead of claiming a transcendent outside perspective, instead of straining (and failing) to get outside, Kant's critique begins inside, internal to reason itself.

His overall strategy is simple enough: let us see what reason can learn about itself when it observes the operations of the understanding within the bounds of experience. While thus discovering the presuppositions, capacities, and limits of knowledge, Kant also discovers that dogmatism and skepticism tried to answer the wrong question by asking "Can reason bridge the gulf between our representations and their dissimilar objects?" Between dogmatic attempts to answer yes and skeptical reminders that the only answer is no, emerged a critical philosophy that did not provide an answer at all but which removed the question: Kant's *Critique of Pure Reason* demonstrates that knowledge and experience do not bridge inside representations and outside objects. The relation between representations and their objects is an internal relation between entities that, far from being radically dissimilar, are actually made for each other.

How can this be? This is not the place to reconstruct, let alone assess Kant's argument. Suffice it to say that he begins with an experiment and that this experiment suggests a notion of experience according to which the objects of experience are already assimilated to the requirements of the mind.

Up to now it has been assumed that all our cognition must conform to the objects; but all attempts to find out something about them . . . on this presupposition come to nothing. Hence let us try whether we do not get farther with the problems of metaphysics by assuming that the objects must conform to our cognition.[7]

Instead of asking how our representations can agree with the objects, Kant proposes that we find out in which ways the objects must agree with our representations. His account is famous for detailing how objects of experience are constituted: we cannot look directly out into

---

[6] Ibid., A738/B766.   [7] Ibid., B xvi.

the world through our senses as if these were transparent windows. Instead, we experience everything as given in time and space, thus susceptible to mathematical treatment. We also experience every event as the effect of a prior event and as the cause of a later event, thus susceptible to scientific or causal treatment. Time, space, causality and other categories do not adhere to the things in themselves, however, but belong to our human mode of representation. They transform what is given to the senses into an object of experience that is given to the mind.

On Kant's account it is still the case that our representations need to agree with the objects of experience. But there is already in the objects of experience a union of what is given to our perception and what is provided by the mind. The objects of experience are constituted in and for the mind, they are made to allow for agreement with other mental constructs, such as our scientific representations of the world. And thus Kant institutes peace on the battlefield of metaphysics. He has pacified the mind, which is no longer vexed by a question that it cannot dismiss but which it cannot answer.

LICHTENBERG'S CRITIQUE OF LANGUAGE

There is little evidence that Wittgenstein thoroughly studied the thought of Kant.[8] At the same time, there can be no doubt that he was familiar with the broad outlines of Kant's philosophy. Though he never quotes and only sometimes mentions Kant,[9] the legacy of Kant informs many of the texts that most influenced him (Schopenhauer, Hertz, even Weininger) and they could be considered general knowledge in the culture of his formative years.

Wittgenstein knew very well, in contrast, the work of a much more obscure contemporary of Kant's: Georg Christoph Lichtenberg (1742–1799).[10] Indeed, that the philosophical acumen of this

---

[8] Wittgenstein discussed Kant in 1916 but appears to have studied the *Critique of Pure Reason* only after completing the *Tractatus*, namely as a prisoner of war in 1918–19. See McGuinness 1988, pp. 252f., Monk 1990, p. 158, and note 1 above.

[9] Wittgenstein refers to Kant in *TLP* 6.36111 and, albeit indirectly, in remark 90 of the *Philosophical Investigations* (*PI* 90). See also *PI* 108.

[10] See Merkel 1988, Janik 1989, Rapic 1999, Nordmann 2002b and 2003.

experimental physicist, Enlightenment writer, and author of aphorisms is appreciated in the English-speaking world at all is due to
one of Wittgenstein's students and to a sometime friend of his.[11] In
1913 Wittgenstein gave Bertrand Russell a selection of Lichtenberg's
works,[12] on various occasions he compared Lichtenberg favorably to
Karl Kraus ("Lichtenberg's wit is the flame that can burn on a pure
candle only"),[13] and in a manuscript chapter devoted to his conception of philosophy, he quotes: "Lichtenberg: 'Our entire philosophy
is correction of the use of language, and therefore correction of a
philosophy, and indeed of the most general philosophy.'"[14]

When Lichtenberg calls himself a critic of language, this label
simultaneously shows his proximity to and his distance from Kant.
Kant's critical philosophy produced a critique of language only in
regard to the mistaken "transcendental employment" of the concepts
of the understanding: the self-critical introspection of reason had
shown that concepts like "causality" are constitutive of experience
but that they have no meaning beyond the bounds of experience.
When objects of experience are given to the understanding, we cannot help but consider them under the aspect of causality as parts
of unbounded causal chains. But when we ask whether there is a
first cause of all things, we are using a term that serves to structure
experience but which applies it to no experience at all.[15]

As before, rather than answer the question "Is there a first cause
of all things," Kant's critique shows that the question is illusory or

---

[11] Georg Henrik von Wright published "Georg Christoph Lichtenberg als Philosoph" and
wrote the "Lichtenberg" entry for the *Encyclopaedia of Philosophy* (von Wright 1942 and
1967). J. P. Stern's *A Doctrine of Scattered Occasions* is still the only book-length study of
Lichtenberg's philosophy in English (Stern 1959).

[12] Wittgenstein, *Cambridge Letters* (*CL*), p. 36.

[13] Wittgenstein, *Movements of Thought* (*MT*), diary, p. 114; cf. pp. 104 and 205, also *Culture
and Value* (*CV*), p. 75.

[14] *Philosophical Occasions* (*PO*), p. 183, also in *The Big Typescript*, vol. XI of the *Wiener Ausgabe*
(*WA11*), p. 285; the passage first appeared in a remark dated October 29, 1931 on p. 139 of
MS 112, published in vol. IV of the *Wiener Ausgabe* (*WA4*), p. 172. Wittgenstein is quoting
remark H 146 from Lichtenberg 1968/71. He elaborates a few lines further down: "Why are
grammatical problems so tough and seemingly ineradicable? – Because they are connected
with the oldest thought habits, that is, with the oldest images that are engraved into our
language itself. ((Lichtenberg.))" For other references to Lichtenberg see Nordmann 2002a
or, for example, pp. 145, 280f., 518, and 636f. of Schulte's critical-genetic edition of *PI*.

[15] Kant 1997, A 293ff./B 249ff.

wrongly posed because it fails to give meaning to the word "cause." Our philosophical perplexity dissolves once we cease to ask illegitimate questions.[16]

This critique of the misuse of concepts is a far cry from Lichtenberg's critique of language. Kant did not consider language itself an object of experience: do spoken and printed words represent "noumenal" things in themselves (concepts, for example) or are words and sentences experienced as phenomena in time and space, under the category of causality – or both?

Though he never produced a system of philosophy, Lichtenberg pursued in a piecemeal manner just such a critique of language and of the most general philosophy which underwrites the colloquial use of language. "What Bacon says about the perniciousness of systems could be said of every word," he remarks: "This means undefining the words again."[17] According to Lichtenberg, not just the categories of the understanding, but every word in our language, every turn of phrase makes some experience possible, opens up a manner of apprehending or questioning the world. Language makes communication possible to the extent that it is conventional, but those conventions also harden conventional ways of thinking about the world and close off opportunities for possible experience. For heuristic purposes and to keep society honest, so to speak, we therefore have to break conventions, undefine words, think and write individually – but in doing so, we may not undermine the conventions, which remain indispensable.[18] Indeed, for the sake of these conventions "philosophy . . . must always speak the language of unphilosophy":

---

[16] In a very "Wittgensteinian" moment, Kant emphasizes that it will never be resolved for good, since reason (the later Wittgenstein would say "grammar") keeps tempting us. The perplexities will therefore have to be removed again and again. As Wittgenstein's readers are well aware, the business of criticism never ends: "there is a natural and unavoidable dialectic of pure reason . . . that irremediably attaches to human reason, so that even after we have exposed the mirage it will still not cease to lead our reason on with false hopes, continually propelling us into momentary aberrations that always need to be removed" (Kant 1997, A298/B354f.).

[17] Lichtenberg 1968/71, C 278. This refers to remark 278 in Lichtenberg's so-called wastebook C. Some of his remarks have been translated, this one in Lichtenberg 1990, p. 49. Compare ibid., A 17 or K 65 (pp. 21 and 167 in Lichtenberg 1990). Remark E 222 provides the epigraph for the current book ("It requires no art . . .").

[18] See Gockel 1973.

To say we perceive *external* objects is contradictory; it is impossible for human beings to go outside themselves. When we believe we are seeing objects we are seeing only ourselves. We can really perceive nothing in the world except ourselves and the changes that take place in us. It is likewise impossible for us to *feel* for others, as it is customary to say we do: we feel only for ourselves. This proposition sounds harsh but it is not when it is correctly understood. We love neither father, nor mother, nor wife, nor child; what we love are the pleasant sensations they produce in us; something always flatters our pride and love of self. It isn't possible any other way, and whoever denies the proposition cannot have understood it.

Thus begins a remark on the relation between our representations and their objects. Lichtenberg continues by giving his reflection a curious, yet decisive twist, which runs counter to the assuredness of his previous philosophical declarations:

Our language, however, must not be philosophical in this respect, just as it must not be Copernican in regard to the system of the world . . . The invention of language preceded philosophy and that is what makes it difficult for philosophy, especially if one wants to explain it to people who don't think much for themselves. When it speaks, philosophy is always compelled to speak the language of unphilosophy.[19]

Despite our knowledge of the solar system, we keep saying that the sun rises and sets. Our language did not, perhaps could and should not become Copernican. And for the same reason we will and perhaps must continue speaking of external objects as if we could perceive them immediately or directly: our language has not, perhaps cannot, become Kantian. Lichtenberg provides a concrete example in another remark from his series of reflections on Kant. It was in this remark that Wittgenstein discovered the similarity between his own and Lichtenberg's conceptions of philosophy:

I and *me. I* feel *me* – that makes two objects. Our false philosophy is embodied in the language as a whole: one might say that we can't reason without reasoning wrongly. People don't bear in mind that speaking, no matter what, is a philosophy. Everyone who speaks is a folk-philosopher, and our academic philosophy consists of qualifications to the popular brand. Our entire philosophy is correction of the use of language, that is, correction of a philosophy, namely the most general kind. But ordinary philosophy has the

[19] Lichtenberg 1968/71, H 151 (pp. 115f. in Lichtenberg 1990); cf. A 130 and A 136 (p. 28 in Lichtenberg 1990).

advantage of possessing the declensions and conjugations. Thus we always teach true philosophy with the language of the false one. Explaining words is no help; for with explanations of words I don't change the pronouns and their declensions.[20]

Lichtenberg distinguishes the "declensions and conjugations" in the use of ordinary language from the philosophical explanation or definition of concepts, that is, nouns. While the conceptual analysis of the philosophers attempts to name the essence of things, always pushing to get beyond the limits of language, ordinary language moves laterally among signs, quite content to stay within our representations.[21]

Lichtenberg's critique of language thus highlights the open-ended interplay between perfectly adapted ordinary language and eye-opening philosophical thought, between analysis of conventions and linguistic innovation: "When using an old word it often follows the channel which the first-grade-primer has dug for reason, while a metaphor makes itself a new one, and often cuts right through."[22] In regard to language, this interplay concerns the relation of the individual and the generic (token and type, as contemporary philosophers might say), in regard to the production of knowledge, it concerns the relation between self-thinking person and community of inquirers, and in regard to the world, it concerns the relation between experimental novelty and our theoretical "pictures."

A lot can go wrong in these relations, and Lichtenberg's satirical remarks show how metaphysics arises when things go very wrong: "A knife without a blade and the handle missing" can raise deep questions concerning the essence of things. And yet it is a rather ordinary object in comparison to the mysterious "*concubinium animae et*

---

[20] Ibid., H 146 (p. 53 in Lichtenberg 1969, partly also p. 115 in Lichtenberg 1990).

[21] Consider, for example, the following remark: "The immeasurable benefit which language bestows on thought consists, I think, in the fact that words are generally signs for things rather than definitions . . . What things are – to find that out is the task of philosophy. The word is intended to be, not a definition, but a mere sign for the definition, which in turn is always the variable result of the collective industriousness of scholars . . . So be cautious about discarding words which are generally understood, and do not discard them if your only reason is that they might convey a false concept of the thing! In the first place, it is not true that a word conveys a false concept, because I know and presuppose after all that the word serves to distinguish the thing; and second, I don't intend to become acquainted with the essence of the thing through the word" (from Lichtenberg 1968/71, K 19, pp. 164f. in Lichtenberg 1990).

[22] Lichtenberg 1968/71, F 116.

corporis," an imaginary machine to explain the interpenetration of body and soul (the soul – it is "entirely, little wings and all, made out of ivory" – is a removable part).[23] Philosophers seem to invent such fanciful devices when they talk about human bodies and minds as if they interacted like a machine, but Lichtenberg also questions what the philosopher is doing who contrasts the living organisms with dead matter: "Perhaps there is no such thing in nature; he kills matter and then calls it dead."[24] And, of course, Lichtenberg's critique of metaphysics extends to ordinary practice: "Some actions are called malicious because they're done by ugly people" or "It is a question whether, when we break a murderer on the wheel, we aren't lapsing into precisely the mistake of the child who hits the chair it bumps into."[25]

Like Kant, Lichtenberg considers the relation between representations and their objects an internal relation: how things appear to us is structured by how we think and speak.[26] While, according to Kant, this relation is constituted in a stable and objective manner by the categories of the understanding, Lichtenberg stands on the shifting ground of linguistic practice. Kant's critique draws the limits of theoretical knowledge, thus curing us of philosophical perplexity. Lichtenberg denies that individuals can ascertain any truth, philosophical or scientific, but this limit also assigns a rôle or defines a duty for every individual. Since everyone is a member in the council of humanity, everyone's reasoned objections have to be addressed by that council: as objections are laid to rest and consensus is formed, scientific truth or objective knowledge emerges from these negotiations.[27] Metaphysical matters, however, encounter a unique fate in the council

---

[23] Both devices appear in a fictional list of items to be auctioned off; see Lichtenberg 1972, pp. 452 and 455f. Wittgenstein discusses the knife in *Philosophical Grammar* (*PG*), part II, §40, in his 1939 lectures on the foundation of mathematics (*LFM*), p. 21, and *WA2*, p. 268 (p. 182 of MS 108).

[24] Lichtenberg 1968/71, F 324 (p. 86 in Lichtenberg 1990); cf. remark D 270: "Just as certain writers, after first dealing their material a rough blow, then say it naturally falls into two parts."

[25] Ibid., F 1020 and J 706 (page 143 in Lichtenberg 1990).

[26] See ibid., J 569: "In the introduction to the 2nd and 3rd editions of Kant's *Critique* (the 3rd is a mere reprint of the 2nd) much occurs that is odd and that I have often thought but not said. We find no causes in the things, but notice only what corresponds into us. Wherever we look, we only see ourselves." Note Lichtenberg's strange, yet precise formulation that might also be translated as follows: "we remark only the correspondence that reaches into us."

[27] See Nordmann 1986 and 1988.

of critical self-thinkers: "I have been thinking for a long time that one day philosophy will devour itself. – Metaphysics has already devoured part of itself."[28] And thus, Lichtenberg's critical method also solves the problems of philosophy.

HEINRICH HERTZ AND THE LIMITS OF SCIENCE

In an age without clear disciplinary boundaries between science and philosophy, Kant taught the sciences, developed a famous cosmological hypothesis, and responded to current scientific developments even in his posthumously published late manuscripts. While elaborating the preconditions for all possible experience, the *Critique of Pure Reason* explains the success of Newtonian mechanics by reconstructing it from so-called synthetic a priori principles, thus showing that it must be true: Newtonian mechanics *is* systematic knowledge of all possible experience of matter in motion. Its success sets a limit for all science, leading Kant to famously declare that there cannot be a proper science of biology since the notions of "organism" and "natural purpose" do not yield to mathematical treatment as do the categories that structure all experience in time and space.[29]

Again, Kant's systematizing interest in science might be contrasted with Lichtenberg's orientation as a prolific experimental physicist. He was known to have demonstrated more than five hundred experiments in one year and took the multiplicity of experimental phenomena as an argument against premature systematization. Science was a project in the making, and his aphoristic style carried the experimental method into philosophy.

---

[28] Lichtenberg 1968/71, J 620 (p. 139 in Lichtenberg 1990). Regarding Lichtenberg's devastating critique of metaphysics, see Zimmermann 1986. Compare Wittgenstein's diary entry of February 7, 1931: "If my name lives on then only as the Terminus ad quem of great occidental philosophy. Somewhat like the name of the one who burnt down the library of Alexandria" (MT, diary p. 64). Remarks like these bring to mind von Wright's comment: "It may appear strange that Schopenhauer, one of the masters of philosophical prose, did not influence Wittgenstein's style. An author, however, who reminds one, often astonishingly, of Wittgenstein is Lichtenberg. Wittgenstein esteemed him highly. To what extent, if any, he can be said to have learned from him I do not know. It is deserving of mention that some of Lichtenberg's thoughts on philosophical questions show a striking resemblance to Wittgenstein's" (1982, p. 34).

[29] He reconsidered this question toward the end of his life in regard to the emerging science of chemistry; see Friedman 1992.

How many ideas hover dispersed in my head of which many a pair, if they should come together, could bring about the greatest of discoveries! But they lie as far apart as Goslar sulphur from East India saltpeter, and both from the dust in the charcoal piles on the Eichsfeld – which three together would make gunpowder. How long the ingredients of gunpowder existed before gunpowder did! There is no natural *aqua regia*. If, when thinking, we yield too freely to the natural combinations of the forms of understanding and of reason, then our concepts often *stick* so much to others that they can't unite with those to which they really belong. If only there were something in that realm like a solution in chemistry, where the individual parts float about, lightly suspended, and thus can follow any current. But since this isn't possible, we must deliberately bring things into contact with each other. We must *experiment* with ideas.[30]

The particular limits of science, too, will be determined experimentally, that is, one hypothesis at a time. Lichtenberg demonstrated this for the purportedly scientific claims of physiognomy: the physiognomists forced ideas into contact with each other and Lichtenberg showed that these did not really belong together and that physiognomy failed to discover anything.

Kant and Lichtenberg are now joined by a third scientist whose critique of language determined the limits of science and knowledge. Heinrich Hertz (1857–1894) never wrote for a general or specifically philosophical audience, but he was well aware of the philosophical significance of his theoretical reflections on the *Constitution of Matter* or on the "philosophical . . . and, indeed, in a certain sense the most important result" of his experiments in electrodynamics.[31] His introduction to the *Principles of Mechanics* begins with the now familiar question how it is possible that science can make representations of nature that allow for successful predictions of future events.

We form for ourselves pictures or symbols of external objects; and we make them in such a way that the necessary consequents of the pictures in thought are always the pictures of the necessary consequents in nature of the things pictured. In order for this requirement to be satisfiable at all, there must be certain agreements between nature and our mind . . . The pictures of which

---

[30] Lichtenberg 1968/71, K 308 (pp. 53f. in Lichtenberg 1969).
[31] Hertz 1962, p. 19. When negotiating his contract for *The Principles of Mechanics*, he wrote to his publisher: "As far as determining the number of copies to be printed, I believe that due to the Introduction you can include some of the philosophical readership" (quoted in Fölsing 1997, p. 509). See Nordmann 1998 and Goldstein 2004.

we are speaking are our conceptions of things; they agree with the things in *one* important respect which consists in satisfying the above-mentioned requirement, but for their purpose it is not necessary that they are in any further agreement with the things. Indeed, we do not know, nor have we any means of discovering whether our conceptions of things agree with them in anything at all but in this *one* fundamental relation alone.[32]

There is *one* fundamental relation between our representations and their objects, and the further development of Hertz's mechanics shows that it is once again conceived as an internal relation. Indeed, he refers to Kant when he declares that the objects of experience are given in accordance with "the laws of the internal intuition."[33] He shows that nature therefore appears to us as a dynamical system: its moving bodies are defined by spatial co-ordinates that are changing over time along certain trajectories. Our representations of the objects also form a kind of dynamical system: our mind makes a model of the system of nature, and in that model certain conceptions will be co-ordinated with certain aspects of the dynamical system, the consequences of those conceptions can then be traced out.

The relation of a dynamical model to the system of which it is regarded as the model, is the same as the relation of the pictures our mind forms of things to these things . . . The agreement between mind and nature can therefore be compared to the agreement between two systems which are models of one another, and we can even account for this agreement by assuming that the mind is capable of making actual dynamical models of things and of working with them.[34]

Since mind and nature, our representations and their objects are two systems that are models of each other, their agreement becomes a matter of simple determination, a question of yes or no: if this is the next state in the development of the dynamical system of nature, the next picture that follows from our dynamical model of that system either is or is not a representation of that state – and thus there either is or is not agreement between our representation and its object. This we can know and this is as much as we can know.[35]

[32] Hertz 1956, pp. 1f.
[33] Ibid., §1. Except for the introduction, *The Principles of Mechanics* is composed as a series of numbered paragraphs.
[34] Ibid., §428.
[35] Janik and Toulmin 1973, pp. 141 and 145f. pointed out already that Hertz, Kant, and Wittgenstein all drew limits to language and knowledge from within our representations.

As in Kant's philosophy, the agreement of mind and nature does not require the comparison of apples and oranges, of two fundamentally dissimilar entities. Indeed, Hertz's immediate juxtaposition of two dynamical systems that are models of each other does not merely illustrate Kant's point, it serves to clarify it splendidly. Though Kant calls time, space, and causality "constitutive" of experience, it remains tempting to think of his categories as intermediaries *between* mind and nature. Kant himself sometimes talks as if the concept of causality, for example, mediates between brute sensation and the understanding. This metaphor would suggest that there is still a distance to be bridged between the sensation and the understanding, and that the categories provide that bridge. This is not what is meant, however, when Kant refers to the categories as constitutive: causality *gives* the object of experience to the understanding. Hertz helps us to understand what this means. The internal relation between the two dynamical systems of mind and nature is immediate. Once the object of experience is constituted, there is no distance whatsoever between the representation and its object – one models the other and in our mind we can hold them directly side by side or superimpose them.

While this helps to clarify Kant's philosophy, Hertz goes beyond it in another respect. From his account of how scientific knowledge is possible, he develops a critique of language that is directed not only against metaphysical philosophy but primarily against the metaphysical confusion inherent in Newtonian mechanics. This confusion, Hertz argues, arises with the concept of force.[36]

Newtonian mechanics had come to represent the pinnacle of science for generations of scientists and certainly for Kant. Indeed, it meets Hertz's criterion for successful science: it is constructed "in such a way that the necessary consequents of the pictures in thought are always the pictures of the necessary consequents in nature of the things pictured." And yet, its appeal to "force" as one of its fundamental concepts is confusing: should we assume that there really *are* forces just because "force" is a crucial element in the construction of that picture? Or, put differently: Newtonian mechanics is a representational system which dynamically models bodies and their

---

[36] In his lectures on the constitution of matter, Hertz subjects to a similar critique other determinations of matter such as the notion of substance; see part II of Hertz 1999.

motions in nature, but does that mean that to every building block of Newtonian mechanics corresponds a real entity in nature? In order to remove conceptual confusion, Hertz therefore requires that we critically examine our representations or pictures of things. They can only be modified and improved, he argues, if we can distinguish in each picture which of its elements serve its constructive purposes and which elements ensure agreement with the objects:[37] "What is ascribed to the pictures for the sake of appropriateness is contained in the notations, definitions, abbreviations, and, in short, all that we can arbitrarily add or take away. What enters into the pictures for the sake of correctness is contained in the results of experience, from which the pictures are built up."[38]

Physicists and philosophers had discussed for two hundred years what "force" *really* is. Hertz's application of the critical method aims to decide whether their question makes sense or whether "force" is perhaps one of those elements that can be arbitrarily added or taken away. If it is, then "force" does not refer to anything real but is merely one of the "confederates concealed beyond the limit of our senses" or one of the "idling wheels, which keep out of the business altogether when actual facts have to be represented."[39]

In order to decide this question, the Newtonian picture of mechanics must be tested: "By varying the choice of the propositions which we take as fundamental, we can give various representations of the principles of mechanics. Hence we can thus obtain various pictures of things; and these pictures we can test and compare with each other."[40] Hertz follows this procedure and devises a picture of mechanics in which "force" does not appear among its fundamental propositions. Since his is also a perfectly good picture of mechanics, we might freely choose between Newton's and his, and the very fact of that choice proves that "force" can be arbitrarily added or taken away from our

---

[37] In B75f./A52f. of his *Critique of Pure Reason*, Kant writes that cognition can arise only from the unification of concepts and intuitions (just as Hertz's images of mechanics unify conceptual apparatus and empirical content). "But on this account," Kant continues, "one must not mix up their roles, rather one has great cause to separate them carefully from each other and distinguish them."

[38] Hertz 1956, pp. 2f. Hertz identifies a third, so to speak, Kantian element. It shares with the criterion of appropriateness that it concerns the construction rather than the empirical content of the picture: "What enters into the pictures, in order that they may be permissible, is given by the nature of our mind."

[39] Ibid., pp. 25, 11f.   [40] Ibid., p. 3; cf. p. 2.

pictures. Hertz therefore shows that, despite its misleading treatment by Newton, "force" is an "empty relation" also in Newton's mechanics. His testing of pictures provides a critique of the language of physics and relieves it of a philosophical perplexity. Now that "force" is eliminated as a fundamental concept of physics, questions concerning its nature no longer arise. Hertz expresses this in a passage that was frequently quoted by Wittgenstein and at one point was to serve as a motto for the *Philosophical Investigations*:[41]

[W]e have heaped upon the signs "force" and "electricity" more relations than can be completely reconciled amongst themselves; we have an obscure feeling of this, demand enlightenment, and express our confused wish by posing the confused question as to the nature of force and electricity. But this question is obviously mistaken in regard to the answer it expects. It cannot be satisfied through knowledge of novel and yet more relations and connections, but by removal of the contradictions among the extant ones; thus perhaps by reduction of the number of extant relations. When these painful contradictions are removed, the question as to the nature [of force and electricity] will not have been answered; but our mind, no longer vexed, will cease to pose what is an illegitimate question for it.[42]

After Kant had set a limit to metaphysical speculation by showing that "causality" has no meaning beyond the bounds of experience, Hertz distanced physics even further from metaphysics by showing that "force" is not a name for something, that it has no meaning beyond its rôle as an empty relation or conceptual glue.

WITTGENSTEIN'S RENEWED CRITIQUE

"What does it mean to *think in the spirit of Kant*?" asked Georg Christoph Lichtenberg, and he suggests the now familiar answer: "I believe it means to find out what the relationships are that obtain between our being, whatever that may be, and those things we say are *outside us*; that is to say, to determine the relationship of the subjective

---

[41] See Schulte's critical-genetic edition of *PI*, p. 741, also the chapter "Philosophy" from *The Big Typescript* (*PO*, p. 182 and *WAII*, p. 285). Compare *PPO*, pp. 379 and 399 and McGuinness 1988, p. 39: "'The whole task of philosophy,' he was fond of quoting from Hertz, 'is to give such a form to our expression that certain disquietudes (or problems) vanish.'"

[42] Hertz 1956, pp. 7f.

to the objective."[43] In this general sense, Ludwig Wittgenstein worked in the spirit of Kant.[44]

In his 1931/1932 lectures, Wittgenstein considered transcendental philosophy, that is, "Kant's critical method without the peculiar applications Kant made of it." This method determines the relationship of the subjective to the objective from within the knowing subject: "This is the right sort of approach. Hume, Descartes and others had tried to start with one proposition such as 'Cogito ergo sum' and work from it to others. Kant disagreed and started with what we know to be so and so, and went on to examine the validity of what we suppose we know."[45] And not long before that, on February 10, 1931, Wittgenstein had noted: "The limit of language manifests itself in the impossibility of describing the fact that corresponds to (is the translation of) a sentence without simply repeating the sentence. (We are involved here with the Kantian solution of the problem of philosophy.)"[46] In these few lines, we find a seemingly paradoxical formulation of Kant's point: the limit of language *is* the solution of the problem of philosophy. Agreement between representations and objects is possible *because* we cannot step outside of experience and of what we know in order to compare our representations to something fundamentally different. Put another way and adopting Hertz's analysis: to the extent that they are models of one another, the

---

[43] Lichtenberg 1968/71 (p. 168 in Lichtenberg 1990).

[44] Wittgenstein was no *doctrinal* neo-Kantian. Rudolf Haller correctly points to "the striking contrast on the one hand between Kant's idea that the conditions of experience, like their possibility, are *given a priori*, and, on the other hand, Wittgenstein's adamant empiricist conviction that no component of experience is *a priori*" (1990, p. 53). Wittgenstein's student Georg Henrik von Wright remembers that "[f]rom Spinoza, Hume, and Kant he said that he could only get occasional glimpses of understanding" (1982, p. 33). And Brian McGuinness reports from an earlier period (the World War I Olmütz discussions): "Wittgenstein made some of them read Frege and he talked to them about Kant and Schopenhauer, with whom they had, like himself, the normal educated man's acquaintance. 'In the words of the great Kant' he would quote from time to time" (1988, pp. 252f.).

[45] *Lectures 1930–1932* (*L30–32*), p. 73. These are lecture notes; the characterization of "transcendental philosophy" was derived by the editors from the text to which Wittgenstein is referring.

[46] *CV*, p. 13. Compare MS 109, p. 31, quoted (and translated) by Hacker 2000, p. 379: "The agreement of thought as such with reality cannot be expressed. If one takes the word agreement in the general sense in which a true proposition agrees with reality, then it is wrong, because there are also false propositions. But another sense [of 'agreement'] cannot be reproduced [or articulated] by language. Like everything else, the (pre-established) harmony between *this* thought and *that* reality is given us by the limits of language."

dynamical systems of nature and mind simply repeat each other; that repetitiveness or mutual mirroring makes objective scientific knowledge possible *and* makes it impossible to describe the facts in any other way.

In the *Tractatus* we find that same emphasis on the need to reflect the problem of philosophy from within the subject or from within language, in other words, to start from what we know or what we have. We find that the discovery of the limits *is* the solution of the problem and that it consists in our inability to step outside our models or pictures:

The book will therefore draw a limit to thinking, or rather – not to thinking, but to the expression of thoughts . . . That limit can . . . only be drawn in language and what lies on the other side of the limit will simply be nonsense . . . I am therefore of the opinion that the problems [of philosophy] have in essentials been finally solved. (*TLP* preface)

The picture, however, cannot picture its form of picturing; it exhibits it . . . the picture cannot place itself outside of its form of representation. (*TLP* 2.172, 2.174)

Though these remarks illustrate the similarity between Wittgenstein and the other three critical philosophers, it is quite another matter to show how Wittgenstein arrives at them, how he defends them. While the formal structure of his argument is the subject matter of the next chapter, the remainder of this one aims to motivate Wittgenstein's proposed solution and to show how his proposal continues and transforms the traditional critiques of metaphysics.

Where Kant inquired about the agreement between representations and their objects, Wittgenstein is interested also in the agreement among people. The example of science and many everyday contexts suggests that those two kinds of agreement are closely associated. We agree among one another, and the views we agree on, agree with reality. Indeed, we may be agreeing with one another just to the extent that the representations we agree on also agree with reality.[47] This

---

[47] The philosophy of science has been haunted by the question whether to give precedence to the epistemological or the ontological sense of "agreement": so-called scientific realists want to explain communicative agreement in terms of empirical agreement ("scientists can agree among one another only if and when they come upon a theory which agrees with

move from the Kantian question "How is experience possible?" to the *Tractarian* "How is agreement possible?" was prompted by the recognition that there is more to contend with than a representation on the one hand and its object on the other: language and logic need to be fitted into the picture. Lichtenberg and some of his contemporaries (Hamann, Herder) were aware of this, but in the nineteenth century a whole new branch of philosophy grew up that was dealing with the relations of language to logic, of logic and language to thought, and of logic, language, and thought to reality. The development of mathematical logic and of conceptual notations allowed for the treatment of these questions in the manner of a formal science in which hypotheses are submitted, counterexamples proposed, thought experiments conducted, theories refined.

Wittgenstein responded to many aspects of this new enterprise,[48] but for our present purposes it is enough to mention two of its most important claims. He rejected both of them.

First, as Lichtenberg pointed out with respect to "*I* feel *me*," natural language seems logically imprecise: here, for example, a sentence that appears to relate two things speaks only of one thing, namely a single human subject. Frege had pointed out how different words may signify the same object ("the morning star is the evening star") and Wittgenstein discusses how the same word signifies in various different ways. In the sentences "The cookie is sweet," "Two plus two is four," and "There is a God," he says, "[T]he word 'is' appears as a copula, as the sign for equality, and as the expression of existence; . . . we speak of *something* but also of *something* happening" (*TLP* 3.323). This gives rise, Wittgenstein adds, to "the most fundamental confusions (of which the whole of philosophy is full)" (*TLP* 3.324).

Such confusions make it difficult, perhaps impossible, to immediately discern from a sentence in ordinary language what its logical structure or the underlying thought is (*TLP* 4.002). Now, some drew from this the further conclusion that there is no immediate internal relation between our representations and their objects: before

---

the facts"); so-called conventionalists and many sociologists of scientific knowledge view communicative agreement as a precondition for empirical agreement ("we need a shared conception of the world before we can ascertain agreement with matters of fact").

[48] For a very readable introduction, see the first chapter of Hacker 1996.

these can be related to one another, the argument goes, our sentences need to be subjected to analysis or a kind of logical clarification. The special language of logical analysis would therefore be an intermediary between ordinary language and the world.

Second, once the new science of logical analysis claims an intermediary language of its own, another set of questions arises. How similar are statements in the intermediary language of logic ("This sentence is true") to statements in our ordinary language ("The cookie is sweet")? Just as sweetness is an attribute of the cookie, we are tempted to assume that truth might be an attribute of a sentence. And just as "cookie," "sweetness," "electron," and "horse" are names which refer to objects or properties in the world, we are tempted to think also of "and," "or," and "if–then" as names that refer to logical objects or types of relations in the world. And if these words refer as names do, "true" and "false" could do the same and refer to basic elements in the realm of logic. Like chemical elements, these might serve as building blocks for more complicated structures. Indeed, the analogy to chemistry might lead to yet another conclusion. In chemistry, elements refer to simple constituents and molecules to compound structures. This might imply for language that entire sentences could also be considered names: instead of naming individual objects, they name situations or complex configurations of objects. Just as simple names refer to simple objects, sentences refer to complex objects (relations), and true sentences refer to the truth. And so, "cookie" names an empirical object, "truth" names a logical object, "The cookie is sweet" names an empirical fact, "The sentence is true" names a logical fact, "All cookies are sweet" might express an empirical law, and "All sentences are true *or* false" expresses a law of thought.

The first claim of the new science introduced the idea of a special language for logical analysis. These further claims introduce a whole new class of objects and facts that are supposed to correspond to the special language. On this account, logic has its own subject matter, and this subject matter – features of human thinking for some, abstract objects for others – has to be considered when we investigate the relation of our representations to their objects. Whatever theory one ends up adopting, this relation will no longer be as direct or immediate as it was envisioned by Hertz. And to the extent that there are interdependencies between our representations and the logical facts, the relation between representations and objects is no longer internal: agreement now requires a proper configuration of natural language, logical form, and objective reality.[49]

Both claims of the new science of logic thus complicate the question to which Kant had provided his simple answer. They challenged any attempt to consider the relation between representations and their objects as an unmediated internal relation. According to Wittgenstein, however, this challenge resulted from the confused view that there is a special substantive relation between language and logic. Once this view is cleared up, we can return to the elegant simplicity of Kant's or Hertz's conception.[50]

Though no one in particular held the two claims precisely as I just caricatured them, these kinds of questions were at issue between the two logicians who most influenced Wittgenstein, Gottlob Frege (1848–1925) and Bertrand Russell (1872–1970). Both sought to provide a theory which would adequately handle this new set of logical questions, objects, and properties. In the manner of the critical tradition, Wittgenstein sought to relieve them of this arduous and perplexing task.

"Logic must take care of itself" (*TLP* 5.473). This sentence opens the notebooks in which he drafted the *Tractatus*, and with this sentence begins his critique of the new science of logic: logic *should* take care of itself, that is, it should not insert itself between our sentences and their correct analysis, and it should not claim for itself a third realm of objects and facts between language and world. It *can* take care of itself, that is, it requires no theory, let alone a science to help it out. "Logic is taking care of itself; all we have to do is watch how it does it."[51]

---

[49] For example, one might establish as a "logical fact" that certain sentences have sense only if they refer to objects that really exist (see the still famous example: "The present king of France is bald"). In that case, the sense of the representation depends on the truth of a statement (there presently is a king of France) even before it can be compared to reality (before one determines whether the "is bald" obtains). These dependencies are external to the direct relation of representation and object. Under these conditions, the agreement of the sentence with reality is not the purely internal relation envisioned by Hertz, that is, a relation immediately determined by the mere juxtaposition or superimposition of two pictures or models.

[50] Compare Carruthers 1990, pp. 31–33.

[51] *NB*, October 13, 1914, compare the earlier formulations on August 8, September 2 and 4, 1914.

Wittgenstein shows this by breaking the apparent symmetry between "The cookie is sweet" and "The sentence is true." The term "sweet" corresponds to or stands in for some property, but "true" does not represent anything. This is Wittgenstein's fundamental idea: "The possibility of sentences is based on the principle that objects are represented by signs. My fundamental idea is that the 'logical constants' do not represent. That the *logic* of facts cannot be represented" (*TLP* 4.0312).[52]

Here is just one of Wittgenstein's illustrations of this fundamental idea. One of the "logical constants" is the word "not." Now, if "not" represented a logical object, there should be a difference of meaning between "It is cold" and the double-negation "It is not the case that it is not cold." After all, the first expression does not refer to the logical object "not" while the second refers to it twice. But this view is at odds with the intuition that the second expression, though a bit more cumbersome, means the same as the first: both assert that it is cold. Indeed, logicians hold that p implies --p ("not not p"), that p, --p, ----p, etc. are logically equivalent to one another.[53]

That from a fact p infinitely many *other* facts should follow, namely --p, ----p, etc. is hard to believe from the start. And it is no less strange that infinitely many sentences of logic (of mathematics) should follow from a half dozen "basic laws."
But all sentences of logic say the same thing. Namely nothing. (*TLP* 5.43)

There is only one fact p and no other facts follow from it.[54] There are various ways of saying that p is the case: we can say "p is the case" or we can say "it is not the case that p is not the case." Logic allows us to move between these different ways of saying that p. But in any

---

[52] See McGuinness 1974.
[53] Again, the two claims of a science of logic might suggest that --p follows from p only by way of a special premise which expresses a general fact about the logical object "not." This premise might state, for example, that the meaning of "not" is such that a second "not" cancels the meaning of the first. Wittgenstein denies that such a special premise is necessary: --p follows directly from p. This does not involve a separate step: --p and ----p are immediately given along with p.
[54] Wittgenstein uses "follows from it" in the narrow logical sense. One can say, of course, that from the fact that it is cold it "follows" that the water is freezing. This is not what Wittgenstein has in mind here. While there is perhaps a causal connection between the two facts "it is cold" and "water freezes," these facts do not logically follow from one another (only experience teaches us that they are connected).

event, we are still saying the same thing and logic itself is not *saying* anything at all. Instead, the propositions of logic *show* something:

The sentence shows what it says; tautologies and contradictions show that they say nothing.

Tautologies leave to reality the whole – infinite – logical space; contradictions take up the entire logical space and leave to reality not even a point. Neither can therefore determine reality in any way whatsoever. (*TLP* 4.461 and 4.463)

But what does logic show? It shows the logical form that is common to language and reality. That there is such a common form rests on a fairly simple observation, one that prompted Wittgenstein to remark in his *Notebooks* on September 29, 1914: "In a sentence a world is put together experimentally. (As when a traffic accident is represented in the Paris courtroom by means of dolls etc.) This must yield the nature of truth immediately (unless I were blind)."[55]

This moment marks the appearance in Wittgenstein's work of the idea that language is a picture of reality. Georg Henrik von Wright fills us in on the background:

It was in the autumn of 1914, on the eastern front. Wittgenstein was reading in a magazine about a lawsuit in Paris concerning an automobile accident. At the trial a miniature model of the accident was presented before the court. The model here served as a proposition; that is, as a description of a possible state of affairs. It has this function owing to a correspondence between the parts of the model (the miniature-houses, -cars, -people) and things (houses, cars, people) in reality. It now occurred to Wittgenstein that one might reverse the analogy and say that a *proposition* serves as a model or *picture*, by virtue of a similar correspondence between *its* parts and the world. The way in which the parts of the proposition are combined – the *structure* of the proposition – depicts a possible combination of elements in reality, a possible state of affairs.[56]

The physical description through the model and a verbal description in a sentence or proposition are just two ways of picturing the accident. The scene of the accident, the courtroom model, and the descriptive sentence all share the same pictorial form. In the case of

[55] The parenthetical remark "*wenn ich nicht blind wäre*" has been translated "were I not blind", which suggests that Wittgenstein does not yet see how the courtroom representation yields the answer. I submit that the translation proposed here is closer to the literal and philosophical meaning: Someone who is not blind can see the relation between model and reality.
[56] Von Wright 1982, pp. 20f.

the accident scene, the red car and the yellow car represent themselves; in the courtroom, a red model stands for the red car, a yellow model stands for the yellow car; and in a verbal description the words "red car" stand for the red car and "yellow car" stands for the yellow car – but all three pictures *show* the same thing, namely that the yellow car impacted the red car from the right. While the sentence, like the model, *is* a picture of how it might have been, the sentence is used to *do* something else, namely to assert that this is actually how it was: the sentence *shows* a possible states of affairs and it *says* that it is actually so and that things really were as they are presented in the sentence. This is Wittgenstein's picture theory of language. After Hertz had pointed out that theories serve to picture systems of bodies in nature, Wittgenstein extended this to the most ordinary descriptive sentence and to the simplest arrangement of objects.

The agreement between thought and reality, between sentences and states of affairs is once again a simply internal relation of likeness between two representations which share the same pictorial form.[57] The sentence offers a picture of reality and says that a state of affairs exists which is pictured by the sentence. If this state of affairs does actually exist, we call the sentence true. If the pictured state of affairs might but does not actually obtain, we call the sentence false. If two persons produce sentences that picture the same state of affairs, their sentences will agree with one another, they say and show the same thing.[58]

---

[57] For the relation between thought and reality compare the quote in note 46 above. Note that, according to Wittgenstein, sentences do not agree with objects but with arrangements of objects. So, our question concerning "agreement between representations and their objects" now requires a qualification to the effect that "the object of a representation" is, strictly speaking, no longer an isolated object but an entire state of affairs.

[58] I have been telling what one might call the Fregean side of the story. Bertrand Russell's objections to Frege overlapped with Wittgenstein's, but Russell's own theory of judgment subverted the strictly internal relation between representation and reality by incorporating the judging mind into this relation. Again Wittgenstein restores the internal relation. James Bogen expresses this nicely: "The mistake, says Wittgenstein, was to analyse 'A believes that p is the case,' 'A thinks p,' etc., as claiming that a proposition p stands in some relation 'to an object, A' (*TLP* 5.541). Properly analysed, 'A judges p' and the rest turn out to be of the form "'p' says p' (*TLP* 5.542) . . . If "'p' says p' is the proper analysis of 'A judges p' then the situation Russell analysed as including a judging subject, the judging, and a Russellian proposition consisting of objects arranged by the judging reduces to a situation consisting just of a picture, sentence, or proposition 'p,' and its expression of its sense. 'p' says that it is the case that p because its elements are 'correlated with' the elements of the putative fact that p (*TLP* 5.5421)" (Bogen 1996, p. 170).

Wittgenstein's investigation of shared logical form does not stop here, however. There is more involved in the comparison of representation and state of affairs than a correspondence between their combinations of parts. The determination of truth through a simple comparison of sentence and state of affairs requires that the sentence is decidable: every descriptive sentence has the logical feature that it can be either true or false, that its truth or falsity cannot be determined by looking at the sentence alone but only by drawing on its agreement, or lack thereof, with reality. Such sentences have the character of contingency. Now, language and reality share the same logical form just to the extent that we consider reality to be contingent also:

> Everything we see could also be different.
> Everything we can describe at all could also be different.
> There is no order of things *a priori*.　　(*TLP* 5.364)[59]

The truth or falsity of empirical sentences depends on whether or not a pictured state of affairs actually obtains. Reality consists of those states of affairs that happen to obtain, and the substance of the world consists of all possible states of affairs. A complete list of all those possible states of affairs that actually obtain would provide a complete description of the world. We arrive at this list of true sentences by picking them from all possible sentences that correspond in perfect symmetry to all possible states of affairs.[60]

So, to our question "What does logic show?" we can now answer more fully that it shows the logical form that is common to language and reality. Logic shows that the relationship between language and reality is symmetrically pictorial, that is, an internal relation as it obtains *between* two pictures or two facts ("The picture is a fact," *TLP* 2.141). Representations are directly in touch with reality: the linkages between the names in a sentence and the objects in a state of affairs provide for the shared co-ordinates of the two systems. Nothing stands between language and reality, since they share logical form

---

[59] Compare *TLP* 6.41, Hertz's "everything could also be different" in Hertz 1956, p. 38, Lichtenberg 1968/71, C 194 and J 942, and Kant's remark that experience cannot teach us that things cannot be different (1997, B 3 and A 734).

[60] Wittgenstein takes this logical ontology a step further to the level of objects and names. Objects are defined by their ability to occur in certain states of affairs. Similarly, names take their meaning from their ability to appear in certain sentences. To fully know an object therefore coincides with apprehending fully the meaning of its name.

and need not pass through a mysterious realm of intermediary logical facts.[61] The traffic accident (which happened or did not happen), its reenactment in a courtroom model (which matches or does not match the actual event), and its verbal description (which is true or false) all exhibit the same structure that establishes an internal relation between them.

> The gramophone record, the musical thought, the score, the waves of sound, all stand to another in that pictorial internal relation, which holds between language and the world.
> To all of them the logical structure is common . . .
> The picture is linked to reality *thus*; it reaches up to it. (*TLP* 4.014, 2.1511)

In a somewhat abstract and roundabout way we once again arrive at the original solution of the original problem. What accounts for the agreement between representations and reality is "the internal similarity between these things which at first sight seem to be entirely different" (*TLP* 4.0141). And as before, Wittgenstein's "*thus*" points to a limit of knowledge: since we cannot step out of our representations and represent how pictures represent reality, all we can do is juxtapose picture and reality and notice that in one respect they join up to each other, namely in that the picture *is* a picture of reality.[62]

Kant had shown that talk of "causality" may lure us to carry that notion beyond the bounds of experience where it loses meaning. Similarly, Hertz showed that the fundamental, though inessential

---

[61] P. M. S. Hacker highlights this by pointing out that the notion of an immediate internal relation is stronger than a correspondence theory of truth (where correspondence relations need to be interpreted, are mediated by rules): "The fact that Wittgenstein speaks of a proposition's agreeing with reality if it is true does not imply any commitment to a 'truth-relation' or 'correspondence-relation' between propositions and facts, of which being true consists. To assert that a proposition '*p*' agrees with reality is to assert that '*p*' says that *p* and it is indeed the fact that *p*" (2000, p. 386).

[62] For more on "internal relations" see *TLP* 4.122–4.1252, in particular. The proximity to Hertz's view is apparent here (for a more detailed discussion, see Nordmann 2002a). It is suggested also in the continuation of the remark on the gramophone, the musical score, and musical thought: "In the fact that there is a general rule by which the musician is able to read the symphony out of the score, and that there is a rule by which one could reconstruct the symphony from the line on a gramophone record and from this again – by means of the first rule – construct the score, herein lies the internal similarity between these things which at first sight seem to be entirely different. And the rule is the law of projection which projects the symphony into the language of the musical score. It is the rule of translation of this language into the language of the gramophone record" (*TLP* 4.0141).

term "force" in a picture of mechanics may tempt us to mistake it for an essential one that refers to something in the world. Wittgenstein similarly warns against the temptation to mistake logical for empirical propositions just because they look alike.

Most of the sentences and questions that have been written about philosophical matters are not false but nonsensical. Therefore, we cannot answer such questions at all, but can only note their nonsensicality. Most of the questions and sentences of philosophers rest upon a misunderstanding of the logic of our language.

(They are of the kind whether the good is more or less identical than the beautiful.)

And it is not astonishing that the deepest problems are really *no* problems. (*TLP* 4.003)

The *Tractatus* shows this not by establishing new sentences but by clarifying the ones we have (*TLP* 4.112). It does not involve translation into a special kind of language of logic, but concludes that "all sentences of our colloquial language are actually, just as they are, in complete logical order" (*TLP* 5.5563).

Wittgenstein has thus drawn in language a limit to the expression of thoughts. On the one hand there are the sentences of logic. Since logic has no subject matter of its own, these sentences are not "about" anything. Therefore they all "say the same thing. Namely nothing." And then there are the sentences that can be true or false. The only thing that can make them true or false is a comparison with reality. All these sentences are contingent, they are the sentences of science, the sentences we use to describe the world. They are "of equal value" (*TLP* 6.4) or on equal footing in that they cannot say anything "deeper" or "higher" than describe contingent states of affairs. Together, the logical propositions (they say nothing because they are always true or always false) and the contingent or empirical propositions (those which are true or false depending on what is the case) delimit language – "and what lies on the other side of the limit will simply be nonsense" (*TLP* preface).

THERAPY AND LIBERATION

This chapter has focused so narrowly on the problem of agreement between representations and reality, on internal relations, and nonsense, that it has neglected other dimensions of the Kantian tradition and the critical method. In conclusion, let us see how some of these other dimensions are also reflected in the works of our four protagonists.

I leave it to Lichtenberg to set the tone, with two remarks about Kant. The first spans the range of positions covered in this chapter so far, the second opens the door to reflections on critical philosophy in the larger scheme of things.

> I really do believe now that the question whether the objects have a reality outside us makes no reasonable sense. By nature we are *compelled* to say about certain objects of our sensations that they are located outside of us, we can't help it . . . The question is almost as silly as whether the blue color is really *blue*. We cannot possibly go beyond the question.

> Mister Kant is certainly deserving of the not inconsiderable merit of having tidied up the physiology of our mind, but this closer knowledge of the muscles and fibers will give us neither better pianists nor better dancers.[63]

All four – Kant, Lichtenberg, Hertz, and Wittgenstein – curb the pretensions of reason. This is the narrowly critical, one might say "negative" result of their investigations. And though the critique of pure reason and language will give us neither better writers nor better readers, there are nevertheless three positives that come with that negative result.

So far, I have only highlighted the first of these positive dimensions. By subjecting to critical scrutiny reason and language, we gain knowledge about the very instruments or tools through which we hope to gain knowledge. This tells us how knowledge is possible as an internal relation between mind and world, which are only apparently dissimilar; it teaches us the limits of science and knowledge, language and reason; in short, it gives us knowledge of ourselves. As opposed perhaps to angels and other divine spirits, who can intuit matters directly, our understanding according to Kant is "discursive, picture-dependent."[64] This dependency is limitation and opportunity at once. Lichtenberg frequently remarks upon this fundamental ambivalence in our tendency to make pictures of things: "The idea that we have of a soul is in many ways similar to the idea of there being

---

[63] Lichtenberg 1968/71, L 277 (p. 189 in Lichtenberg 1990) and L 911.
[64] Kant 2000, p. 277 (page 408 of the Akademie edition).

a magnet in the earth. It is a mere picture. To conceive of all things in this form is a heuristic device innate to man."[65] We have also seen how Hertz characterizes the search for scientific and technical knowlege in terms of the pictures we form ourselves of external objects. And Wittgenstein, of course, gives us a picture theory of language.

With this knowledge of ourselves as creators of pictures comes a second positive effect, which is sometimes called therapeutic but which may also be liberating.[66] Knowledge of our limits cures us from the temptation to ask nonsensical questions to which there cannot be any answers. Kant frequently invokes the metaphor of creating a lasting peace on the battlefield of metaphysics. Lichtenberg encourages restless speculation but not where "we cannot possibly go beyond the question."[67] Hertz maintains that after the elimination of "force" as a fundamental concept "our mind, no longer vexed, will cease to ask what for it is an illegitimate question." And Wittgenstein promises that we will notice "the solution of the problem of life when this problem vanishes" (*TLP* 6.521).

This therapy saves us from bad philosophy, indeed it invites laughter at the misguided endeavors of metaphysics, and this laughter can set us free from the oppressive hold on mind and body by certain metaphysical conceptions. We have already seen how Kant makes fun of the interminable battles of the metaphysicians.

It is already a great and necessary proof of cleverness or insight to know what one should reasonably ask. For if the question is absurd in itself and demands unnecessary answers, then, besides the embarrassment of the one who proposes it, it also has the disadvantage of misleading the incautious listener into absurd answers, and presenting the ridiculous sight (as the ancients said) of one person milking a billy-goat while the other holds a sieve underneath.[68]

Knowing quite well how "to play a couple of pieces on the metaphysic," Lichtenberg notes about an anonymous metaphysician:

[65] Lichtenberg 1968/71, J 568 (p. 136 in Lichtenberg 1990).
[66] Compare Ostrow 2002, p. 1.
[67] "With greater majesty never a mind stood still" (C 25, p. 42 in Lichtenberg 1990). Compare these remarks on peace of mind: "Nothing can contribute more to peace of mind than the lack of any opinion whatever." "You ask me, friend, which is better: to be plagued by a bad conscience or with mind at peace to hang from the gallows?" (E 63 and C 247, pp. 67 and 48 in Lichtenberg 1990).
[68] Kant 1997, A58/B82f.; see also B xivf. and A4f./B8f.

"When he philosophizes he usually throws pleasant moonlight over the objects, which is pleasing on the whole but fails to distinctly show one single object."[69]

Heinrich Hertz ridicules in a long passage the intellectual contortions of traditional mechanics as it attempts to explain no physical action at all:

We see a piece of iron resting upon a table, and we accordingly imagine that no causes of motion – no forces – are present there. Physics . . . teaches us otherwise. Through the force of gravitation every atom of the iron is attracted by every other atom in the universe. But every atom of the iron is also magnetic, and is thus connected by fresh forces with every other magnetic atom in the universe. But bodies in the universe also contain electricity in motion, and this exerts further complicated forces which attract every atom of the iron. And in so far as the parts of the iron themselves contain electricity, we have yet again different forces to take into consideration; and in addition to these various kinds of molecular force. Some of these forces are not small: if only a part of these forces were effective, this part would suffice to tear the iron to pieces. But, in fact, all the forces are so adjusted among each other that the effect of this immense arsenal is zero; that in spite of a thousand existing causes of motion, no motion takes place; that the iron, after all, simply rests. Now if we place these conceptions before unprejudiced persons, who will believe us? Whom shall we convince that we are still speaking of actual things and not of fabrications by a freewheeling power of imagination?[70]

And though there are many who suspect that Wittgenstein has no humor at all – certainly not in the terse *Tractatus*! – we already saw him make light of a logical theory which requires that from the fact p follow infinitely many other facts. The *Tractatus* also offers some amusing asides like the following remark: "By the way: To say of *two* things that they are identical is nonsense, and to say of *one* that it is identical with itself, says nothing at all" (*TLP* 5.5503).[71]

Beyond humor, however, lies the final, perhaps most important shared concern of our four critical philosophers. Even as they draw so

---

[69] Lichtenberg 1968/71, J 507 and L 320 (pp. 133 and 190 in Lichtenberg 1990). See also, for example, L 298, F 1022, or the following remark, G 71 (pp. 317, 99, 108 in Lichtenberg 1990): "He marveled that cats had two holes cut in their coat just at the place where their eyes would be."

[70] Hertz 1956, p. 13.

[71] Compare *TLP* 3.323, 4.003, or 4.1272, and the verbal puns in 4.128, 5.1362, 5.5303, and 5.553; perhaps also 2.0232, 4.002, 4.014, 4.113, 4.115, 4.461, 5.61, and 6.43.

carefully the limits of knowledge and reject the metaphysical aspirations of reason, none of them imposes a limit on human imagination, yearning, or feeling. Once again, Kant formulates this most concisely when he emphasizes the "positive utility of critical principles." Since knowledge is always knowledge of objects or appearances, he argues, the attempt to gain knowledge of God, for example, would transform God into just another object. But surely, believers and unbelievers agree, this is not how one should think of God. It is more adequate therefore and even more pious to draw the limits of knowledge so narrowly that God is beyond them:

I cannot even *assume God, freedom and immortality* for the sake of the necessary practical use of my reason unless I simultaneously *deprive* speculative reason of its pretension to extravagant insights; because in order to attain to such insights, speculative reason would have to help itself to principles that in fact reach only to objects of possible experience, and which, if they were to be applied to what cannot be an object of experience, would always actually transform it into an appearance . . . Thus I had to deny *knowledge* to make room for *faith*.[72]

Lichtenberg provides a more general and in this instance also more poetic formulation of this point: "I imagine that where we reach the limits of things as they have been set for us, or even before we reach them, we can see into the infinite, just as from the surface of the earth we look out into immeasurable space."[73]

Such praise of limits can even be found in the narrowly scientific context of Heinrich Hertz's work. He notes that his mechanics cannot account for "even the lowest process of life":

That this is so seems to me not a disadvantage but rather an advantage of our law. Precisely because it affords us to synoptically view the whole of mechanics, it also shows us the limits of this whole. Precisely because it gives us only a fact without attributing to it the semblance of necessity, it lets us recognize that everything could also be different.[74]

---

[72] Kant 1997, B xxixf.

[73] Lichtenberg 1968/71, D 312 (p. 58 in Lichtenberg 1990), but see also the following variant on the theme: "Reason now peers from above on the realm of dark but warm feelings as the Alpine peaks do above the clouds. They behold the sun more clearly and distinctly, but they are cold and barren. Boasting of their height." And regarding the interplay between critical self-limitation and hope of something more: "To be sure, I can't say whether things will be better, once they are different; but this much I can say, they have to be different if they are to be good" (L 406 and K 293, p. 191 in Lichtenberg 1990).

[74] Hertz 1956, p. 38.

Related to this, Hertz offers another reason for limiting his mechanics in this manner. That reason is very similar to the one given by Kant: the term "force" blurs the boundary between living beings and dead matter; it therefore invites the treatment of the living being as just another mechanical object. This, Hertz says, would "offend against a feeling which is sound and natural. It is therefore more cautious to limit the probable validity of the law to inanimate systems."[75]

Wittgenstein will have the last word, of course. He, too, "denies *knowledge* to make room for *faith*." Those who believe that they can talk just as sensibly about absolute or ethical value as they can about cars and cookies are actually conflating them. According to them, "that an experience has absolute value *is just a fact like other facts*." Wittgenstein rebels against this conflation since it diminishes the intent of our ethical or religious tendencies (just as "God" is diminished when transformed into a mere object of experience by our claims to have knowledge in matters of faith):

My whole tendency and I believe the tendency of all men who ever tried to write or talk Ethics or Religion was to run against the boundaries of language. This running against the walls of our cage is perfectly, absolutely hopeless. Ethics so far as it springs from the desire to say something about the ultimate meaning of life, the absolute good, the absolute valuable, can be no science. What it says does not add to our knowledge in any sense. But it is a document of a tendency in the human mind which I personally cannot help respecting deeply and I would not for my life ridicule it.[76]

---

[75] Ibid., § 320.
[76] "Lecture on Ethics" (LE), p. 44. Compare *PI*, p. 119: "The results of philosophy are the discovery of some or another plain nonsense and bruises that the understanding has got by running up against the limits of language. The bruises let us recognize the value of that discovery."

CHAPTER 2

The argument

We have now seen why one might want to declare nonsensical all sentences except for the propositions of logic and science and our ordinary descriptions of the world. Within the critical tradition this amounts to a perfectly sensible determination of the limits of language and knowledge. What we have not seen as yet is why we should draw those limits where Wittgenstein draws them.

The previous chapter presented an assortment of sometimes compelling philosophical convictions, it suggested motivations and showed how the views of Kant, Lichtenberg, Hertz, and Wittgenstein reenforce each other, but it did not give us more than hints of how to defend their critical conclusions. We might agree, for example, that it is better to dismiss certain questions as nonsensical rather than to remain haunted forever by the inadequacy of all proposed answers. But do we really have a credible account of the agreement between representations and reality, and does it really make us see how all metaphysical matters are evidently nonsensical?

We must therefore begin to investigate how Wittgenstein makes his case in the *Tractatus*, how he establishes his conclusions about sense and nonsense, and then, of course, whether his argument is invalidated because, on his own terms, he writes philosophy in the nonsensical language of unphilosophy.

STRICTLY PHILOSOPHICAL AND
SIMULTANEOUSLY LITERARY

In two famous letters to a prospective publisher of the *Tractatus*, Wittgenstein provides a few hints to the novice reader of his book. The first of these letters inquires only whether Herr Ludwig von

Ficker, editor of the journal *Der Brenner*, would want to look at the manuscript:

> About a year before becoming a prisoner of war I finished a philosophical work on which I had worked for the preceding seven years. It is essentially the presentation of a system. And this presentation is *extremely* compact since I have only recorded in it what – and how it has – really occurred to me . . . The work is strictly philosophical and simultaneously literary, and yet there is no blathering in it.

A little later, in October or November 1919, he submitted the manuscript to von Ficker and added more detailed instructions:

> But now I am counting on you. And there it may be of some help to you if I write you a few words about my book: since – I am quite sure of that – you won't get very much at all out of reading it. For, you won't understand it; its subject matter will appear entirely foreign to you. But in reality it isn't foreign to you, for the sense of the book is an ethical one. I once wanted to include a sentence in the preface which doesn't in fact appear there now. But I am writing it to you now because it might serve you as a key: For I wanted to write that my work consists of two parts: the one you have in front of you and all that I have *not* written. And just that second part is the important one. Because the ethical is delimited by my book as it were from within; and I am convinced that *strictly* it can *only* be delimited like that. In short, I believe: Everything that *many* are *blathering* about today, I settled by being silent about it. And that's why this book, unless I am very mistaken, says much that you yourself want to say, but perhaps you won't see that it is said in it. I would now recommend that you read the *preface* and the *conclusion*, since these express the sense most immediately.[1]

Aside from suggesting that the *Tractatus* presents an overarching train of thought which is announced in the preface and carried to a conclusion at the end, these letters emphasize that Wittgenstein's presentation records only what occurred to him and also *how* it occurred to him. By presenting what occurred to him, his book is "strictly philosophical." By preserving how and under what conditions this occurred to him, the book is "at the same time literary." This emphasis on the dual character of the book, philosophical as well as literary, can also be found in the preface of the *Tractatus*:

---

[1] "Letters to Ludwig von Ficker" (LvF), pp. 32–35. The first of these two letters is extensively quoted and the second reproduced in its entirety also in von Wright 1982, pp. 81–83.

If this work has a value it consists in two things. First that in it thoughts are expressed, and this value will be the greater the better the thoughts are expressed. The more the nail has been hit on the head. – Here I am conscious that I have fallen far short of what is possible. Simply because my powers are insufficient to cope with the task. – May others come and do it better.

On the other hand the *truth* of the thoughts communicated here seems to me unassailable and definitive. I am therefore of the opinion that the problems have in essentials been finally solved. And if I am not mistaken in this, then the value of this work secondly consists in that it shows how little has been achieved when these problems are solved.

Though Wittgenstein claims here to solve once and for all the problems of philosophy, the value of his book does not consist in this. Its philosophical value consists in showing that almost everything remains untouched by this solution. And its equally important literary value consists in the fact that thoughts are expressed in it, hopefully without blathering and hopefully well.

This and the next chapter follow Wittgenstein's lead and treat the philosophical and the literary character of his book separately. Only in chapters 4 and 5 will we pursue the suggestion that the book really "has *a* [single] value," which "consists in *two* things." Before considering the interplay, perhaps mutual dependency of the literary and philosophical dimensions of the *Tractatus*, let us begin by considering the thoughts that occurred to Wittgenstein and how they add up to an overarching train of thought.

IDENTIFYING THE CONCLUSION

The *Tractatus Logico-Philosophicus* clarifies the business of logic, it proposes the picture theory of language, details the internal relation between representation and reality, offers a philosophy of science, and includes reflections on ethics, aesthetics, and the will. With all this and more going on, how can we even speak of an overarching argument in the *Tractatus*?[2]

Only interpretive success can establish the plausibility of the claim that from the preface to the concluding remarks Wittgenstein

---

[2] By arguing for a linear overarching argument, this chapter also takes issue with Eli Friedlander's suggestion that the *Tractatus* does not move from the preface to a conclusion, but that it has a circular structure (2001, pp. 17 and 22f., but see p. 15).

expresses a single, perhaps "ethical" sense. In the meantime, it may serve us to recall that in the critical tradition all the particular philosophical points are subservient to the critical task of delimiting reason or language from within, and of showing that what lies on the other side of the limit is unknowable or nonsensical. If delimitation is the critical goal, our reconstruction of Wittgenstein's argument might begin by specifying this goal: where is the conclusion that states the intended limitation and that is established by the overarching argument of the *Tractatus*?

We naturally look for the conclusion at the very end of a book, and there we find the remark that carries the number 7: "Whereof one cannot speak, about that one must be silent." Our suspicion might be confirmed by Wittgenstein's remark to von Ficker that preface and conclusion "express the sense most immediately." Also, in the preface we find Wittgenstein announcing his conclusion:

The book deals with the problems of philosophy and shows, as I believe, that the formulation of these problems rests on a misunderstanding of the logic of our language. Its entire sense could be summed up somewhat as follows: what can be said at all can be said clearly; and whereof one cannot talk about that one must be silent.

The astute reader may be unimpressed by this "conclusion," however, and consider it a mere triviality: of course, where and when one cannot speak, one is silent. The apparent triviality becomes meaningful only if one sees it as a corollary to remark 6.522: "There is indeed the inexpressible. This *shows* itself; it is the mystical." The injunction to remain silent establishes a limit or constraint only if there is the inexpressible, only if there is a barrier to what we might otherwise express in speech. I therefore propose that we should consider as the conclusion of Wittgenstein's overarching argument that "There is indeed the inexpressible" or, translated more accurately, that "There is indeed the inexpressible in speech."

These few words deserve closer scrutiny, if only because they are carefully crafted to admit of various interpretations. First of all, there is that curious construction "inexpressible in speech," English for "*unaussprechlich.*" In ordinary contexts, the German "*aussprechen*" concerns our ability to clearly speak, pronounce, or articulate words. As such, the German word is a hybrid of sorts between "*ausdrücken* (to express, quite literally in the sense of squeezing out)" and "*sprechen* (to speak)." Wittgenstein's use of "*aussprechen*" and the translation "express in speech" therefore reflects that the word refers to a particular mode of expression. When we express something in a gesture, sentence, or song, we give it an external manifestation of sorts: we make a feeling or an idea public by putting it into that gesture, sentence, or song. "*Aussprechen*" is a special case of "*ausdrücken*" or expression: it concerns what we put into words or language, thus suggesting yet another translation of *TLP* 6.522: "There is indeed what cannot be put into words."[3]

Why does it matter whether we get this translation just right, why can we not simply write "There is indeed the unsayable"? Though "to say" and "to express" can be used interchangeably, Wittgenstein employs them very differently and reserves "to say" for a rather narrow context. Saying has nothing to do with expression and need not involve a human subject at all, as when Wittgenstein writes: "'p' says p" (*TLP* 5.542). Taken by itself, a sentence is merely a picture of a possible state of affairs – only when it is said or asserted does that sentence become a claim, true or false, concerning some particular state of affairs. So if "saying" only relates to sentences in the first place and as it were switches them on, the statement that there is indeed the unsayable would have to mean that there are otherwise impeccable sentences which, for some reason or another, cannot be asserted. This is not at all what Wittgenstein's conclusion is about, however. We notice that something is "inexpressible in speech" when we fail in our efforts to create a sentence in the first place, when we fail to give meaning.[4]

---

[3] Thus, in this book, "express" is a more general term and not shorthand for "express in speech." By way of translation, one might also try "There is indeed the unspeakable," were it not for the many meanings of indescribable horror or moral offense that have accumulated around the "unspeakable" in English. Compare also Engelmann 1967, p. 7, which translates "*unaussprechlich*" as "unutterable."

[4] To be sure, there is a passage in the *Tractatus* (*TLP* 4.113–4.116) which suggests a conflation of the "sayable" and the "expressible in speech" (and the "thinkable"). It elaborates the two aspects of the critical task of philosophy – delimiting the unthinkable from within the thinkable and indicating the unsayable by clearly presenting the sayable. Diamond 2000, pp. 149f. points out that these two aspects of the task are not identical (see the preface of the *TLP*). They overlap, however, in that the clear presentation of the sayable provides a paradigm for what can be clearly thought and also for what can be clearly expressed in speech. Now, this use of "unsayable" does not bear on whether the construction "there is indeed the unsayable" is

So, rather than involve Wittgenstein's technical notion of saying, *TLP* 6.522 concerns what can or cannot be expressed, pronounced, or articulated in speech. What we produce or make manifest in the act of speaking are words, sentences, pictures, and facts (since sentences are pictures and pictures are facts; *TLP* 4.021, 2.141). One example of what we cannot produce or make manifest in the act of speaking is things:

> I can only *mention* the objects. Signs represent them. I can only speak *of* them, *express them in speech* I cannot. (*TLP* 3.221)

> What if there were something outside the *facts*? Which our sentences are unable to express? But there we have the *things*, for example, *and we feel no desire at all* to express them in sentences.[5]

While we may feel a desire to express thoughts, feelings, values, ideas, and somehow ourselves in speech, it does not even occur to us that we should express things or objects in speech: we are quite content merely to express their names, that is, to refer to them, to name or mention them. But what is important to Wittgenstein is that facts can be expressed in speech, and we do so by producing particular configurations of words that share a logical form with configurations of objects and that can therefore picture them, agree with them, and so on. So, things are one example of what is inexpressible in speech. While we have no desire to do so in their case, the concluding remarks of the *Tractatus* suggest that there are other cases where we may have

---

possible. *TLP* 4.115 states only that the clear presentation of the sayable creates a contrast-class of the unsayable ("[philosophy] will indicate (*bedeuten*) the unsayable by clearly presenting the sayable"). In other words, philosophy tells us what is required for a sentence to be assertible; ungrammatical sentences and logical truths are "unsayable." Even if one chose, less plausibly, a mystical translation of "*bedeuten*" ("[philosophy] will hint at (*bedeuten*) the unsayable") this would not yet imply that the realm hinted at is a realm of being. Incidentally, *TLP* 4.115 is the only occurrence of "sayable" and "unsayable" in the *Tractatus*. This stands in striking contrast to the liberal use of these terms in interpretations of the *Tractatus*.

5 *NB*, May 27, 1915. *TLP* 3.221 juxtaposes "*sprechen* von (to speak *of*)" and "*sie* [*die Dinge*] *aussprechen* (to express them [the things] in speech)." The second passage from the *Notebooks* provides a context for the formulation of *TLP* 3.221 on which it elaborates by asking what our sentences cannot express ("*was unsere Sätze nicht auszudrücken vermögen*"). Together, the four remarks of May 17, 1915 clearly indicate that Wittgenstein equates "*aussprechen*" with "*in Sätzen ausdrücken* (to express in sentences)." (Remember that the contrast to expressible in speech is expressible in music, expressible through a gesture, expressible through the life one leads, etc.)

a desire to do so: "There is indeed the inexpressible in speech. This shows itself; it is the mystical."[6]

At this point arises a second question of interpretation, and this one relates to the two words "there is." One straightforward way of reading *TLP* 6.522 adds another word to it: "There is indeed *something* inexpressible in speech." This interpretation takes the remark to have what logicians call existential import: it tells us that something exists in the world, namely the mystical or the higher. Though we may not know what these terms refer to (they are not names of objects), they do refer to *something*. And while we cannot speak of the mystical or the higher, we are literally silent *about* it, indeed, our silence gestures toward this ineffable realm of being.

Another way of reading Wittgenstein's remark avoids existential import or a claim about the existence of a something that is inexpressible in speech. *TLP* 6.522 may just be the denial of the sweeping assertion "Everything I desire to express in speech *is* expressible in speech." In this broadly confident statement, the "everything I desire to express" is not limited to existing somethings but corresponds to a perfectly generic "whatever it may be that I desire to express." Against this confidence, Wittgenstein's remark answers "No, not everything you desire to express in speech is expressible in speech: there is indeed the inexpressible in speech. The failure of your sweeping claim shows itself, and what you run up against in your failure is what we might call the mystical." In other words, when *TLP* 7 requires that "whereof one

---

[6] The second half of this remark casts a curious light on the example of things: we can see how things might show themselves, but in which sense are they mystical? If we assume that they are inaccessible like Kant's thing in itself, this would echo the considerations of chapter 1: the circumstance that things are inexpressible in speech while facts are expressible, exemplifies that agreement between object and representation is an internal relation. Things are very different from thoughts, feelings, values, ideas, Kant's phenomena, or Wittgenstein's facts. Only the things are strictly "out there," we have no direct acquaintance with them, etc. Also, while things cannot be expressed in speech, we can speak *of* them, that is, we need not be silent about them. In order to construe *TLP* 7 as a corollary of 6.522, the latter must concern the nontrivial case of what is inexpressible in speech and neither named or referred to in a sentence. In other words, the example of things does not suffice to establish Wittgenstein's conclusion. As we will see, the case of ethics does establish it. It also illustrates just how important it is to distinguish between "expression" in general and the special case of "expression in speech." While sentences cannot express (*ausdrücken*) ethics or anything higher (*TLP* 6.42), and while ethics cannot be expressed in speech (*aussprechen*, *TLP* 6.421), the *Tractatus* nowhere suggests that ethics cannot be expressed at all, for example through conduct or action.

cannot speak, about that one must be silent," the notion of "about-ness" carries no promise: our silence may well be a silence about nothing.

While there has been some debate about choosing the correct reading of *TLP* 6.522 and 7,[7] the matter might have to remain open. Indeed, we should consider that in the tradition of critical philosophy the issue is undecidable – and rightly so: we would go beyond the limits of language or reason if we attempted to determine whether or not a something corresponds to what is inexpressible in speech. On this account, *TLP* 6.522 and 7 are artfully or systematically ambiguous – noncommittal by design.

There is one more problem regarding Wittgenstein's conclusion in *TLP* 6.522. He anticipates that problem in *TLP* 4.127: "The question concerning the existence of a formal concept is nonsensical. For no sentence can answer such a question. (Thus one cannot ask, for example: 'Are there unanalyzable subject–predicate sentences?')" Surely, if one cannot ask, let alone answer whether there are subject-predicate sentences that cannot be analyzed,[8] then one cannot ask, let alone decree whether there is what is inexpressible in speech. Wittgenstein's remark thus appears to be intriguingly self-exemplifying – nonsensical, a failure to express something, or a sign of there being the "inexpressible in speech"?[9]

While this last problem refers us to chapters 4 and 5, our next step is to show how the *Tractatus* establishes its conclusion.

[7] See, for example, Conant 1989, Diamond 1991 and 2000, and Hacker 2000.
[8] The example refers to a discussion (with or against Russell) at the very beginning of the *Notebooks*. The statement "There is (no) subject-predicate sentence of this kind" does not relate a predicate to a subject. While we can decide for any given subject-predicate sentence whether it has sense and, if yes, whether it is true or false, there are no such decision procedures for "there is" sentences. Unrestricted claims of existence like these do not concern what is or is not the case; they concern what shall count as, say, an "unanalyzable subject-predicate sentence" – and this depends entirely on what we mean by our terms. Instead of a determination of truth or falsity, we are getting into a dispute about definitions.
[9] I will spare the reader a digression regarding the only unscrutinized word in remark 6.522 – the "indeed" which is a translation of "*allerdings.*" This term does not necessarily provide emphasis, it can also qualify a remark. One can ask "*gibt es das?* (does this exist?)" and answer "*das gibt es allerdings* (yes, indeed, it exists)." One can also say "*es ist allerdings wahr, dass es das gibt, aber* (while it is true that such a thing exists)" or "*dann gibt es allerdings noch* (then, however, there is also this)." Again, Wittgenstein's remark admits of both readings. Such issues of translation are the reason why, starting with the first English edition of the *Tractatus* in 1922, all of his works have been published bilingually with German and English on facing sides – a treatment usually reserved for dead poets.

THE PERFORMANCE OF FAILURE

We have just discovered the systematic ambiguity of the statement that there is indeed the inexpressible in speech – does it refer to a really existing, yet inexpressible something, or does it contradict our supreme confidence that we can express in speech whatever we wish to express? Accordingly, one might think that two rather different strategies are required to establish this conclusion.

If one wanted to establish that there is something that is inexpressible in speech, a suitable argument would appeal to some kind of evidence: *here* is something that is inexpressible in speech. Such an argument would consist of two parts. First one identifies a thought or feeling that supposedly stands for something real. Then one produces a proof of the limits of language. Properly put together (ensuring that the meanings are clear and stable over the course of the entire argument), the two parts might establish that the thought or feeling lies *beyond* the limits of language and is therefore inexpressible *in* speech.

Now if someone wanted to deny once and for all that everything is expressible in speech, a suitable argument would proceed quite differently. It would begin with an illusion,[10] namely the hopeful conviction that I can express in speech whatever it may be that I desire to express. Sooner or later, and try as one may, one will encounter failure while attempting to follow through on that conviction, and this failure establishes the conclusion. Instead of piecing together various parts of an argument, this strategy consists of a single movement that starts out with an illusion and ends in disillusionment, a movement that requires no interpretation but only the frustration of confidence.

As different as they appear, these two strategies combine fairly easily, and their combination allows Wittgenstein to establish both versions of his conclusion at once. Wittgenstein illustrates this especially well in his "Lecture on Ethics," where he begins with an appeal to evidence, namely a meaningful experience, then tries to put that experience into words and finds that he succeeds only to the extent that he strips his experience of its essential content. What he therefore runs up against

[10] This is Cora Diamond's term in Diamond 2000.

is a failure to express that essential content in language. A reflection
on the nature of sentences then shows why this failure is inevitable.

Wittgenstein begins this argument in the "Lecture on Ethics" by
describing certain experiences of the absolute, for example the feeling
of absolute safety in a Vienna theatre. He then turns to another feeling,
namely his desire to express in language that something is absolutely
good: "the *absolute good*, if it is a describable state of affairs, would
be one which everybody, independent of his tastes and inclinations,
would *necessarily* bring about or would feel guilty for not bringing
about."[11] The absolute good does not just happen to be good, it cannot
be otherwise. Its goodness does not depend on anything, it is not a
matter of choice which would allow us to say: "This state of affairs
could be good or not good, let's call it (absolutely) good."

But try as he may, Wittgenstein cannot express this notion of "absolute goodness" in language. After all, any sentence in our language has
the feature that it is easily negated – all we need to do is add a "not"
to it and "This state of affairs is (absolutely) good" becomes "This
state of affairs is not good." There is thus an ineluctable element of
choice in asserting or negating the sentence, since language moves
easily between both. Like all sentences, therefore, "this is absolutely
good" is contingent and not absolute. Whether we actually assert or
negate it will depend on something, and this something is what can
make the sentence true or false. Indeed, as with all sentences, the
meaning or significance of this one will come from knowing what
would make it true: we will call something absolutely good if such
and such conditions are satisfied (our mood is right, a standard has
been met, and so on) and, accordingly, our assertion "this is absolutely
good" will end up meaning "the mood is right" or "the standard has
been met." But yet again, the whole point of "absolutely good" is that
it is unconditionally good, that nothing is required to make it so – it
just is.

Our desire to express this sense of absolute value in language thus
ends up with sentences that can only express contingency and what
happens to be. They never express what absolutely must be just as it
is. Is there really no way out of this dilemma "that we cannot express
what we want to express"?[12] Someone might suggest "that after all

[11] LE, p. 40.   [12] Ibid., p. 44.

what we mean by saying that an experience has absolute value *is just a fact like other facts.*" But this is exactly the point: a fact just like other facts can be expressed in language, but we would strip the notion of "absolute good" of its essential content if we considered it a fact just like other facts: "no statement of fact can ever be, or imply, a statement of absolute value."[13] Facts are what happen to be the case, they are contingent and not absolute. And statements of fact are significant or have sense because we can tell what would make them true or false. "Now when [it] is urged against me," Wittgenstein therefore continues, that the experience of absolute value is just a fact,

I at once see clearly, as it were in a flash of light, not only that no description that I can think of would do to describe what I mean by absolute value, but that I would reject every significant description that anybody could possibly suggest, *ab initio*, on the ground of its significance . . . For all I wanted to do . . . was just *to go beyond* the world and that is to say beyond significant language.

All of this illustrates how in 1929 Wittgenstein combined the two strategies: he used for evidence a familiar experience or desire and then subjected it to a motion that began with confidence and ended in failure, proving moreover that this failure was unavoidable: the desire is at odds with the world, and its failure establishes the inexpressibility of absolute value in language. And to say that absolute value is indeed inexpressible in speech leaves quite open whether absolute values are somethings such as, for example, objects in a Platonic realm of eternal ethical ideas. Indeed, it leaves open whether there are absolute values or whether the notion of absolute value makes sense in the first place.

Unlike the "Lecture on Ethics," the *Tractatus Logico-Philosophicus* does not tell a story of how we start and what happens then, nor does it adopt the strategy it recommends as the right method of philosophy.

The right method of philosophy would really be this: to say nothing but what can be said, that is, the sentences of natural science – that is something that has nothing to do with philosophy – and then always, whenever others want to say something metaphysical, to reveal to them that they had failed to give meaning to certain signs in their sentences. (*TLP* 6.53)

[13] Ibid., p. 39.

The "right method of philosophy" would also frustrate the desire to express what cannot be expressed. Following this method, however, Wittgenstein would not be demonstrating why it is impossible to express a notion of absolute value in a language that renders everything contingent. Instead, he would let the desire of others run up against his constant question "What do you mean?" And whenever we would think that we had succeeded in creating a meaningful sentence, Wittgenstein would show us either that it is still not meaningful, or – if meaningful – that it expresses something rather different from what we had been trying to express, namely a contingent matter of fact and not some unassailable metaphysical truth.[14]

Wittgenstein's description of the right method of philosophy remains programmatic, of course. While this is how it should be, it cannot be like that in a book. The *Tractatus* thus recommends a method of philosophy that it itself cannot pursue.

Instead of telling a story about the failure to express the absolute, and instead of listening silently while others fail to give meaning, the *Tractatus* uses the picture theory of language to show "that we cannot express what we want to express." Or perhaps one should say that the discovery of the picture theory showed Wittgenstein that we cannot remain confident about being able to express in speech any sense whatsoever. Omitting only a brief technical aside, here in its entirety is the passage from Wittgenstein's *Notebooks* in which the picture theory makes its dramatic appearance (which Wittgenstein accentuated here and in the continuation via a liberal use of exclamation marks).

26.9.14
What is the basis of our – surely well-founded – confidence that we shall be able to express any sense whatsoever in our two-dimensional script?

27.9.14
After all, a sentence can only express its sense by being its logical depiction! . . .

29.9.14
The general concept of the sentence carries with it also a completely general concept of the co-ordination of sentence and state of affairs: the solution to all my questions must be *extremely* simple!

---

[14] He does this in ibid., p. 38: "the word good in the relative sense simply means coming up to a certain standard. Thus when we say that this man is a good pianist we mean that he can play pieces of a certain degree of difficulty with a certain degree of dexterity."

In a sentence a world is put together experimentally. (As when a traffic accident is represented in the Paris courtroom by means of dolls, etc.)

This must yield the nature of truth immediately (unless I were blind).

Consider hieroglyphic scripts in which every word represents its meaning! Consider that *actual* pictures of states of affairs can be *correct* and *incorrect*.

≫ㅅㅊ≪: If in this picture the figure on the right represents the man A, and the one on the left designates man B, then the whole might state something like "A fights with B." The sentence in pictorial script can be true and false. It has a sense independent of its truth or falsity. Everything essential must be demonstrable in regard to it.

One can say that while we are not certain that we can put all states of affairs as pictures onto paper, yet we are certain that we can depict all the *logical* properties of states of affairs in our two-dimensional script.

We are still very much on the surface, but apparently on a good trajectory.[15]

Wittgenstein's exploration of the "surely well-founded" confidence that any sense whatsoever can be expressed in the two-dimensional script of our language thus leads him to the realization that we can be confident only that the logical properties of states of affairs can be so expressed: his original confidence was not so well founded, after all.[16] Indeed, the very first step of his exploration spells doom for his initial confidence: it introduces a notion of "sense" so narrow that it cannot possibly accommodate "any sense whatsoever."

When Wittgenstein takes note of our confidence that we shall be able to express in language any sense whatsoever, he uses the term "sense" in a general, nonlinguistic manner. This notion of sense (the German is "*Sinn*") encompasses our ideas concerning the meaning of life, the significance of a gesture, custom or action, the meaning of an artwork or feeling – in short, everything that either makes sense or is meaningful (has sense). About all these kinds of sense

[15] For more exclamation marks see the subsequent entries on September 30 ("A picture can represent relations that do not exist!!!"), October 2 and 3.
[16] In earlier discussions, Wittgenstein is less clear about the difference between "a language which *can* express everything" and "a language which can express or *say* everything that *can* be said"; see his "Notes dictated to G. E. Moore" from April 1914 included in *NB*, p. 108. In contrast, *TLP* 4.002 presupposes an already established notion of specifically linguistic sense when it declares that human beings have the ability to construct languages "capable of expressing every sense."

Wittgenstein asks why we are so confident that we can express them in language.

His answer begins with the reminder that sentences can only express what they (logically) depict. The sense of a sentence is therefore limited from the very beginning to what is depictable. While we can picture how things are or might be, we do not picture the meaning of life, what sense an action makes, and so on. Indeed, if a sentence puts a world together experimentally, it is not a suitable vehicle to express what does not resemble a world and is not put together or assembled like a factual or hypothetical state of affairs. The characterization of what a sentence is draws a narrow limit to what counts as "sense" in the realm of language: "In the sentence a situation is as it were put together experimentally. One can just about say: instead of, this sentence has this or that sense; this sentence represents this or that situation" (*TLP* 4.031).[17]

Just as the attempt to express absolute value in language always finds itself expressing contingent but not absolute matters, so the attempt to express any sense whatsoever in two-dimensional script will always end up expressing a picturable state of affairs or nothing at all.

In the "Lecture on Ethics," according to the "right method of philosophy," and also in this crucial passage from the *Notebooks* we begin with the confident pursuit of a desire and find that it runs up against certain limits that contradict our confidence. In all three cases we are therefore dealing with variants of an argument known as *reductio ad absurdum*. We will see that the *Tractatus* also adopts this style of argument to establish its conclusion. Indeed, I will argue that it does so in a rather precise manner.[18]

---

[17] The second half of *TLP* 4.031 appears in the *Notebooks* on October 2, 1914 – still in the wake of the newly discovered picture theory.

[18] I will point out below that my reconstruction of the argument differs from extant *reductio*-interpretations (which emphasize the self-defeating aspect of the *Tractatus*, see p. 8 above and Sullivan 2004, p. 38) by considering a method of indirect proof that establishes a conclusion. Meredith Williams lists three familiar approaches: "The standard interpretation construes *T* 6.54 as Wittgenstein's acknowledgement that his theory of meaning undercuts the mean- ingfulness of the sentences used to state that theory. Here Wittgenstein tolerates paradox, using the doctrine of showing to ameliorate its irrationality. The austere interpretation con- strues the passage as the key to understanding the *Tractatus* as a whole. Paradox is no part of the *Tractatus*, but is an illusion created by the meaningless word strings that constitute the corpus of the text. The *reductio* interpretation makes paradox the point of the work, which

INDIRECT PROOF

Here is an example of a typical *reductio ad absurdum*, what logicians also call indirect proof. It starts with the claim that Ludwig Wittgenstein died in World War I. From this claim it follows that the *Tractatus* was never published. This then implies that these words about the argument of the *Tractatus* would not have been written. And from this it finally follows that you are not reading these words. But this is absurd since you *are* reading them. We thus arrive at a contradiction: you know that you are reading these words and our claim implies that you are not. But when a deduction leads into a contradiction, we know that there is *something* wrong with the premises – they cannot all be true. (A valid deductive argument with premises that are all true must have a true conclusion; a contradiction, however, cannot be true, it cannot be the case that you are and are not reading these words now.) So, if the premises cannot all be true, which one is the culprit? In this case, there appears to be only one candidate, namely the claim that Wittgenstein died in World War I. By "reducing this claim to absurdity," that is, by showing that it leads us to a contradiction, we establish that it cannot be true and provide an indirect or negative proof that Wittgenstein did not die in World War I.

Here is a formal representation of this argument as one might find it in a textbook of logic.[19]

is to repudiate the entire picture theory of language on the grounds that it is self-defeating" (Williams 2004, p. 26). The following adds a fourth or "indirect proof" interpretation where paradox serves to establish a conclusion regarding the limits of language. (David Stern 2003 provides a more comprehensive taxonomoy of readings: logical atomist, logical positivist, metaphysical, irrationalist, and therapeutic – the current approach reconciles the therapeutic reading with the logical positivist and metaphysical ones.)

[19] Each letter represents a sentence (p: Wittgenstein died; q: the *Tractatus* was published, etc.), "⊃" means "if-then" and "¬" means "not" (p ⊃ ¬q: if p then not q). Our hypothesis is designated as H. For each subsequent step of the argument we indicate whether it represents a background assumption (B) or whether it was derived from previous statements by some standard rule of inference (MP, C, RAA). Background assumptions are supposedly unproblematic statements that could be logical theorems, truisms, or undisputed matters of fact. The rule MP ("*modus ponens*," sometimes translated "affirming the antecedent") allows us to infer q from the two premises p ⊃ q and p. The "conjunction" rule C allows us to combine any two premises (p and q on separate lines become p & q on one line). RAA (*reductio ad absurdum*) states that ¬H can be inferred once a contradiction is shown to follow from the hypothetical assumption H (if necessary, with the help of one or several Bs).

(1)	Ludwig Wittgenstein died in World War I.	p	H(ypothesis)
(2)	If Ludwig Wittgenstein died in World War I, the *Tractatus* was never published.	p ⊃ ¬q	B(ackground assumption)
(3)	So, the *Tractatus* was never published.	¬q	M(*odus*) P(*onens*) from lines 1 and 2
(4)	If the *Tractatus* was never published, these words were not written.	¬q ⊃ ¬r	B
(5)	So, these words were not written.	¬r	MP from 3 and 4
(6)	If these words were not written, you are not reading them.	¬r ⊃ ¬s	B
(7)	So, you are not reading these words.	¬s	MP from 5 and 6
(8)	You are reading these words.	s	B
(9)	You are and you are not reading these words.	s & ¬s	C(onjunction) of 7 and 8
(10)	Therefore, Wittgenstein did not die in World War I.	∴ ¬p	RAA (*reductio ad absurdum*) from 1 to 9

All *reductio*-arguments begin with a claim or hypothesis (H). The vertical line indicates that a hypothesis has been introduced and that we are temporarily relying on it. The vertical line thus signals a change of the grammatical mood in a deductive argument that ordinarily proceeds in the indicative mood where one assertion prepares for or follows from another. For example, an ordinary deductive argument sounds like this: "Since it *is true* that all critical philosophers establish limits of meaningful expression and that Wittgenstein was a critical philosopher, it *follows* that Wittgenstein established such limits."[20] In contrast, the hypothetical character of the *reductio ad absurdum* places the argument into a subjunctive "what if" mood, as indicated by the vertical line: "What *would follow*, if the hypothesis *were true*?"

---

[20] This formulation presents a particular instance of an argument that has the general form *modus ponens*. In this instance, the truth of the premises is asserted. Logicians typically study only the forms themselves and these are indifferent to the actual truth or falsity of the premises (a valid argument will continue to be valid even if the premises are false). In other words, instances of deductive arguments (other than *reductio*-arguments) typically occur in the indicative mood.

All successful *reductio*-arguments culminate in a contradiction that immediately establishes the falsity of the hypothesis. At this point, we leave the hypothetical mode, the vertical line ends, and we reach a positive conclusion.

The *reductio*-argument or indirect proof demonstrates the impossibility of maintaining a hypothesis: one can no longer uphold it once the implied contradiction reveals its absurdity. Since a contradiction is utterly meaningless (one cannot mean what it professes to say), we would obviously fail to preserve the meaningfulness of our thoughts were we to add the hypothesis to the stock of our beliefs. While we might discover this problem by ourselves as we subject H to a "what if" test, we could also be taught through the "right method of philosophy": one person confidently maintains a hypothesis or belief, the other does not offer an opposing point of view but through a series of questions elicits that the hypothesis is untenable. Whether by ourselves or through dialogue, the procedure resembles a thought experiment: "So this is what you think; let's try this out and see where it takes us." The thought experiment thus provides an internal critique of the hypothesis, a criticism from within. It presupposes only what we take to be the shared beliefs B and does not invoke a different point of view or any opinion that stands outside the hypothesis and our shared beliefs.

While these features of *reductio*-arguments are familiar by now from our various examples, other features will become important later on. We might note, for example, that the conclusion of this argument is only as strong as our faith in the background assumptions B. The contradiction tells us nothing more than that one of the premises must be wrong: it points to H as the culprit only if we can be quite sure that our background assumptions are true. The *reductio*-argument will persuade only those who have already agreed that the hypothesis is much weaker, far more vulnerable than any of the other premises.[21]

---

[21] For the sake of illustration, imagine someone who believes that the weakest premise in our example is (4): "If the *Tractatus* was never published, these words were not written." This person firmly believes that Wittgenstein died in World War I and, consequently, that the *Tractatus* was never published. But she has no problem imagining writers who disguise their own views by taking as their subject a fictitious philosophical work. She will argue that the *reductio*-argument exposes the absurdity of the assumption that just because the book

The contradiction reveals at once a definitive conclusion only thanks to this antecedent agreement. And only thus, once the hypothesis is consumed in contradiction, does its negative after-image immediately appear: it shows itself.

Finally, the *reductio*-argument is peculiar in that it moves in two directions at once: it proceeds forward from the hypothesis, deducing its consequences or articulating its implications. All the while, however, it aims to reflect back on the hypothesis and evaluates it. In this way *reductio*-arguments resemble the so-called transcendental arguments of Kant and the Kantian tradition. These are arguments that begin with something given (science, experience, language, and so on) and develop, analyze, or articulate it by reflecting on its preconditions. A transcendental philosophy such as Kant's therefore provides a theory of science and experience as well as (simultaneously) a theory of what must be the case if science and experience are to be possible in the first place. One might say that the hypothesis of a successful *reductio*-argument has failed to pass a transcendental test: as we articulate its implications, we discover that its condition of possibility is not satisfied.[22] And unlike any other deductive argument, once the hypothesis has failed this test, we may never appeal to it again. Indeed, the whole *reductio*-argument must be thrown out and none of the inferential steps that led to its conclusion can ever be cited again.[23] We may as well erase them from memory: every inference was tainted by the fact that in light of our concluding contradiction, the hypothesis was not even possible to start with.

THE HYPOTHESIS OF THE *TRACTATUS*

A *reductio*-argument serves as a ladder enabling us to reach our conclusion, and once we arrive, the ladder must be thrown away.

does not exist, I could not sit down and pretend to write these words about it. (Maybe we can persuade her by showing her a copy of the *Tractatus*, thus producing another contradiction . . .)

[22] To be sure, this "transcendental test" cannot be identified with Kant's "transcendental method," which seeks to identify and explicate conditions of possibility (whereas the *reductio ad absurdum* can only detect impossibility).

[23] While the unproblematic background beliefs B can be reintroduced at any time, none of the lines that rely on the hypothesis (in our example, lines 3, 5, 7, 9) may be cited or used again.

Wittgenstein uses this metaphor in *TLP* 6.54 to describe how he proceeds in the *Tractatus*: "My sentences serve as elucidations in the following way: anyone who understands me eventually recognizes them as nonsensical, having climbed through them – on them – beyond them. (One must, so to speak, throw away the ladder after one has climbed up on it.) One must overcome these sentences and then see the world right."

The metaphor of the ladder suggests that there is, in the *Tractatus*, a linear development of an overarching train of thought. Climbing the ladder rung by rung, the readers come to reach a new philosophical plateau. Upon arrival they must conclude that from the ladder, which was obviously instrumental in getting them there, they saw the world wrong. With the conclusion of the *Tractatus*, the reader has assumed a vantage-point from which at least some of its premises appear nonsensical. This is just as in indirect proof: the hypothesis of a *reductio*-argument helps establish the conclusion, but one sees the world wrong while entertaining it.

We have now identified the systematically ambiguous conclusion of the *Tractatus* and we have strong indications that it is established by indirect proof or *reductio ad absurdum*. This leaves us finally with the task of identifying the hypothesis, how and where Wittgenstein leads it into contradiction such that the conclusion immediately shows itself.

Of course, if the *Tractatus* employs a *reductio*-argument we already know what the hypothesis is: it is the opposite of the conclusion. The opposite of "there is indeed the inexpressible in speech" is the "surely well-founded" confidence that any sense whatsoever is expressible in speech. According to this hypothesis, the limits of language – if there are such things – are wide enough to accommodate anything that may have meaning: the world, an action, an artwork, a claim about what is the case, a feeling or intention, an ethical attitude, and so on. All this is supposed to be representable in language, that is, it can be recognized when put into words. Aside from denying any effective limits of language, this confidence admits of no distinction between expression and representation: when a feeling, a value, a belief is properly expressed in the medium of language, it will be recognizably represented there. We can put this in very simplistic terms that appear

quite familiar since, on some level, all of us would like to believe in
the possibility of this: according to the hypothesis, our feelings can
move into a sentence and from the sentence others can recover the
feeling; our linguistic expression *is* an objective representation of what
is expressed.[24] All sense or all meaning is therefore within the limits
of language and, as such, also within the world: it is externalized and
objectively contained in a sequence of words – a person can die and
what she expressed can live on in the sentence.[25]

This, then, is the hypothesis of the overarching argument of the
Tractatus.

(o) We are able to express any sense whatsoever in our two-dimensional script, that is, nothing is inexpressible in speech and all sense is in the world and within the limits of language.	H(ypothesis)

This fundamental trust in the power of language applies to the
hypothesis itself. Since it admits of no distinction between expression and representation, sentence (o) is a representation of our surely
well-founded confidence, and this confidence is the sense that is supposed to be expressed in (o). Along with the assertion of (o) comes,
therefore, the conviction that (o) and philosophical sentences like it
are not nonsensical. This corollary should be included with a more
complete statement of the hypothesis:

---

[24] Even Wittgenstein himself kept experiencing the pull of this naïve supposition. "In the
correctly written sentence, a particle detaches from the heart or brain & arrives as a sentence
on paper," he noted in his diary on October 31, 1931 (MT, diary p. 114). He immediately
adds a remark that qualifies and criticizes this supposition: "I believe that my sentences are
mostly descriptions of visual images that occur to me." His own sentences are not particles
from the heart but descriptions of images, and this is true also of the one in which he speaks
about particles that detach from the heart and arrive on paper – for what else is this but a
visual image?

[25] This account of the seemingly well-founded hypothesis deliberately avoids a problematic
middle term: "thought." Does all thought have a linguistic character and is all our thinking
therefore a kind of quiet speaking? And is "any sense whatsoever" first and foremost a
thought? In the preface of the *Tractatus* and in *TLP* 4.002 Wittgenstein makes it quite clear
that we cannot solve our problem quite so simply (see below, pp. 81–94). And in his diary
he notes on May 9, 1930: "One often thinks – and I myself *often* make this mistake – that
everything one thinks can be written down. In reality one can only write down – that is,
without doing something stupid & inappropriate – what arises in us in the form of writing.
Everything else seems comical & as it were like dirt. That is, something that needs to be
wiped off " (MT, diary p. 27).

(o$_A$) We are able to express any sense whatsoever in our two-dimensional script, that is, nothing is inexpressible in speech and all sense is in the world, within the limits of language.	H(ypothesis)
(o$_B$) Statements such as sentence o$_A$ are not nonsensical.	Corollary of hypothesis

Now, before we go on to show how and where this hypothesis (o$_{A\&B}$) is led into contradiction, an urgent objection must be addressed. "This is all well and good," the objection reminds us, "but this hypothesis is nowhere stated in the *Tractatus*." Indeed, the *Tractatus* does not offer these formulations anywhere, but is this to say that the *Tractatus* does not begin with this hypothesis?

Most readers would maintain (and the appearances obviously speak in their favor) that the *Tractatus* begins with *TLP* 1: "The world is everything that is the case." Attached to the numeral "1" is a footnote: "The decimal figures as numbers of the separate propositions indicate the logical importance of the propositions, the emphasis laid upon them in my exposition." Thus it would seem that *TLP* 1 marks a thunderous beginning, laying down the law. Hans-Johann Glock, for example, declares in his *Wittgenstein Dictionary* that "[t]he famous beginning of the *Tractatus* is the climax of a realist tradition which assigned importance to facts as mind-independent constituents of the world."[26] On Glock's account, the rest of the *Tractatus* proceeds from this realist commitment. And even if it does not develop with the stringency and clarity of a deductive argument, it shares with standard deductive arguments that everything follows from here. What comes after this first premise moves unidirectionally forward toward *TLP* 2, 3, and ultimately 7.

Upon closer scrutiny, however, the *Tractatus* begins right in the middle of things and *TLP* 1 is not really its beginning at all. The sentence "The world is all that is the case" presupposes our hypothesis (O$_{A\&B}$); it is an expression or manifestation of the seemingly well-founded confidence that such metaphysical verdicts are expressible in speech. Indeed, "The world is all that is the case" can open the *Tractatus* only by implicitly claiming about itself that it is not nonsense.

---

[26] Glock 1996, p. 115.

Elaborating on Wittgenstein's ladder metaphor, one might say that *TLP* 1 is the first rung of the ladder and *TLP* 7 the last, but that only the two parts of our hypothesis ($O_{A\&B}$) provide the rails that support the rungs and turn them into a ladder.

As one reads on, the *Tractatus* soon provides another indication that *TLP* 1 is not properly a beginning from which everything else flows in a forward direction. This appears in a famously difficult passage, which is so puzzling precisely because the remarks seem to move forward and backward at once:

2.02 The object is simple.
2.0201 . . .
2.021 The objects form the substance of the world. Therefore they cannot be composite.
2.0211 If the world had no substance, whether a sentence has sense would depend on whether some other sentence is true.
2.0212 It would then be impossible to form a (true or false) picture of the world.

This progression of remarks can be seen, firstly, as the continuation of a forward movement that began with "The world is all that is the case." Briefly put, this progression articulates the ontology of the *Tractatus*: the world consists of facts and not of things, since "what is the case" is always a factual configuration of things in a state of affairs. The elements of these configurations (the things or objects) are simple. Since these simple elements form the substrate or material out of which the facts are composed, they are the substance of the world. This relation between objects and their configuration in states of affairs makes it possible to form pictures of the world (since sentences are configurations of names of objects that can picture the configurations of objects).[27]

---

[27] Here is a closer ontological reading of 2.02 to 2.0212. Quite in line with Glock's comment about Wittgenstein's realist commitment, the series of remarks begins with an ontological claim (laying down the law again: the object is simple) and its elaboration in 2.021. In a somewhat cryptic manner, 2.0211 further elaborates this view: if simple objects form the substance of the world, whether a sentence has sense does not depend on the truth or falsity of some other sentence. This may be clarified by an example of the kind that would have been familiar to Wittgenstein's contemporary "technical" readers: if simple objects did not form the substance out of which facts are composed, our sentences might refer to composite things ("the present king of France") and form sentences like "the present king of France is bald." However, the truth or falsity of this sentence can be decided only if France has a

Significantly, however, the series of remarks also forms a backward movement that may have begun with *TLP* 2.1, "We make pictures of the facts," or on September 29, 1914, when Wittgenstein noted that "a traffic accident is represented in the Paris courtroom by means of dolls." The series of remarks makes explicit what are the implicit preconditions for our ability to form pictures. The ability itself is simply a given, but what must the world be like so as to be representable by pictures that are true or false?[28] For example, it must have discrete elements of which we can clearly say whether or not they stand in such-and-such a relation to one another, that is, it must have a substrate of simple objects that can enter into possible states of affairs. The states of affairs that actually obtain are the facts, and all the facts are all that is the case. This epistemological or transcendental reconstruction of the preconditions of our ability to make pictures leads to the necessary ontological supposition that the world is always what at a given moment just happens to be the totality of facts (*TLP* 1, 1.1).[29]

king. Therefore, another sentence must be true ("France has a king") for our sentence to have sense. But if we allowed only simple objects like "France" and "king," we could only form sentences like "France has a king and that king is bald." In this case, if France had no king, the conjunction would simply be false but perfectly sensible as it stands.

The remarks continue with 2.0212, which performs a shorthand *reductio ad absurdum* on the denial of this consequence: if one assumed that the sense of a sentence relied on the truth of another one, what we do all the time should be impossible to do, namely to form pictures of the world (we might refer here to 2.1 or simply to the newspaper article about the model used in a Parisian traffic court). Taken together, 2.0211 and 2.0212 show by indirect proof that from 2.02 and its elaboration 2.021 follows something true: the proposed ontology is consistent with our ability to form pictures of the world.

This interpretation skirts the controversial question of what, exactly, Wittgenstein means by "simple object." While he sometimes appears to require that simple objects would have to be discovered through a drawn-out logical analysis (and that logically simple objects should be physically simple, too), I adopt for present purposes his suggestion that the simplicity of objects is relative to the state of affairs in which they occur. See, for example, the entry on June 14, 1915 in the *Notebooks*: "It seems that the idea of the SIMPLE is already to be found in that of the complex and in the idea of analysis, and in such a way that we come to this idea quite apart from any examples of simple objects, or of sentences which mention them, and we realize the existence of the simple object – *a priori* – as a logical necessity." (Compare the entire discussion on June 14 to 18.)

[28] See *NB*, October 10, 1914: "A statement cannot deal with the logical structure of the world, for in order for a statement to be possible at all, in order for a sentence to be *capable* of having *sense*, the world must already have just the logical structure that it has. The logic of the world is prior to all truth and falsehood."

[29] This "backward" reading of the series of remarks further highlights why *TLP* 1, "The world is all that is the case," could not serve as a solid beginning or foundation for a philosophical work, even in the realist tradition: according to *TLP* 1, the facts are not mind-independently

While this only begins to properly contextualize *TLP* 1, the discussion so far suggests that the opening of the *Tractatus* can be reconstructed as in table 1.

INDIRECT PROOF OF THE CONCLUSION

Since the *Tractatus* does not explicitly state the premise of its overarching argument, it took some work to establish it. Matters become a good deal easier when we turn to its conclusion. We can safely bypass many intricate particulars along the way and find ourselves well prepared to recognize how and where the hypothesis of the *Tractatus* is led into contradiction, thus yielding the conclusion that "there is indeed the inexpressible in speech."

This and the previous chapter have indicated already how 2.1 and 2.01 will be developed, how the epistemological fact that "We make pictures of the facts" is related to the ontological posit "A state of affairs is a connection of objects. (Items, things.)" Agreement between our representations and their objects is possible because our sentences are true or false pictures of the world: the relation between these pictures and the world is an internal relation because both sentences and states of affairs are configurations of simple things (names, objects) that can be correlated to one another, one serving as a model for the other. As we have seen, both therefore share the character of contingency. Each state of affairs either obtains or does not obtain. Each sentence can be negated and it is always the case that either its assertion or its negation is true – and which of these is true depends

in the world and the world is not the succession of what is the case at any given time. Instead, the facts *are* the world and there is a constant succession of worlds, each by itself perfectly static and unchanging (see below, chapter 4, note 9). According to *TLP* 1, when I cross out "new" and instead write "different" fact, a new world has come into being: the previous totality of facts contained my sentence about a "new fact," the current world my sentence about a "different fact." *TLP* 1 thus posits a very peculiar and not at all trivial or intuitive (realist) ontology, namely the one that is implicit in our attempts to picture the world. Indeed, this ontology may not be philosophically defensible at all (when an action occurs and produces a change in the world that action cannot be part of a world even if, say, it instantiated an empirically observed constant conjunction of cause and effect). However, on the transcendental interpretation Wittgenstein does not and need not defend this bad ontology, only explicate it as an implicit presupposition of our representational practice. As opposed to the ontological interpretation of these remarks, the transcendental or epistemological one establishes more than the consistency of the posited ontology and our ability to form pictures of the world. Instead, it explicates a necessary precondition.

Table 1 *The opening of the* Tractatus

O$_A$	We are able to express any sense whatsoever in our two-dimensional script, that is, nothing is inexpressible in speech and all sense is in the world, within the limits of language.	H(ypothesis)
O$_B$	Statements such as sentence O$_A$ are not nonsensical.	Corollary of hypothesis
1	The world is all that is the case.	Ontological posit presupposing O$_B$ and, by extension, O$_A$; necessary precondition for 2.1
1.1	The world is the totality of facts, not of things.	Elaboration of 1
. . .	. . .	. . .
2.02	The object is simple.	Elaboration of 1 etc., restatement of the conclusion in 2.021
. . .	. . .	. . .
2.021	The objects form the substance of the world. Therefore they cannot be composite.	Elaboration of 2.02 and conclusion of RAA in 2.0211 to 2.1
2.0211	If the world had no substance, whether a sentence has sense would depend on whether some other sentence is true.	H* of nested *reductio*-argument and a first implication of H*
2.0212	It would then be impossible to form a (true or false) picture of the world.	From 2.0211, leading H* into contradiction with 2.1
. . .	. . .	. . .
2.1	We make pictures of the facts.	A given fact (as in traffic court); consequence of and occasion for 1 etc.
. . .	. . .	. . .
4.031	In the sentence a situation is as it were put together experimentally.	Further development of 1, 2.01, 2.1, etc., still presupposing O$_{A\&B}$

entirely on whether, in fact, the state of affairs does or does not happen to obtain. In the language of philosophy, one would therefore say that the truth of the sentence is contingent upon what is the case. And inversely, the world that is presupposed by this account of the agreement – a world that is picturable – is one in which everything is as it is and happens as it happens, a contingent world where nothing *has* to be and nothing *has* to happen: the existence or non-existence of a state of affairs does not logically depend on anything else.[30]

This account delimits language from within by singling out the descriptive or representational function of language. Only when we use a sentence to picture a state of affairs can we specify the truth-conditions and thus the meaning of what we say. For, our sentences have sense just to the extent that they are internally linked to states of affairs. This linkage unambiguously decides whether the sentence is true or false: if this state of affairs obtains, the sentence is true, if it does not, then the sentence is false. If we can specify what will make the sentence true or false, then the sense expressed by that sentence is contingent; if we cannot specify such truth-conditions, the sentence has no sense.

This limitation of language from within therefore implies that only descriptive sentences have sense. Since the (complete) description of the world is the task of science, Wittgenstein remarks: "The entirety of the true sentences is the entire natural science (or the entirety of the natural sciences)" (*TLP* 4.11). When we inspect this entirety of true sentences with the analytical tools provided by Wittgenstein, we will find that each of them represents a fact, that none of them is necessarily true, that all are contingent, and finally that none of them logically implies the other, that each is independent (1.21, 2.062, 4.211, 5.134).[31] There is, therefore, no hierarchy or rank ordering among these sentences, all of them are equivalent or, literally, of equal value: "All

[30] To be sure, Wittgenstein needs to grapple with an obvious objection: what about science and the causal laws of nature, don't they show that when one thing is the case (the cause) another must follow (the effect)? Wittgenstein dismisses this objection in section 6.3. He has Hume on his side when he insists that only logic tells us "what must be": there is nothing in between the two poles of logical necessity and (empirical) contingency. "The investigation of logic is the investigation of *all lawfulness*. And outside of logic everything is contingent" (6.3). Accordingly, "that the sun will rise tomorrow is a hypothesis; and that means: we don't *know* whether it will rise" (6.36311). Science with its laws is "the attempt to construct all the *true* sentences that we require for the description of the world according to one plan" (6.343) and these true sentences include everything we *know* to be true about the position of the sun relative to the earth.

[31] Wittgenstein admits, of course, that certain composite sentences can imply more elementary ones. So, the sentence "p and q" implies "q." Much of the *Tractatus* is devoted to the question of how we might arrive at a set of elementary sentences such that (i) all the true sentences in that set produce a complete description of the world, and (ii) all the sentences in that set are truly independent of one another, the truth or falsity of one not affecting the truth or falsity of any other. Compare *TLP* 4.26, 4.51, 5.13ff. Wittgenstein's requirement of "independence" has

sentences are of equal value" (*TLP* 6.4). Since all sentences express facts, there can be no hierarchy among them such that some express what ranks logically, metaphysically, or ethically higher (*TLP* 5.556f., 6.42).[32]

So, should anyone believe that values, feelings, meanings are something other than contingent facts, any attempt to express these will fail. This failure can take two forms. Either the attempt yields no sensible sentence at all and out comes a kind of gibberish that is poetic at best. In this case, instead of speaking clearly and sensibly, one speaks in riddles, enigmatically, perhaps "mystically" (also in the pejorative sense of that term). Or, a sensible sentence is produced, but in virtue of its having sense, this sentence presents a contingent fact, after all, and thus not what it was meant to express. One is left then with the feeling that there may be an ineffable, mystical something that eludes all attempts to adequately express it in speech (where this "something" may refer to a "higher" realm of being or, more likely, to an uncertain hunch, sentiment, impulse, hope, feeling, and so on). Having arrived at 6.4, Wittgenstein describes both kinds of failure, thus leading the hypothesis into contradiction.

6.4 All sentences are of equal value.
6.41 The sense of the world must lie outside the world. In the world everything is as it is and happens as it happens. *In* it there is no value – and if there were, it would have no value.
  If there is a value that has value, it must lie outside everything happening and being-so. For all happening and being-so is contingent.
  What makes it non-contingent cannot lie *in* the world, for then this would be contingent again.
  It must lie outside the world.

Wittgenstein formulates the contradiction twice: if there were value in the world, it would have no value; if something that lies in the world turns what is contingent into something noncontingent, this noncontingent thing would be contingent again. (If there were value

been taken very seriously by certain interpretations, such as those of Griffin 1964, Graßhoff 1997 and 1998, and Lampert 2000 and 2003. Ricketts 1996, p. 84 reduces it to an implicit requirement rather than an explicit metaphysical commitment.
[32] Compare *NB*, October 30, 1914: "*Every sentence* can be negated. And this shows that 'true' and 'false' means the same for all sentences. (This is of the greatest possible importance)." See also the entry dated October 12, 1916 and *PT*, an unnumbered remark on facsimile page 86 (p. 238 of the edition by McGuinness *et al.*).

in the world, it would be the "value" of contingency, a value without value that makes all sentences equivalent, *"gleichwertig"* or of
equal value). Following the pattern of most *reductio*-arguments, the
penultimate draft of the *Tractatus* delivers its conclusion (the denial
of the hypothesis) just as soon as the contradiction of the hypothesis
appears:

Therefore also there can be no propositions of ethics. Sentences cannot
express anything higher.
    There is indeed the inexpressible in speech. This *shows* itself, it is the
mystical.[33]

That same draft preserves the logical structure of Wittgenstein's overarching argument even more tightly when, a few pages earlier, it
takes the reader straight from "All sentences are of equal value" to
"Whereof one cannot speak, about that one must be silent" in the
very next line.[34] When Wittgenstein reshaped this arrangement, he
did so in two steps that preserved the relation between hypothesis,
contradiction, denial of hypothesis, and the final statement of the
Tractatus (see table 2).[35] First, he numbered the remarks of his penultimate draft and thereby widened the gap between "all sentences
are of equal value" and "whereof one cannot speak, about that one
must be silent." The latter statement now took its place as its ultimate
conclusion at the very end of the *Tractatus*. Wittgenstein used the gap
to make explicit the connection between the two statements, that is,
by inserting first of all the final two steps of the *reductio*-argument
(the statement of the contradiction and the conclusion that there is
indeed the inexpressible in speech). He also inserted various remarks
that explore the far-reaching implications of the insight that sentences cannot express anything higher. This left the final remark of the
Tractatus rather detached from the argument that led up to it. In a
second step, Wittgenstein changed the numbering of the remarks.
By moving "there is indeed the inexpressible in speech" into the

---

[33] See p. 75 in the facsimile reproduction of *PT*, also p. 230 of the edition by McGuinness *et al.*
[34] Page 71 in the facsimile edition of *PT*.
[35] Wittgenstein added a numbering system to the *Prototractatus* and edited that system for
the *Tractatus*. Therefore, two different numbers are assigned here to "There is indeed the
inexpressible in speech." The critical edition by Graßhoff and Lampert of the various typescripts of the *TLP* shows that Wittgenstein made no subsequent changes to the order of
these remarks.

Prototractatus (order of text)	Prototractatus (numbering)	Tractatus
All sentences are of equal value (6.4)	6.4 6.41	6.4 6.41
Whereof one cannot . . . (7) . . .	6.42 6.43 (will be *TLP* 6.522)	6.42
The sense of the world must lie outside the world . . . (6.41)	. . . 6.431 to 6.521 . . .	. . . 6.421 to 6.521 . . .
Sentences cannot express anything higher (6.42)	6.53 (The right method of philosophy) 6.54 (My sentences elucidate through this)	6.522 (was 6.43 in *PT*) 6.53 6.54
There is the inexpressible in speech (6.43/6.522)	7	7

immediate vicinity of the concluding remark, he tied the whole conclusion of the *Tractatus* back into the *reductio*-argument. In this final
version of the *Tractatus* (see table 3) the general reflections about the
problems of life in 6.42 to 6.521 are bridged by an arch that extends
from "sentences cannot express anything higher" (*TLP* 6.42) to "there
is indeed the inexpressible in speech" (*TLP* 6.522). Also, 6.522's denial
of Wittgenstein's hypothesis that "we are able to express any sense
whatsoever in our two-dimensional script" is now closely followed by
a corollary that denies the corollary of this hypothesis: while 6.522
rejects O_A, 6.54 rejects O_B and its claim that, surely, the statements
that make up the *Tractatus* are not nonsensical.[36]

This detailing of Wittgenstein's *reductio*-argument closes as it
began, namely by emphasizing the artful construction of the text.
As we saw, Wittgenstein's conclusion leaves undecided whether or
not there is a something that we must be silent about. Now we see

---

[36] More precisely, 6.522 can be read as the denial of O_A: there is something (namely, the mystical)
that cannot be expressed in speech, and thus we are not able to express any sense whatsoever
in two-dimensional script. With 6.54 as its corollary, 6.522 can also be read as the denial
of O_B: some attempts to produce sense result in failure (that is, in an enigmatic or mystical
way of talking); thus, the trust that anything we believe to be expressible can be expressed
in speech breaks down just as soon as Wittgenstein's attempt to express that trust is shown
to be nonsensical.

Table 3 *The closing of the* Tractatus

6.4	All sentences are of equal value.	From 1, 2.01, 2.02, 2.1, etc., still presupposing $O_{A\&B}$ – epistemological corollary of 6.41B
6.41A	The sense of the world must lie outside the world.	Contrary to O_A's "all sense is in the world," anticipated consequence of 1 to 6.41E
6.41B	In the world everything is as it is and happens as it happens. *In* it there is no value –	From 1, 2.01, 2.02, etc. – ontological corollary of 6.4
6.41C	– and if there were [value in the world], it would have no value.	From O_A, 6.4, 6.41B; $O_{A\&B}$ is led into contradiction
6.41D	If there is a value that has value, it must lie outside everything happening and being-so. For all happening and being-so is contingent.	Elaboration of 6.41B
6.41E	What makes [all happening and being-so] noncontingent cannot lie *in* the world, for then this would be contingent again.	From O_A, 6.41B&D; restatement of the contradiction in 6.41C
6.41F	It [that is: what makes all happening and being so noncontingent; what has value; the sense or meaning of the world] must lie outside the world.	From 6.41B&D; ground for the rejection of O_A, but still dependent on O_B
6.42 to 6.521	[Beginning with "therefore also there can be no propositions of ethics," elaboration of sense that *also* wants but fails to realize adequate expression in speech: "Sentences cannot express anything higher."]	Expansion of 6.41F
6.522	There is indeed the inexpressible in speech. This *shows* itself . . .	RAA $O_{A\&B}$ to 6.41A–E shows the denial of O_A
6.53	The right method of philosophy would really be this: To say nothing but what can be said, namely the sentences of natural science . . .	Corollary of 6.522 (preparing for 6.54 and 7 with a reminder of 4.11)
6.54	My sentences elucidate through this: who understands me recognizes them in the end as nonsensical . . .	Corollary of 6.522; denial of O_B
7	Whereof one cannot speak, about that one must be silent.	Corollary of 6.522

that he uses the *reductio*-argument not only to refute our fundamental trust in the power of language to express whatever we please. He uses it also to refute the implicit faith shared by the author with his readers that at least we can express in language what belongs to the philosophical investigation of our fundamental trust.

RESOLUTELY ANTIMETAPHYSICAL LIMITS OF LANGUAGE

Only scholars of Wittgenstein's work want to know how this reconstruction of Wittgenstein's argument relates to extant interpretations. To conclude this chapter here are a few remarks directed at them. Others may safely skip these pages.

To be sure, many philosophical commentators have remarked that the *Tractatus* undercuts traditional metaphysics, that more or less credibly it subverts the language in which it was written. However, only Max Black proposed explicitly that it was the overall aim of the *Tractatus* to produce a self-defeating argument in analogy to a negative proof or *reductio ad absurdum*:

Our problem is that of understanding how a terminology can have a rational use, even if the ultimate verdict has to be that there is nothing better to do with that terminology than to discard it. In mathematics, as it happens, we can find many examples of this sort, which may provide the clue that has so far been lacking . . . A simple example would be the attempt to assign a meaning to division by zero (i.e. to a symbol of the form x/o), consistent with the antecedently given rules for the division and multiplication of numbers. It very quickly appears that no such meaning can be assigned, since $x/o = y$ would imply $x = y \cdot o$ . . . and so we could infer $x = y \cdot o = o$, which could not hold in the general case. Here the problematic symbol x/o is used in *determinate* ways in the calculations that lead up to its rejection . . . The investigation might therefore be called an instance of "the indirect proof of nonsense." That the desired extension is inadmissable, though a negative result, is as valuable as such other negative results in mathematics as the impossibility of trisecting the angle, and the like. The work done to reach this result cannot reasonably be regarded as wasted – nor the method employed in reaching it as irrational . . . A negative metaphysics, such as that of the *Tractatus*, has its own rules of procedure: the ladder must be *used* before it can be thrown away.[37]

---

[37] Black 1964, pp. 382 to 386. Black's notation does not include a sign for multiplication: if x divided by o equals y, then x equals y multiplied by o; thus x would equal o. Imagine putting any number whatsoever in the place of x, and the general (absurd) result would be

These remarks make Max Black one of the few critics who takes literally Wittgenstein's claim that the sentences in the *Tractatus* are nonsensical: "Their absurdity is irredeemable, and their ultimate fate must be rejection." This interpretation differs from the one advanced here in that it finds the hypothesis in the proclamations of the *Tractatus* itself rather than in the underlying fundamental trust in the power of language. Also, on Black's account, aside from exposing the incoherence of its own metaphysical doctrine, the *Tractatus* has no conclusion – "through severe mental labor" Wittgenstein's assumptions are finally defeated in 6.54 with its verdict concerning their nonsensicality. Wittgenstein thus ends up merely revealing the "incoherence" of his own "new vision" of the world.[38] The price for taking literally Wittgenstein's final verdict therefore seems to be that we can no longer take the *Tractatus* seriously – all this severe mental labor only to learn that it was a complete waste of time?[39]

In his discussion of *reductio*-interpretations, Logi Gunnarsson elaborates this point.[40] On Black's account, we discover that the sentences of the *Tractatus* are nonsensical, but this affords no inference as to whether any other sentences are nonsensical, too – the *Tractatus* does not allow us to see *why* its sentences are nonsensical since, due to their nonsensicality, they cannot tell or teach us this. Black's difficulty is therefore that a sentence like *x*/0 means nothing and can teach us nothing – except solely that it is illegitimate. In contrast,

---

that all numbers equal 0. Black gives credit to pp. 444f. of Ambrose 1959. Her use of the term "conversion-analysis" (as opposed to "actual analysis") also suggests a form of indirect proof. More recently, Kremer 2001 entertained the notion.

[38] Black 1964, pp. 382 and 386, see note 18 above, and Sullivan 2004, p. 38. Compare the following passage from Stenius 1960, pp. 224f.: "What is of lasting value in the *Tractatus* is not the philosophical system which is its alleged result, but the views proposed in the different steps of the argument 'leading' to it, that is, of the ladder which according to 6.54 is to be thrown away after one had climbed up on it . . . an essential aim of the philosophical activity in the *Tractatus* actually was to *make* philosophy aimless. The 'definitiveness' of the truth of the thoughts expressed in the book thus meant that Wittgenstein considered this aim to be reached."

[39] According to Black the accomplishment of the *Tractatus* consists in providing a quasi-mathematical proof of the impossibility of philosophizing about "the world." Brockhaus 1991, pp. 6 and 330f. appears to make a similar point: "seeing that we must fail constitutes a considerable philosophical victory which frees us forever from pseudo-ethical rhetoric." For Brockhaus, however, this victory signals an "ineffable solution" to a metaphysical problem. His is therefore a "vain attempt to have it both ways," or, to use Diamond's term, his interpretation serves as an example of "chickening out" (Diamond 1988, pp. 20ff.).

[40] Gunnarsson 2000, pp. 41f., 45.

Wittgenstein's sentences are to elucidate in spite of being nonsensical (*TLP* 4.112, 6.54). Indeed, their being nonsensical is not the first and only thing we learn from them. There is only one way in which they can teach us their nonsensicality, and that is by first teaching the workings and limits of language and logic. Before we can appreciate the illegitimacy of division by zero, we need to know how division and multiplication work. This is overlooked also by Cora Diamond's remark that we understand the *Tractatus* and its author when we understand where they go wrong.[41] For how have we learned to recognize where they go wrong if not by reading the *Tractatus*? P. M. S. Hacker puts the question as follows:

> The predicament is serious. It is not merely . . . that Wittgenstein deliberately saws off the branch upon which he is sitting, since if the account of the conditions of representation given in the book is correct, then the sentences of the book are mere pseudo-propositions. But rather, if that is so, then the account of the conditions of representation is itself nonsensical. And that seems a *reductio ad absurdum* of the very argument that led to the claim that the sentences of the book are one and all pseudo-propositions.[42]

In order to get ourselves out of this predicament, what we need to understand is how – as opposed to x/o – Wittgenstein's sentences are nonsensical without being utterly self-defeating, nonsensical *and* instructive or elucidatory.

Cora Diamond and James Conant have taken on this rather more difficult task. Separately developed and formulated, their views so intimately reenforce one another that for our present purposes they can be taken to provide a unified interpretation. While it offers important cues for the account developed here, it fails to fully explore these cues and ends up with a rather narrow, curiously entangled view of Wittgenstein's philosophy. In particular, though it recommends an austere or resolute reading of the *Tractatus*, it attributes metaphysical doctrines precisely where Wittgenstein remains radically agnostic and antimetaphysical.[43]

---

[41] Diamond 2000, pp. 155f.   [42] Hacker 2000, p. 356.
[43] Since their interpretation has proven to be enormously influential, the following discussion of Conant's and Diamond's views establishes a kind of undercurrent or countercurrent to my investigation. On various occasions I develop the similarities and differences further. See

The most notable point of contact with Conant and Diamond's interpretation is that they also construe the *Tractatus* as a *reductio*-argument of sorts. What are reduced to absurdity are not just the sentences of the *Tractatus* itself but also the reader's illusion that these sentences make sense. This illusion corresponds to the hypothesis in our reconstruction of the argument, though it renders this hypothesis rather differently.[44] Here is how James Conant summarizes the overall structure of the *Tractatus*:

The *Tractatus* aims to show that (as Wittgenstein later puts it) "I cannot use language to get outside language." It accomplishes this aim by first encouraging me to suppose that I can use language in such a way, and then enabling me to work through the (apparent) consequences of this (pseudo-)supposition, until I reach the point at which my impression of there being a determinate supposition (whose consequences I have throughout been exploring) dissolves on me . . . On this reading, first I grasp that there is something which *must* be; then I see that it cannot be said; then I grasp that if it can't be said it can't be thought (that the limits of language are the limits of thought); and then, finally, when I reach the top of the ladder, I grasp that there has been no "it" in my grasp all along (that that which I cannot think I cannot "grasp" either) . . . Thus the elucidatory strategy of the *Tractatus* depends on the reader's provisionally taking himself to be participating in the traditional philosophical activity of establishing theses through a procedure of reasoned argument; but it only succeeds if the reader fully comes to understand what the work means to say about itself when it says that philosophy, as this works seeks to practice it, results not in doctrine, but in elucidation, not in [philosophical sentences] but in [the becoming clear of sentences]. And the attainment of this recognition depends upon the reader's actually undergoing a certain *experience* – the attainment of which is identified in 6.54 as the sign that the reader has understood the author of the work: the reader's experience of having his illusion of sense (in the "premises" and "conclusions" of the "argument") dissipate through its becoming clear

the final section of the introduction above; chapter 4, notes 47 and 58; chapter 5, beginning of the first section, notes 5 and 86; the third section of the conclusion; and throughout.

44 Like Black, Diamond and Conant leave us with a rather narrow vision of the *Tractatus*. Ultimately, the illusion we are to be cured of is that some nonsense is more substantial than other nonsense. Unlike the fundamental trust that all sense whatsoever is expressible in speech, theirs is not a widespread or dangerous illusion but confined to a small group of interpreters of Wittgenstein. Also, we learn that those and just those propositions are "nonsensical" that help advance us on Wittgenstein's ladder, namely the elucidatory propositions that are essential to philosophy. See Diamond 2000, p. 163f. and Conant 2000, pp. 196, 198, and 216.

to him that (what he took to be) the [philosophical sentences] of the work are [nonsense].[45]

As described by Conant – and here is another important point of contact – the *reductio* does not consist in the establishment of a sentence or doctrinal conclusion but rather in the failure of an activity that leads to an experiential recognition:[46] under the spell of our illusion we attempt to give meaning or grasp a sense that keeps eluding us until we realize that it cannot be grasped. Conant and Diamond go a step further, of course, when they say that it cannot be grasped *because* there is nothing there that could be grasped in the first place: "I grasp that if it can't be said it can't be thought (that the limits of language are the limits of thought); and then, finally, when I reach the top of the ladder, I grasp that there has been no 'it' in my grasp all along (that that which I cannot think I cannot 'grasp' either)." This is the most contentious aspect of their proposal and it is here where they attribute too readily a substantial metaphysical doctrine to Wittgenstein.

Their interpretation relies heavily on two sentences of Wittgenstein's preface, on remarks 4.112, 4.113 to 4.116, 5.61, and also on the concluding remarks of the *Tractatus*. These (and perhaps some other remarks) they refer to as the "frame" of the work because they contain instructions to the reader which Diamond and Conant exempt from the verdict that the sentences of the *Tractatus* are nonsensical.[47]

---

[45] Conant 2000, pp. 196f. The bracketed terms are English translations where Conant uses the original German expressions. Compare Diamond 2000, pp. 159f.

[46] Chapter 5 will show in greater detail how significant it is that the *reductio*-argument is an activity.

[47] See Conant 2000, p. 216: "Question: *which* sentences are (to be recognized as) nonsensical? Answer: those that elucidate. 4.112 does not say 'A philosophical work consists *entirely* of elucidations.' It says 'A philosophical work consists *essentially* of elucidations.' Not every sentence of the work is (to be recognized as) nonsense. For not every sentence serves as an elucidation." Conant suggests that the elucidations will be recognized as nonsense while we learn that we cannot give sense to them. This would imply that we experience no such failure with sentences that are taken to belong to the nonelucidatory frame, for example, "the limits of language are the limits of thought." Logi Gunnarsson makes explicit the further consequence of Conant's view, namely that only in the frame of the *Tractatus*, in the instructions to the reader, are thoughts expressed (2000, pp. 51–53 and 103). See Williams's critical challenge (2004, p. 19) and the reply by Conant and Diamond 2004, pp. 57–62. Hacker 2000, p. 360 criticizes this approach as "methodologically inconsistent." The inconsistency is not that some sentences of the *Tractatus* are considered nonsensical elucidations and others not. Instead, the inconsistency is that Conant and Diamond take

However, if one takes the sentences of natural science as a paradigm of meaningful sentences (as in *TLP* 4.11, for example) and the elucidations of the *Tractatus* as paradigms of nonsense, it is hard to comprehend how we can grasp successfully the sense of the following passage that belongs to the frame and figures prominently in Diamond and Conant's interpretation:

> The book will therefore draw a limit to thinking, or rather – not to thinking, but to the expression of thoughts: For, in order to draw a limit to thinking, we would have to be able to think both sides of this limit (we would have to be able to think what cannot be thought).
>
> Therefore the limit can only be drawn in language and what lies on the other side of the limit will simply be nonsense. (*TLP*, preface)

Assuming for now that this passage makes sense (or that nonsensical sentences can be interpreted), how are we to understand it? While it agrees rather precisely with the interpretation developed earlier in this and in later chapters, it does not support Diamond and Conant's interpretation. The passage does not assert what they take it to signify, namely (i) that the limits of language are the limits of thought, (ii) that what is simply nonsense cannot reach for, gesture, allude to something that is inexpressible in speech, and, therefore, (iii) that there is only one kind of nonsense, namely "plain nonsense".[48]

---

    great pain (see below) to show how one fails to grasp anything at all in certain uses of the term "object," while they take the sentences of the frame to be unproblematic, indeed, to authorize profound metaphysical commitments. The present proposal attempts to treat all the sentences of the *Tractatus* on a par while showing how these (literally) nonsensical sentences manage to elucidate.

[48] Instead of translating "will simply be nonsense" Conant and Diamond insist on "will be plain nonsense," which underscores their contention that one should not distinguish between kinds of nonsense (mere nonsense and a profound nonsense that gestures at the ineffable). As a rule for interpretation (difficult enough to satisfy even for Conant and Diamond themselves), their contention is warranted. However, it cannot be justified in reference to this passage of Wittgenstein's preface. Instead of emphasizing – as Conant and Diamond assume – that beyond the limit in language lies "*einfacher Unsinn* (simple or plain nonsense)," Wittgenstein here uses "*einfach* (simply)" as a procedural term that characterizes his strategy: once the conditions are specified that make sentences meaningful, whatever fails to meet them is simply or automatically nonsense ("*was jenseits der Grenze liegt, wird einfach Unsinn sein*"). Or, once certain attempts to express something in speech produce a contradiction and thereby come up against the limits of language, the recognition follows simply or automatically that such attempts can produce nothing but nonsense. To translate "will be plain nonsense" would require an adverbial construction that ordinarily occurs only as an exclamation in the present tense "*das ist doch einfach Unsinn!*," as in, "that's just nonsense!" (Incidentally, in *PI* 119 Wittgenstein does speak of "plain nonsense," namely "*schlichter Unsinn*.")

The preface states that the primary value of the *Tractatus* is that in it thoughts are expressed, thoughts that will be understood perhaps only by those who have already thought them themselves.[49] Judging from this context alone, the quoted passage claims only the following: (i) one cannot draw a limit to thought; however, (ii), one can draw limits to the expression of thought; (iii) one such limit will be drawn in the *Tractatus*, namely the limit to expression in speech; and (iv) once it is drawn, other speech that lies beyond this limit is simply nonsense. In this passage Wittgenstein sets up an instructive and programmatic contrast. As opposed to an envisioned limit of thought beyond which there is no thinking, one *can* speak on both sides of the limit of language, namely sense on this side, nonsense on the other. (Indeed, we might take this passage to suggest that in order to draw a limit to the expression of thought, Wittgenstein will have to speak on both sides of this limit, that is, speak nonsensically with sentences that cannot express thoughts – but in the course of doing so he will, by way of a *reductio*-argument, manage to express thoughts concerning the limits of language.)

Taken by itself, this passage contradicts Conant's strong interpretive claim "that the limits of language are the limits of thought," which prepares for the next rung of the ladder, namely "that that which I cannot think I cannot 'grasp' either." Conant could object by pointing out that in the body of the *Tractatus* (3 to 3.01, 3.2, 4.01, perhaps 5.61)[50] and in associated texts Wittgenstein does appear to equate the

<hr>

[49] That is, the preface begins and ends with comments about the thoughts that are expressed in the *Tractatus*. It states that one cannot draw a limit to thought. This makes very puzzling, indeed, the interpretations proposed by James Conant or Logi Gunnarsson. The latter writes, for example: "The *Tractatus* aims to draw a limit to the expression of thought; beyond that limit there are no thoughts" (2000, pp. 59f.). Surely, the second part of his remark is not implied by the first – the first part states only that beyond that particular limit there is no expression of thought in speech.

[50] Less circumspect than Conant, Logi Gunnarsson claims explicitly that *TLP* 4.114 and 4.115 "seem to repeat" the passage of the preface: "[Philosophy] is supposed to limit the thinkable and thereby the unthinkable. It is supposed to delimit the unthinkable from within through the thinkable. It will indicate the unsayable by clearly presenting the sayable." Gunnarsson goes on to suggest that the shared meaning of these passages is that "nothing counts as a thought when it cannot be said" and then refers the reader for further support to 5.61: "Therefore we cannot say in logic: This and that is in the world, but not that. [For that would require that] logic must get outside the limits of the world ... What we cannot think, that we cannot think; we therefore cannot *say* either what we cannot think" (2000, pp. 51 and 101f.). Gunnarsson's comments disagree with the statement of the preface that one cannot

limits of language with the limits of thought, after all.[51] However, the required reconciliation undermines his all-important distinction between a meaningful "frame" and the nonsensical elucidations in the main body of the text. Also, it is telling that Conant would resolve the issue toward the strong claim that the limits of language are the limits of thought. He could have adopted a weaker interpretation: at best, the tension between Wittgenstein's various statements about limits of thought and language testifies to his critical agnosticism, and at worst it indicates an unresolved ambiguity in his use of the term "thought." Either way, Wittgenstein does not on this weaker interpretation pretend to deliver in the *Tractatus* a metaphysical theory of mind.[52]

draw a limit to thought. They also disagree with 5.61, which implies only that logic cannot draw a limit to thought, that thought has to take care of itself – what can be thought, can be thought, and what cannot be thought, cannot be thought and cannot be said either.

[51] In a letter to Russell, for example, Wittgenstein writes: "The main point is the theory of what can be expressed (*gesagt*) by sentences – i.e. by language – (and which comes to the same, what can be *thought*) and what can not be expressed by sentences but only shown (*gezeigt*); which, I believe, is the cardinal problem of philosophy" (*CL*, p. 124, see also 125). And in the *Notebooks* we find an entry dated December 9, 1916: "Now it is becoming clear why I thought that thinking and language were the same. For thinking is a kind of language. For a thought is, of course, *also* a logical picture of the sentence, and therefore it just is a kind of sentence." But note the ambiguities in this entry (he once *thought* that thinking and language were the same; the thought is *also* but perhaps not only a logical picture) and see the conflicting entries of October 5 and December 8, 1914.

[52] Here is my proposal of how to resolve this tension. Wittgenstein uses the preface to orient the reader toward the expression of thought in speech. As he enters the body of the text he thus leaves behind the more general question whether or not something is a thought only if it can be expressed. He does hold on to the intuition, however, that if a thought is not expressed clearly, it remains in effect unexpressed. While this intuition holds for musical thought as well as for propositional thought about the world, *TLP* 3 introduces "thought" as it is to be used for the present purposes (namely to determine the limits of expressibility in speech): "The logical picture of the facts is the thought." This curious expression falls short of a general definition of what thoughts are (Wittgenstein does not write: "Thoughts are logical pictures of the facts"). However, he also does not restrict the statement to a subset of "thoughts" by writing "Logical pictures of facts are thoughts (and other things may be thoughts, too)." One reason for the peculiar construction may be found in the history of its composition. In the *Prototractatus* (p. 3 of the facsimile) he changed "The logical picture of the facts is the sentence" into "is the thought." Another reason for exhibiting so peculiarly "is the thought (*ist der Gedanke*)" may have been that this alludes to Frege. Indeed, the two passages quoted in the preceding note suggest that, as opposed to the preface, a far more specific notion of "thought" is operative in them, namely Frege's nonpsychological representation of representations. Thought thus stands in a particular relation to the world, like a sentence it "says" something about it, and whatever can merely be shown has nothing corresponding to it in thought. As a representation of a representation, thought is "expressed" only by becoming "perceptible to the senses" (*TLP* 3.1, 3.2) in an actually produced sentence.

It was already suggested that a similar criticism applies to the next and last rung of Wittgenstein's ladder. According to Conant, we realize here that that which we cannot think we cannot grasp either, that is, that there never was an "it" that we meant to express but failed to. In this instance, Conant and Diamond, along with their critic Hacker overstep critical bounds. Conant and Diamond maintain that the *Tractatus* undermines the illusion of ineffable truths that can only be shown. The mandate of silence in *TLP* 7 is therefore a "symptom of philosophical discourse," that is, a silence signifying nothing but emptiness.[53] In contrast, Hacker maintains that this silence can be pregnant with meaning regarding the essence of the world and the nature of the sublime.[54] We have seen that Wittgenstein's "There is indeed the inexpressible in speech" (*TLP* 6.522) artfully skirts existential import and therefore leaves these metaphysical options open: whether or not there is something to be silent about is precisely what lies beyond the limits of language and knowledge.

Diamond and Conant are right that all nonsense involves the same failure, namely that of "giving no meaning to certain signs of the sentence" (*TLP* 6.53). If nonsense can show anything at all, it surely shows no facts, no features or aspects of the world, or anything that can be described. But this does not mean, as James Conant maintains, that it cannot show anything at all. In his criticism of their work, Hacker provides a long list of what the nonsensical sentences of the *Tractatus* purport to show (and chapter 5 below will adduce arguments of its own).[55] Diamond and Conant exclude this possibility in order

---

An expressed thought just *is* the meaningful sentence (*TLP* 4) just as it *is* a logical picture of the facts. In contrast, the preface asks what – of all the things that occur in our minds, that is: thoughts – can find adequate expression in speech. On my interpretation, just as Wittgenstein shifts from a generic, unspecifiable "any sense whatsoever" to "sense expressible in two-dimensional script" (also in *TLP* 4.002, of course), so he shifts from a generic and unspecifiable thought (which may include musical, propositional, evaluative, desirous thought) to a restricted notion of nonpsychological, propositional, representational thought. Wittgenstein later remarks: "'Thought' sometimes means a particular mental process which may accompany the utterance of a sentence and sometimes the sentence itself in the system of language" (*PG*, part I, I, 13; cf. *PI* remarks 339–342).

[53] See Conant 1992, p. 216.   [54] See Hacker 2000, p. 382.

[55] Ibid., pp. 353–355. To be sure, Hacker also maintains that "Wittgenstein's own propositions . . . are, by the lights of the *Tractatus*, nonsensical pseudo-propositions. They show nothing at all" (p. 356). A few pages later, he writes: "But one may, the author of the *Tractatus* thought, deliberately and self-consciously flout the rules of logical syntax [that is, talk nonsense] with the intention of bringing one's readers to apprehend something that cannot be said but

to defend their austere conception of only one kind of nonsense. As we have seen, through this exclusion they inadvertently take on less than austere metaphysical commitments. A final example will show that this pertains not only to matters beyond the stated scope of the *Tractatus*, namely the relation of thought to language and what there is to be silent about. It also pertains to questions at the heart of the *Tractatus*. Indeed, it was for these questions that Cora Diamond first developed her interpretation.[56]

Diamond, Conant, and their critic Hacker agree that Wittgenstein holds that "one cannot, for example, say 'There are objects' as one says 'There are books'" (*TLP* 4.1272). They agree, moreover, that ordinarily it would be plain nonsense to say "There are objects." They even appear to agree why this is so, namely that this is a misuse of language which mistakes formal concepts for names – as if the word "object" had in this context an object to which it refers. This misuse amounts to a failure to give meaning: we would be hard-pressed to specify what "object" refers to, what state of affairs is pictured by "there are objects" and what would make this statement true or false. Their disagreement arises in a rather peculiar manner, namely in that Hacker liberally assumes that there are objects, or at least that there is nothing in Wittgenstein's argument about sense and nonsense which precludes their existence. It is just *that there are objects* cannot be expressed by the statement "there are objects." Instead, it is expressed by perfectly sensible sentences such as "The gloves are

is shown" (p. 367). While the first of these statements refers as it were to Wittgenstein's doctrine (to the verbal provisions of the *Tractatus*), the second refers to his philosophical practice. While this distinction between doctrine and practice renders Hacker's interpretation consistent, his interpretation of the *Tractatus* claims no consistency for Wittgenstein: "It is a mistake of Diamond to suppose that the *Tractatus* is a self-consistent work" (p. 370). That Conant and Diamond (and I) make this supposition and that Hacker does not make it marks a decisive difference between hermeneutic strategies. Like any (philosophical) text, the *Tractatus* becomes fruitful and challenging precisely in that it demands of its readers to render it self-consistent. For the same reason, however, I agree with Hacker that it is "hermeneutically unsound" to interpret the *Tractatus* in isolation (as Conant and Diamond do) and to leave this interpretation inconsistent with other documents pertaining to the creation of the *Tractatus* (Hacker 2000, p. 371). The most interesting defense of the notion that the *Tractatus* is not self-consistent but tolerates paradox was provided by Williams 2004, p. 27. On this interpretation, the *Tractatus* becomes a *reductio*-argument only when viewed from the point of view of *PI*.

[56] Diamond 1991 characterizes the procedure of the *Tractatus* as follows: it proposes statements like "A is an object," then strips them of any meaning that one might conceivably assign to them, and thus shows that there cannot be a science of logic.

in the box" as well as by perfectly nonsensical (pseudo-)sentences such as "These keys are the cousins of the cook."[57] Hacker finds the liberal acknowledgment of objects also in remarks by Wittgenstein, for example: "The formal concept ['object'] is already given with the object[!] which falls under it" (*TLP* 4.12721). Indeed, Wittgenstein's injunction to silence is philosophically *more* significant rather than *less* so once we allow that, of course, *there are objects* except to say so is to say nothing at all.

Conant questions this liberality: "Hacker is untroubled by the lack of difficulty he encounters in telling us *what* it is that cannot be said."[58] Of course one should not and cannot be untroubled by this, but one needs to explore how the statement "there are objects" retains its semblance of intelligibility even after we discover that it neither says nor shows anything except our failure to express something with it. Our lack of difficulty in speaking of what cannot be said is a curious fact, indeed. However, Conant's treatment cuts us off even from raising this question.

Imagine someone saying "Electromagnetic fields are objects" or "Reality is no figment of the imagination since there are objects other than myself." Imagine further that she is subsequently pressed by the questioner envisioned by Wittgenstein in *TLP* 6.53. This questioner says nothing having to do with philosophy, but merely wants to know from the speaker whether she has given meaning to all the signs in her sentence, in particular to the word "object." Under pressure from the questioner, she will ultimately come to a point of exasperation that is captured by Conant: "Just forget about the logical rôle that the term appears to have in my use of it, damn it all! What I mean to refer to is just *that* which is represented by a variable [such as the term 'object'] and don't begrudge me the requisite pinch of salt!" Conant shrewdly exposes the inadequacy of this strenuous, desperate effort to consider an idea in the mind as a representation of something in the world, in other words, to reach out with a concept in the hope

---

[57] See Hacker 2000, p. 363: as opposed to A's being in the box, "we do not take A's being an object to be something that is the case and might not be the case, we take it as something that could not be otherwise. And of course that is *one* reason why Wittgenstein does not think that these sentences express genuine propositions: they do not satisfy the essential requirement on a proposition with a sense, namely bipolarity. They attempt to say something that cannot be said."
[58] For this and the following, see Conant 2000, pp. 206–208.

of touching reality. "What is the reference of 'that' here?" Conant asks, and continues: "Can a sufficiently emphatic use of the word 'that' reach all the way to the '___which is expressed by a variable'?" Conant denies this and points out that one would miss the point of the *Tractatus* by thinking "that meaning can thus be conferred on an expression through a pyschological act" of intending something or projecting an inner feeling of sense.[59]

Indeed, any such attempt at conferring meaning must fail: only those sentences have sense that represent a state of affairs. Sentences can express facts only and no effort of the will can squeeze a feeling or an idea into a meaningful sentence (other than by substituting for them a representation of objects and events). The fundamental trust that any sense whatsoever can be expressed in a sentence thus runs up against the limits of language. But is this to say that there was nothing at stake in this failure, that there was no intention or feeling of inner sense that we did not manage to express? And after experiencing this failure, must we clean house among our feelings, ideas, values to make sure that we never find ourselves in the position of intending to express them again? Conant suggests just that.[60] According to him, the ultimate aim of the *Tractatus* is to lead us "to the point where our conviction that we understand what a sentence such as 'A is an object' is even attempting to say completely dissolves on us (and all we are left with is a string of words in which we are no longer able to discern even an abortive attempt to mean something)."

This formulation of Wittgenstein's ultimate aim mistakes austerity for severity. According to a more modest statement of its aim, the *Tractatus* prevents us from doing something inappropriate. It teaches us to be aware that some of the things that occur to us cannot be adequately expressed in language, that at best they become distorted in the attempt and therefore better remain unspoken. To be sure, our inability to articulate them and to take them for a representation of any kind, renders their status highly questionable. But that may

[59] Note that Conant learned this point of the *Tractatus* not from the frame but from the body of the work.

[60] To be sure, this is how Conant would consider Wittgenstein's injunction to silence to be philosophically *more* significant rather than less so. It silences also the pretensions of the mind according to which there is more to it than what it can express in speech. On Conant's interpretation of Wittgenstein, there is nothing to the mind and certainly no thought that exists independently of what is expressible in speech.

be all there is to the matter – any more definite verdict regarding the existence or nonexistence of what we had been trying to express would transgress the limits of knowledge and language.

Given Diamond and Conant's interpretation of 6.54, it is odd that they would adopt such a more restrictive, severe, and, indeed, substantial stance.[61] They emphasize Wittgenstein's remark in 6.54 that "anyone who understands *me* eventually recognizes *them* [my sentences] as nonsensical." On Diamond and Conant's reading, Wittgenstein's sentences are plainly nonsensical and therefore cannot be understood at all. Even the sentences that elucidate or expose the illusion of an intelligible philosophical argument are such incomprehensible nonsense. Though we cannot understand any of his sentences, Conant and Diamond pick up on Wittgenstein's suggestion that we can nevertheless understand their author.[62] They only begin to explore, however, what it means to understand the author as a person and how this can be done without understanding the sentences that were produced by him.[63] But even their suggestion of this possibility offers yet another important cue for the present investigation: an understanding of the author of the *Tractatus* involves the discernment of character, personality, intentions, and perhaps of values, feelings, and convictions. That is, in order to understand the author one must discern some kind of sense that Wittgenstein manages to express in or through the *Tractatus*, even if he does not do so in the particular sentences of which it is composed. Hereby, Diamond and Conant implicitly attribute to Wittgenstein a distinction between two kinds

---

[61] They acknowledge as much in Conant and Diamond 2004, p. 93. As opposed to Williams 2004, I do not accuse Conant and Diamond of assuming that there are certain logical conditions on legitimate sentence construction (Conant and Diamond 2004, p. 58). On the contrary, I suggest that their restraint in this regard amounts to throwing the baby out with the bathwater: Conant and Diamond make metaphysical commitments by insisting too adamantly on the impossibility of stating conditions of grammaticality, of identifying limits of sense, of contrasting assignments of meaning in descriptive and expressive modes of speech.

[62] See Diamond 2000, pp. 155f., Conant 2000, p. 198.

[63] The urgency of this matter is amplified by Gunnarsson 2000, p. 101: "To understand the book (or its author) is not the same as understanding the sentences in the book. They are nonsense and cannot be understood." Since Conant and Diamond both exempt certain sentences of Wittgenstein's from the charge of nonsensicality (they are not elucidatory but set the frame), they might argue that one can learn to understand the author from the frame he devised and expressed intelligibly. As we have seen, rather than save Wittgenstein by rendering his view self-consistent, this suggestion diminishes the scope of his critical philosophy.

of sense: the sense of a sentence (its truth-conditions) and whatever is encompassed by the broader notion of "any sense whatsoever." When Conant writes that the *Tractatus* takes us to the point where "all we are left with is a string of words in which we are no longer able to discern even an abortive attempt to mean something," this still allows that we can understand the author of this string of words and that, for example, we may discern in it Wittgenstein's abortive attempt to express himself. The failure to express oneself in speech is a failure of someone who wishes to accomplish something – and such a failure does not make this someone or something go away.[64]

Everyone can, therefore, agree that "there are no different *senses* of the word 'nonsense.' Nor are there *kinds* of nonsense — nonsense no more comes in kinds than it comes in degrees." However, Hacker and the present investigation part company from Diamond and Conant by continuing as follows:

But the nonsense of the pseudo-propositions of philosophy, in particular of the philosophy of the *Tractatus*, differs from the nonsense of "A is a frabble," for it is held to be an *attempt to say what cannot be said but only shown*. In this sense it can be said to be "illuminating nonsense." It is the motive behind it and the means chosen for the objective (e.g. the illegitimate use of formal concepts) that earmarks the nonsense of the *Tractatus*.[65]

A trivial example can bring this discussion to a close. Even after Max Black's *reductio*-argument, I still understand "division by zero"

---

[64] This insistence that failure does not extinguish motive is a far cry from a substantial interpre-tation according to which failure teaches us precisely what we have been looking for. See Fann 1969, p. 38: "although the 'question' of the meaning of life is strictly speaking not a question, the *process* of raising the question, trying to answer it and finally realizing the non-sensicality of the question *shows* the meaning of life to the one who has gone through the process. He is better off for it, the sense of life becomes clear to him." This is what Conant and Diamond rightly criticize as an "irresolute" ineffability-interpretation that wants to have it both ways. Here is another example of such an interpretation: "The ascent over the ladder alludes to the mystical ascent; the world that one sees from the height of this ascent, is the world seen from outside the world (*ekstasis*); and the throwing away of the ladder and transcending of the propositions establishes the function of the *Tractatus* as a *via negativa*" (Nieli 1987, p. 118).

[65] Hacker 2000, p. 365. Conant and Diamond recognize and reject Hacker's distinction as a psychological one. Conant writes that "the *Tractatus* is not concerned to argue that there are *no* ways to distinguish between kinds of nonsense . . . but only that there are no *logically* distinct kinds of nonsense" (2000, p. 209). According to Conant, the point of the *Tractatus* is that logic teaches a lesson to psychology, namely that the psychological distinction evaporates. Compare Conant 2000, p. 196 and the somewhat different take in Diamond 2000, p. 161.

in a rather peculiar way even though I cannot find it intelligible. I may ask myself, for example, "Why is it again that there cannot be division by zero?" Answering my own question, I remind myself by rehearsing Black's argument: "Ah yes, if I allowed division by zero and placed different numbers in the numerator, each of these different numbers would equal 0 and this is a patently absurd consequence." Like any activity, the instructive failures that are rehearsed by the *Tractatus* have a definite temporal structure and can be repeated any number of times (as Wittgenstein suggests in *TLP* 6.53). The "somethings" that are to be expressed remain a pawn in the game; they can and perhaps need to be conjured up again and again: "In philosophy we are deceived by an illusion. But this illusion is also something, and I must at some time place it completely and clearly[!] before my eyes, before I can say it is only an illusion."[66]

---

[66] MS 110, p. 239, quoted (from Stern 1995) by Conant 2000, p. 197. In the manuscript Wittgenstein changed "But this illusion" into "But an illusion."

CHAPTER 3

Thought experiments

Wittgenstein's short preface to the *Tractatus* emphasizes twice that thoughts are expressed in his book:

This book will be understood perhaps only by those who themselves have thought at one time or another the thoughts that are expressed in it – or at least similar thoughts. . . . If this work has a value it consists in two things. First that in it thoughts are expressed, and this value will be the greater the better the thoughts are expressed.

As we have seen in the previous two chapters, the thoughts expressed in the *Tractatus* concern a limit to the expression of thought, namely the limit of expression in language. At the very end of his book, Wittgenstein points out that sentences like these lie beyond this limit – and what this means is that the thoughts to be *expressed by* his sentences are not *contained in* them. Indeed, they have no meaningful content at all because we cannot specify how the world would have to be different in order for these sentences to be considered false. They cannot properly be understood since they are nonsensical. However, Wittgenstein allows that the person who utters them can be understood: "anyone who understands me eventually recognizes [my sentences] as nonsensical" (*TLP* 6.54).

This sounds puzzling, indeed: supposedly, we are able to understand the thought of a person who produces nonsensical sentences. And lest we imagine that Wittgenstein speaks loosely here, he makes the very same suggestion in his preface. Why *can't* we draw limits to thought? Because that would require thinking both sides of the limit, that is, "we ought to be able to think what cannot be thought."[1]

---

[1] Compare *TLP* 3.03: "We cannot think anything unlogical, because we would then have to think unlogically."

Why *can* we draw the limit to the expression of thought in language? Because we can speak and write on both sides of the limit: what is within the limit are meaningful sentences, "and what lies beyond the limit, will simply be nonsense." So here again Wittgenstein suggests that nonsensical sentences may be required for the expression of his thoughts that concern the limits of language. The difficulty that lies ahead for him is the task of expressing thoughts, of making himself understood through the employment of nonsensical sentences. This helps to explain why he values success in this difficult task on a par with the definitive solution of the problems of philosophy: "If this work has a value it consists in two things. First that in it thoughts are expressed . . . the value of this work secondly consists in that it shows how little has been achieved when these problems are solved."

How, then, are readers to understand Wittgenstein and to finally understand that his sentences are nonsensical? The most straight-forward path to understanding is precluded: we cannot learn to understand him by grasping the content that is communicated by his sentences. Since his sentences are nonsensical, they have no content to be grasped. Some of Wittgenstein's critics fear that this leaves only a philosophically unacceptable alternative, namely a mystical harmony between Wittgenstein and "those who themselves have thought at one time or another the thoughts that are expressed" in the *Tractatus*. Fortunately, however, the previous chapter has suggested a third possibility: we can gain an understanding of Wittgenstein by appreciating what he attempts to do but fails to achieve. We can appreciate this by participating in what he does, that is, by sharing with him the fundamental and ultimately illusory trust in the power of language, and then by running up, along with him, against the limits of language. On this account, the *Tractatus* performs an experiment of sorts, and through their participation in the experiment Wittgenstein's readers are prompted to think for and by themselves the thoughts expressed in the book. Having experienced what Wittgenstein experienced, they are in a position to understand him – even as they are realizing that it was only an illusion when they thought that they were understanding his sentences.

The previous chapter reconstructed Wittgenstein's argument as a *reductio ad absurdum* or indirect proof. In the course of this,

reductio-arguments were already shown to be thought experiments
of sorts. And while that chapter focused on the philosophical or
rationally persuasive character of the argument, this one deals with
his manner of writing it down – how does Wittgenstein prompt his
readers to enact his thought experiment and to "actually undergo a
certain experience"?[2] Furthermore, in order to achieve this goal, why
on earth would he choose a style of presentation of which Alexander Maslow said that it constitutes "the most formidable obstacle to
understanding the *Tractatus*"?[3]

By the end of chapter 5 we will see why his chosen style is just
the right one, perfectly adequate to his task in that it allows for
his sentences to be nonsensical and yet for the *Tractatus* to express
thoughts. But instead of anticipating this conclusion or answering
from hindsight, this chapter makes a first approach by considering
the character, structure, and precedents of his method of writing. The
first section arrives at Wittgenstein's own description of the method,
one that explains why he considered his writing clear as crystal and at
the same time feared that no one would understand it. We will then
see that Wittgenstein's method proceeds in close analogy to what
he calls "the only strictly correct method" of philosophy. The third
section details how, instead of developing an idiosyncratic system of
belief, Wittgenstein's remarks – all of them together and each on its
own – engage the reader in a thought experiment. The final section
shows how this deliberate initiation of thought experiments did not
create a crisis of faith in the power of language. Instead it responded in
a moderating manner to an already existing crisis of faith in language.

A RECORD OF OCCURRENCES

As early as 1912, Bertrand Russell worried about Wittgenstein's philosophical style. In a letter to Lady Ottoline Morrell he notes:

I told him he ought not simply to *state* what he thinks true, but to give
arguments for it, but he said arguments spoil its beauty, and that he would
feel as if dirtying a flower with muddy hands. He does appeal to me – the
artist in intellect is so very rare. I told him I hadn't the heart to say anything
against that, and that he had better acquire a slave to state the arguments.

---

[2] Conant 2000, p. 197.   [3] Maslow 1961, p. ix.

I am seriously afraid that no one will see the point of anything he writes, because he won't recommend it by arguments addressed to a different point of view.[4]

Seven years later, after reading the manuscript of the *Tractatus*, Gottlob Frege echoed Russell's concern in a letter to Wittgenstein:

What you tell me about the purpose of your book is alien to me. According to you it can only be accomplished when others have already thought the thoughts expressed in it. The joy of reading therefore cannot be awakened through its already familiar content, but only through its form that carries the stamp of, say, the peculiarity of the author. Through this the book becomes more of an artistic than a scientific achievement: what is said in it takes the backseat to how it is said. In my remarks I had assumed that you wanted to convey some novel content to me. And in that case the greatest distinctness would indeed make for greatest beauty.[5]

Two of Wittgenstein's teachers worried that aesthetic or artistic ambitions might get in the way of argument, intelligibility, clarity, even beauty. However, as much as Wittgenstein resisted their recommendations, and as much as he defended his style, he did so in terms of "scientific" rather than aesthetic values. Not the artist's interest in beauty but a philosophical concern for intellectual integrity eventually led him to the aphorism.

As for the alleged failure to give arguments, the previous chapter and many other investigations of the *Tractatus* show that it provides an overarching argument and along the way various particular arguments. These, to be sure, are arguments of a particular kind. In a *reductio*-argument, for example, one learns from the experience of failure in the course of a thought experiment. This deviates from standard conceptions of the "philosophical argument," according to which premises are first justified, then elaborated, and for each subsequent step established, how it follows from the preceding ones. Wittgenstein's refusal to give arguments of the latter kind accords with his conception of philosophy (no doctrine, but an activity that requires the reader to think the thoughts him- or herself) and his conception of logic (entailment relations must be seen, they cannot be explained). While this refusal diminished Wittgenstein's expectation

[4] May 28, 1912, quoted by McGuinness 1988, p. 104.
[5] Frege 1989, p. 21 (September 16, 1919).

that anyone would in fact understand the thoughts expressed in the *Tractatus*, it did not diminish his desire to be understood, or his conviction that he had expressed himself with utmost clarity. Various statements testify to this.

In fact you would not understand it [the *Tractatus*] without a previous explanation as it's written in quite short remarks. (This of course means that *nobody* will understand it; although I believe it's all as clear as crystal. But it upsets all our theory of truth, of classes, of numbers, and all the rest.)
    I'm now afraid that it might be very difficult for me to reach any understanding with you. And the small remaining hope that my manuscript may mean something to you has completely vanished . . . It's galling to have to lug the completed work round in captivity and to see how nonsense has free rein outside! And it's equally galling to think that no one will understand it even if it does get printed!
    I also sent my MS to Frege. He wrote to me a week ago and I gather that he doesn't understand a word of it all. So my only hope is to see *you* soon and explain all to you, for it is *very* hard not to be understood by a single soul! . . . I suppose you don't understand the notation "ξ". It does not mean "for all values of ξ . . .". But all is said in my book about it and I feel unable to write it again. Try to understand it till we meet . . .
    [Y]ou won't get too much out of reading it. For you won't understand it; the subject matter will appear totally foreign to you. In reality it isn't foreign to you at all . . . I would recommend that you read the preface and the ending since these express its sense most immediately.[6]

A common thread runs through these and similar remarks – that the book is short, perhaps too short, that verbal explanations might be possible, but that he is "quite incapable of writing a commentary on the book" or "to write it again."[7]

[S]ome of your questions want a very lengthy answer and you know how difficult it is for me to write on logic. That's also the reason why my book is so short, and consequently so obscure.
    As to the shortness of the book I am *awfully sorry for it; but what can I do*?! If you were to squeeze me out like a lemon you would get nothing more out of me . . . So don't be angry that I cannot make my book bigger. I would if I could.[8]

[6] *CL*, pp. 111, 115–117, and 124–126 (letters to Russell, March 13, June 12, and August 19, 1919); LvF, pp. 94f. (October/November 1919, German edition, p. 35).
[7] *CL*, pp. 115f. and 126.
[8] *CL*, p. 124; letter to C. K. Ogden (*LO*), the first translator of the *Tractatus*, p. 46 (May 5, 1922).

Some might view this as the conceit of an author who claims for himself the artist's prerogative to be difficult by refusing to explain his work. However, Wittgenstein himself offers a much more straightforward account of why his remarks cannot be elaborated, explained, or repeated, why he believes that it is all as clear as crystal, and why his thoughts are nevertheless difficult, if not impossible to understand.

In his letters to prospective publisher Ludwig von Ficker, Wittgenstein referred to the worthiest books as those "that are written honestly through and through." The characterization of his own book indicates how it demands the honesty of a faithful reporter or even recorder: "It is essentially the presentation of a system. And this presentation is *extremely* compact since I have only recorded in it what – and how it has – really occurred to me."[9] This suggests that the *Tractatus Logico-Philosophicus* is a record of separate mental events. Many of these first appeared in the wartime notebooks, where they are dated like entries in a diary. On some days he notes privately (using coded script) that he has worked but there are no corresponding philosophical entries, and even where he remarks that he "worked quite a lot. Not entirely without success" he has very few short remarks to show for it.[10] It appears that while he works, Wittgenstein is waiting for something to occur to him, then to write down what and how it really did occur to him. The German word for this is "*einfallen*," which means "have an idea" but also, literally, "fall into" or "invade." Indeed, his diary shows that Wittgenstein was waiting for such occurrences or ideas before he jotted down what was to become the first philosophical remark of his wartime notebooks:

---

[9] LvF, pp. 92 and 96 (December 4 and October 1919, German edition, pp. 38 and 32).

[10] Compare, for example, remarks from September and early October 1914 in the "Secret" Diaries (SD) with the entries in the *Notebooks 1914–1916* (*NB*) – these separately published remarks, coded and uncoded, were culled from the same notebooks. He reports that he has been working on September 10, 15, and 28 but there are no philosophical remarks recorded on those days. On September 24, October 2 and 6, he reports that he has worked quite a bit. There are 1 to 4 remarks recorded on those days. A coded remark from September 15 sheds light on this situation: "I can work best now while peeling potatoes. I always volunteer for it. It is for me just what lense-grinding was for Spinoza" (SD, p. 21; cf. p. 29). This would suggest that "working" neither involved note-taking nor drafting on paper, with only a few resulting remarks transcribed into the notebooks. "Working" meant thinking, hoping that something would occur to him, namely some idea to write down in his notebooks.

21.8.14

Is my working over with once and for all?!! The devil knows! Will nothing ever occur to me again? I am completely "unfamiliar" with all the concepts of my work. I *see* nothing!!!

22.8.14

Have been stuck on a sandbank for 3 days now. Work frequently with many interruptions and up until now without any success at all. Still can't come upon anything solid. Everything dissolves into smoke. Take heart!!!

Logic must take care of itself.[11]

We witnessed another prominent instance of such an *Einfall* in the notebooks when we saw how the picture theory of language occurred to Wittgenstein on the basis of a newspaper report (see above, pp. 37 and 59).[12]

The task of recording what and how something really came to mind implies its own standards of precision and clarity. When he *sees* something, Wittgenstein attempts to capture succinctly just what he is seeing, mindful of the special conditions under which it occurred to him.[13] These special conditions are just the ones that set the stage for his thought experiment – the works of Russell and Frege, the problems they raise, the previous discussions he had with them, and their implicit faith or fundamental trust in the hypothesis that such reflections are surely not nonsensical but within the limits of language

---

[11] Except for the last line that opens *NB*, this text was written in coded script and was published on p. 18 of SD. "Stuck on a sandbank" was the riverboat on which Wittgenstein was stationed. "Take heart" is a translation of "*nur zu*," an injunction to confidently take a leap ("Go ahead! What are you waiting for?"). In these "Secret" Diaries Wittgenstein repeatedly returns to the question of whether anything will ever occur to him again (see pp. 42, 55, and 60). They also show him waiting for the magic word ("Yesterday it was on the tip of my tongue. But then it slides back again") or a flash of illumination (see pp. 42 and 57, also 28, 31f.). See also *NB*, the entries of January 20 and June 3, 1915.

[12] Compare the following observation by one of Wittgenstein's friends, J. P. Stern: "'What I invent are new *similes*,' he wrote in 1931. This ability of pictorial thinking in parallels (which could be called 'lateral thinking') has something in common with Goethe's 'object-oriented thinking'; and it is this that he admired in Lichtenberg (even though he hardly thanked one, when this was pointed out to him). This gift, one of the main sources of his philosophical insights, was fully developed already when the *Tractatus* assumed its final shape. The core thought of this book consists in the insight, after all (or, to use Lichtenberg's word, in the '*Einfall*') that sentences are pictures; that the relation of language and world loses its puzzling character once we recognize that language has a structure which in a meaningful way resembles that of the world" (Stern 1990, p. 25 and see *CV*, p. 16 for the Wittgenstein quote from 1931).

[13] On February 9, 1931 Wittgenstein remarked: "My thoughts are so evanescent, evaporate so fast, like dreams which must be recorded immediately upon awakening if they are not to be forgotten right away" (MT, diary p. 65).

and the world. Pursuing a general account of linguistic significance and the relation of language and world, it occurred to Wittgenstein that the world is all that is the case. Proposition 1 of the *Tractatus* is thus a prominently placed faithful record of such a real occurrence. Its manner of presentation also exhibits the remark as a relatively isolated mental event, separate from all others but one that arose in the context of a single systematic thought experiment – this latter aspect indicated by the system of numbering.[14] The somewhat opaque consecutive numbering of otherwise more and less isolated remarks indicates also that Wittgenstein's thought experiment is not grounded in secure first premises that confer validity on everything that comes after them. Instead, the reader is confronted merely with the implicit claim of systematicity and thus with the promise that, in the end, all will actually hang together and form a consistent body of thought. For the time being, however, the reader knows only that "This book will be understood perhaps only by those who themselves have thought at one time or another the thoughts that are expressed in it." (Many years later, in the preface to the *Philosophical Investigations*, Wittgenstein echoed and varied this warning: "I should not like my writing to spare other people the trouble of thinking. But, if possible, to stimulate someone to thoughts of his own.")

In this chapter we will therefore entertain the proposal that Wittgenstein produced the *reductio*-argument of the *Tractatus* along these, surely somewhat idealized lines: if speaking about language and its relation to the world had sense, he may have begun asking himself, what thoughts about this relation would occur to me? With the hypothetical "if speaking about these matters had sense" he put himself in a leisurely, idling mood, granting himself a temporary philosophical holiday.[15] His hypothetical scenario thus set the stage for a thought experiment: from the thoughts which in the course of the experiment invaded or fell into ("*einfallen*") his consciousness,

---

[14] Regarding *TLP* 1 as an "occurrence," see page 123 and note 70 below. LvF, p. 39 (p. 97 of the translation, December 5, 1919): "And by the way, the decimal numbers of my sentences would absolutely have to be printed, too, for they alone lend perspicuity and clarity to the book which would be an incomprehensible mess without this numbering."

[15] Wittgenstein thus readies himself for the thought experiment and gives himself a break from the ordinary employment of language by adopting his hypothesis and an unquestioned faith in the supposedly unlimited expressive power of language. This is not unlike Descartes's deliberate retreat from the world in the preface to his *Meditations*: a thorough investigation of the foundation of all belief requires a leisurely setting at the fireplace. Concerning the metaphor of language idling during a philosophical holiday, compare *PI* remarks 38 and 132.

he preserved the best, precisely observing, recording, and ordering what really occurred to him. His descriptive acuity thus produced a narrative of real, though isolated, mental events. And the resulting series of remarks shows, among other things, that sentences dealing with language and its relation to the world are nonsensical.

INVENTION AND REFLECTION

So far, Wittgenstein's manner of writing was considered merely an effort to produce honest descriptions of actual mental events. I have so far refrained from using for his short remarks the label "aphorism," which suggests that each of these remarks is a small artwork in its own right. Just as we do not need to view Wittgenstein as an "artist in intellect," we do not need to appreciate his writing aesthetically.[16] And yet, much more needs to be said about his choice of the peculiar method of recording only what – and how it has – really occurred to him. After all, Wittgenstein's pursuit of this method explains not only why his remarks cannot be elaborated, explained, or repeated, and why he believes that it is all as clear as crystal. It also suggests that he deliberately chose an approach that renders his thoughts hard, if not impossible to understand.

He cannot elaborate, explain, or repeat his remarks since as records of isolated mental events each is unique unto itself. The best and only thing to be done for each thought is to capture it succinctly. He considers his thoughts to be precise and clear since they are mere descriptions – faithful and accurate – of real moments of clarity and insight. Yet, no one can understand them since, as opposed to most philosophical writing, his remarks do not persuade by force of their established content and its implications. Only the experience of conducting or reenacting the thought experiment can provide an understanding of Wittgenstein's thinking – though not of his sentences.

In order to know why Wittgenstein would choose a method of writing that carried such a risk of misunderstanding, one needs to know first what, if any, alternatives there were. Wittgenstein considered only one alternative for the *Tractatus*, and this has the drawback

---

[16] "Those commentators who have called these sentences 'aphoristic' hold that aphorism is a tool of style and that it may safely be ignored by the philosophical interpreter" (Goff 1969, p. 58).

that it cannot ordinarily be practiced within the confines of a book.

The right method of philosophy would really be this: To say nothing but what can be said, that is, the sentences of natural science – that is something that has nothing to do with philosophy – and then always, whenever others want to say something metaphysical, to reveal to them that they had failed to give meaning to certain signs in their sentences. This method would be unsatisfactory for the other – he wouldn't have the feeling that we were teaching him philosophy – but it would be the only strictly correct method. (*TLP* 6.53)[17]

On this strictly correct method of philosophy, Wittgenstein himself would not be saying anything nonsensical at all. He would leave this to those who still maintained a fundamental faith in the power of language to express any sense whatsoever. His prodding would help them to the experience that their attempts to express philosophical ideas has led them to utter nonsensical sentences.[18]

While Wittgenstein did not choose this method, the one he did adopt proceeds in analogy to it. By embarking on a thought experiment that begins with hypothetical premises that are then led to absurdity, he leaves open whether we should consider the text of the *Tractatus* as something that *he* is saying or writing. For all the reader knows, it results from the adoption of the hypothetical premises and an experimental "what then?" – where the tentative adoption of these premises does not require an author who is personally committed to them. To understand Wittgenstein is merely to understand that he conducted a thought experiment in the course of which an attempt to express philosophical thoughts ran up against the limits of language and thus resulted in failure.

This brings to the fore another question concerning Wittgenstein's method of writing. On the one hand, readers are never drawn into a continuous stream of thought, never allowed to participate in the

[17] The later Wittgenstein moved the method of recording mental occurrences or *Einfälle* toward the dialogical situation envisioned by *TLP* 6.53. In the *Philosophical Investigations* the conditions under which thoughts occurred to him were no longer part of a single overarching thought experiment, but arose in the course of an ongoing conversation with hypothetical interlocutors.

[18] The availability of this method explains why Wittgenstein was ready to engage with Russell and many others in conversation about the *Tractatus* – just as long as he did not have to elaborate it in writing.

thought processes of the author, never given the illusion that they are listening to Wittgenstein's inner voice. On the other hand, the systematic numbering of the remarks suggests the presence of a system of thought, and the remarks themselves have a rather authoritative sound: "The world is all that is the case." So, when Wittgenstein states that he records what and how it really has occurred to him, are we to imagine that he is listening to some voice of inspiration or that he is merely paying attention to his own thought processes? In other words: who is speaking when a thought occurs to Wittgenstein and is recorded by him? Wittgenstein's remarks are systematically ambiguous in this regard. Each is personal in that it records something that occurred to *him*; in that sense it reflects *his Einfälle* or ideas. At the same time, each remark is impersonal and absolute, not because it is proven or justified, but on the contrary because it seems to come from nowhere with oracular or apodictic certainty, that is, it sounds like the voice of God laying down the law: "By the way: Objects are colorless" (*TLP* 2.0232).[19]

Here we approach for the first time a definition of Wittgenstein's writing as specifically "aphoristic." All writing has to negotiate the gulf between the particular and the universal, between the author's idiosyncratic voice and the printed word's claim to objectivity. While most writing seeks to blend these opposites, Wittgenstein's remarks dramatize their opposition. According to Gerhard Neumann, this defines the aphorism, and his definition therefore focuses not on literary or stylistic features but on the procedure of aphoristic thinking.

[The aphorism] insists upon the *presentation of the conflict* between the singular and its subsumption under the general. It presents the conflict between on the one hand what's observed, remarked, apprehended by the senses and on the other hand what has the character of a maxim, of the

---

[19] See, for example, Hampshire 1991, p. 3: "The non-argumentative, aphoristic style of the *Tractatus* is designed to show that the deliverances of genius are to be accepted as 'perceptions' (his later word), and not as the testable and reversible conclusions of argument. Russell described the assertions in the *Tractatus* as being like the *Ukases* of the tsar. Either the *Tractatus* contained the final truth about philosophy, which need be no longer discussed, as Wittgenstein believed at the time, or the whole conception of the relation between language and reality in that work was mistaken . . . There is no halfway success, and that is why it does not help to read even the great philosophers of the past, who are only a distraction from direct vision, or epiphany." Compare Monk 1990, p. 156.

reflected or abstracted by the mind. Individual experience and system of thought, the orders of feeling and thought, the capacities to detail and to abstract, all present themselves in the aphorism in their non-dissociable confrontation.

From this results a special relation between the aphorism and its creator or reader (who are often one and the same person): this reader always completes anew the "presentation" of the conflict between sensed particularity and thought universality, either by "supplying" a given general sentence with individual experience or inversely by "extrapolating in thought" from a detailed observation that is recorded in the aphorism. The reader thus alternates between situating a reflection given in the text and reflecting the situations created by the text. This gives central significance to the arrangement of aphorisms in smaller and larger groups, as practiced by many authors: through the confrontation of the texts within the group the reader is drawn into the reciprocal play of inducing and deducing. In a sense, the reader is thereby only created as a partner for the given situation of thought and representation.[20]

Gerhard Neumann established this definition of the aphorism without consideration of Wittgenstein, but by reflecting on authors whose aphorisms were read and appreciated by Wittgenstein. These include Lichtenberg and Goethe, Schopenhauer and Nietzsche, Hugo von Hofmannsthal and Karl Kraus (but also Francis Bacon, Angelus Silesius, Marie von Ebner-Eschenbach, perhaps Novalis, Schlegel, Schnitzler, Musil, and others). Though he did not arrange his aphorisms in groups, Georg Christoph Lichtenberg's remarks provide the paradigm for Neumann's focus on the aphorism's procedure of thought. Indeed, Lichtenberg's aphorisms have been taken as thought experiments that inaugurate a reciprocal interplay of *Einfall* (the idea that occurs to the author) and *Klärung* (the articulation of that idea).[21] In order to further appreciate Wittgenstein's method of conducting a thought experiment for and with his readers, it is useful to establish in greater detail the method of *Einfall* and *Klärung* in Lichtenberg and Wittgenstein.

---

[20] Neumann 1976b, pp. 5f; cf. Neumann 1976a and Gockel 1973. After rejecting the treatment of Wittgenstein's aphorism as mere "tools of style" (see note 16 above), Robert Goff maintains that "[i]t is not philosophically appropriate to distinguish his style from meaning, nor his use of language from theories he is alleged to have about language" (1969, p. 70).

[21] See the 1933 article that may be credited with founding modern-day investigations of the aphorism as a literary genre, Mautner 1976.

EXPERIMENTS WITH IDEAS

In his diaries of 1930–1932, Wittgenstein frequently remarks on his method of writing. Here, for example, is a remark dated May 9, 1930: "One often thinks – and I myself *often* make this mistake – that everything one thinks can be written down. In reality one can only write down – that is, without doing something stupid & inappropriate – what arises in us in the form of writing."[22] Again, Wittgenstein refers to a seemingly impersonal process of something arising or originating in him, something that already has the right form, one that is amenable to being written down. Anything that can be described, for example, can be described in writing.

On October 31, 1931 Wittgenstein expands on this and continues with a remark about Lichtenberg: "I believe that my sentences are mostly descriptions of visual images that occur to me. Lichtenberg's wit is the flame that can burn on a pure candle only."[23] In the context of these diaries, Wittgenstein's worries about the distorting effects of vanity on his own writing and on the aphorisms of Karl Kraus, this remark on Lichtenberg's purity thus harks back to the statement that the worthiest books are those "that are written honestly through and through."[24]

This is only one of various instances where Wittgenstein appealed to Lichtenberg's model. As early as 1913, he presented Bertrand Russell with "a secondhand copy of Lichtenberg": "I hope you'll

---

[22] MT, diary p. 27. Wittgenstein used wavy underlining to indicate his dissatisfaction with the formulation "arises in us." The remark continues: "Everything else seems comical & as it were like dirt. That is, something that needs to be wiped off." Compare p. 101: "That something occurs to you is a gift from heaven, but it depends on what you make of it"; also the diary entries on pp. 98f. and 120 and the following remark by Karl Kraus: "Language doesn't clothe the thought but thought grows into language; this is something of which the modest creator can never convince the brazen tailor" (1955, pp. 325f.). See Nordmann 2001 for a more extensive discussion of Wittgenstein's diaries and his philosophical method.

[23] MT, diary p. 114.

[24] On March 10, 1937 Wittgenstein writes to Ludwig Hänsel (*PPO*, p. 301): "Someone who writes aphorisms, remarks, must have *digested*, otherwise the aphorism is a fraud. (I know of course how much the aphoristic way of writing – especially through Kraus – is part of our time. And how much I am myself influenced by him. Also in the bad sense.)" Wittgenstein placed Lichtenberg above Kraus, noting that "the greatness of what one writes depends on everything else one does," see *CV*, p. 75. For remarks on Kraus and vanity in his later diary, see MT, diary pp. 104 and 205, also 30, 101. (Note that Kraus 1955, pp. 132 and 168 anticipates accusations of vanity.)

enjoy some of it at least."[25] To facilitate Russell's enjoyment, Wittgenstein highlighted a few of Lichtenberg's remarks. Perhaps he thought that Russell would find them especially congenial and delightful. Or perhaps he was using them to convey something to Russell. This, at any rate, is one of the highlighted remarks: "The question 'Should one philosophize for oneself?' is like the question, 'Should one shave oneself?' the answer is, Yes, if one can do it well." Wittgenstein isolated this remark within a larger thought experiment of Lichtenberg's and thereby helped to create it as a free-standing aphorism.[26] It works in isolation precisely because it does not exhaust itself in its punch line. On the contrary, Lichtenberg's two throw-away lines only initiate what can become a sustained movement of thought. One who shaves badly should not shave himself or else he may just cut his head off. But what are the dangers of philosophizing badly? Philosophy is too important and too dangerous, the remark appears to suggest, as to be entrusted entirely to the Enlightenment's slogan that everyone should think for themselves and its facile corollary that everyone can have their own philosophy. And yet, Lichtenberg himself is an exemplary representative of the Enlightenment, an advocate of self-thinking (rather than reading and learning what to think), a proponent of philosophy as an activity rather than a doctrine. The only alternatives to thinking for oneself are equally unpalatable – either not to think at all or to grow a long beard and let someone else think for you. Moving on from there, however, the remark also suggests that philosophizing is dangerous even when done properly: since this activity involves sharp tools of analysis and criticism, it threatens to cut off the long beards of tradition and prejudice as well as the heads of those whose livelihood relies on the perpetuation of tradition and prejudice.[27] So, does this remark endorse self-thinking or discourage it? Is philosophy more dangerous when it is badly done and leaves our misconceptions intact, or when it is done well and thereby draws blood? On the one hand, this activity is understood only by those who think the thoughts themselves, and on the other

---

[25] Quoted from Wittgenstein's inscription, see *CL*, p. 36.

[26] Lichtenberg 1968/71, C 142 (p. 44 in Lichtenberg 1990). The question highlighted by Wittgenstein is part of a longer reflection on how to usefully teach philosophy.

[27] In another remark Lichtenberg notes that "it is nearly impossible to carry the torch of truth through a crowd without someone's beard getting singed" (Lichtenberg 1968/71, Mat I 153).

hand, self-thinking needs to be done well, co-ordinated by a shared set of tools and perhaps the shared context of a thought experiment that is staged for the readers by the author.

This remark by Lichtenberg exemplifies how a reader gets drawn into a procedure of thought and is prompted to take what J. P. Stern calls a "double look."[28] The remark begins with the contrivance of analogizing a very abstract and a very concrete notion (to think for oneself, to shave oneself). It then posits – without argument! – a startling commonality between them, and thus inaugurates an open-ended reflection about the analogy. This reflection is not controlled by the remark itself but relies on the reader to supply individual experience and critical reflection. Indeed, it is characteristic of Lichtenberg's aphoristic procedure of thought that this open-ended reflection may well culminate in a rejection of the analogy. No – someone might conclude – philosophy is not dangerous but always beneficial, and as opposed to the case of shaving, there is no harm done when one does not do it well. The startling analogy between shaving and philosophizing functions as a hypothesis that sets in motion a critical thought experiment that may or may not end up endorsing the hypothesis: Lichtenberg is not trying to convince us but to get us going, perhaps to recognize, perhaps to criticize or clarify something. In the words of Stern: "The aim of all aphorisms, we recall, is not to give a coherent account, but to elicit a response of thought."[29]

The method of writing aphoristically is therefore nothing other than the apt and, literally, provocative expression of isolated thoughts ("the more the nail has been hit on the head"). Indeed, Gottfried Gabriel suggests that for Wittgenstein, following Karl Kraus, "to express thoughts" meant as much as "to write aphorisms."[30] To be sure, Gabriel's provocative formulation blurs the distinction between those thoughts that can be expressed in sentences and those others that can only be expressed through the procedure of a *reductio*-argument

---

[28] Stern 1959, pp. 200–217.

[29] Ibid., p. 112. Compare his extended discussion, on pp. 121f., of Lichtenberg's five-word "aphoristic experiment": "God, who winds our sundials" (Lichtenberg 1968/71, F 1022; p. 99 in Lichtenberg 1990). For the justification of such discussions, see Kraus: "My barbs require commentary. Otherwise they are too easily understood" (1955, p. 287). Or compare Nietzsche 1998, the very end of his preface to the *Genealogy of Morality*: "An aphorism, righteously minted and cast, has not been 'deciphered' yet when it has been read; rather, its *exegesis* only begins there and it requires an exegetical art."

[30] See Gabriel 1991, pp. 26–29. Compare Janik and Toulmin 1973, pp. 198–200 and throughout.

or an aphorism. But his point can be taken as follows. At times a great admirer of his contemporary Kraus, Wittgenstein saw in the work of the Viennese journalist, essayist, writer of aphorisms, and critic of language that the *Einfall* or sudden appearance in language of a thought can be identified with "aphorism." And as with all aphoristic writing, the thoughts that occur to Kraus, his *Einfälle*, are not to be mistaken for his opinions or beliefs:[31]

Because I take its word for it, the thought comes. –
The thought provoked language. One word led to another. –
Between the lines there is room for meaning, at best. Between words there
  is room for more: for the thought. –
The thought is a child of love. Opinion is accepted in bourgeois society.[32]

So far, we have seen two reasons why Wittgenstein's method of writing suits the thought experiment of his indirect proof or *reductio ad absurdum*. First, instead of recommending the author's own system of belief, it allows for a system of thought to seemingly articulate *itself* with the help and investment of the reader. Second, Wittgenstein's remarks, even when taken by themselves, might challenge his reader to enter into the experimental mode by providing the necessary commitments, establishing the relevant connections, and raising the critical questions. This would ensure that the reader can actually undergo that particular experience of failing to express any thought whatsoever in language. What remains to be shown is how Wittgenstein's remarks, like those of Lichtenberg, do in fact engage the reader in thought experiments even when taken by themselves. How, for example, do the following two remarks provoke and afford a "double look"?[33]

4.031 In the sentence a situation is as it were put together experimentally . . .
4.0311 One name stands for one thing, another for another thing and among them they are connected, so the whole presents – like a living picture – the state of affairs.[34]

---

[31] Witness his frequent remarks to the effect that he has no mastery of language but that language masters him. See, for example, Kraus 1955, pp. 116, 134, 164, 291, 326, 334, and 338.
[32] Ibid., pp. 464, 292, 325, 112; cf. 116, 134f.
[33] Other examples will be presented in note 47 and pp. 123f. below.
[34] The two remarks follow almost immediately upon one another. Omitted here is only the second part of *TLP* 4.031: "Instead of, 'This sentence has such and such a sense,' we can just about say, 'This sentence represents such and such a situation.'" In the *Prototractatus* the two parts of 4.031 occur as separate *Einfälle*. *TLP* 4.0311 does not appear in the *Prototractatus* at all, but occurs in the earlier *Notebooks 1914–1916*, dated November 4, 1914.

As for the first of these remarks, we can expand its meaning by considering its variants or drafts, by noting, for example, that "situation" replaced "world" or that this sentence was originally followed by a parenthetical remark about the model of a car accident in a Paris courtroom. But even when taking it just as it stands, we may wonder what is meant by "experiment" here, or what kind of experiment is being referred to. One might first think of a scientific experiment. Read in this manner, the remark states that every sentence is a hypothesis that is tested against the world: if the situation obtains, the sentence or hypothesis turn out to be true; if it does not obtain, the sentence or hypothesis represents only how the world would or could have been if it were true.[35] But, of course, this is not how it goes in science. In science, true and false hypotheses do not come in symmetrical pairs, the true a denial of the false one and vice versa, with nature just happening to agree with one and thereby not the other. Instead, some hypotheses are false because they refer to nonexistent entities or processes, others are true not because they happen to represent the world accurately but because they organize our representations in the first place (see *TLP* 6.343, 6.35). But even if there were no problem with the conception of sentences as hypotheses, should we be speaking of a scientific experiment here? We think of scientific experiments as manipulations of nature, while *TLP* 4.031 refers to the manipulation of words, an experiment that is performed well before one finds out what the world is really like.

   What does it mean, then, to put together a situation, and what is experimental about it? Consulting the various English translations (all of them correct) of Wittgenstein's *"probeweise,"* we find "for the sake of experiment," "as an experiment," and "by way of experiment."[36] Taken together, these terms introduce us to a whole set of apparently competing, perhaps complementary analogies – the analogy to science

---

[35] If what matters here is the obtaining or nonobtaining of a situation (*Sachlage*), why doesn't Wittgenstein employ "state of affairs" (*Sachverhalt*) for the sake of consistent usage? Could it be that, despite numerous interpretive attempts to the contrary, Wittgenstein does not really distinguish between *Sachlage* and *Sachverhalt* after all? (He speaks of a state of affairs in 4.0311. Daniel Kolak chose to translate both terms as "elementary fact" and in 4.031 simply as "fact," see his edition, p. 52: "To go beyond this is, in my opinion, mere translational pedantry.")

[36] These are the translations by C. K. Ogden (1922) and Kolak (1998) on the one hand, and on the other hand by Pears and McGuinness (1961) who translate 4.031: "In a proposition a situation is, as it were, constructed by way of experiment."

is joined by analogies to engineering and art. To say that the sentence puts a situation together "for the sake of experiment" and "as an experiment" underscores the analogy to science. Indeed, it addresses our previous concern by stressing the purpose of sentences. Sentences picture the world, after all, and in virtue of that they bring about a decision concerning truth or falsity, that is, we put them together *for the sake of* an experiment. On this interpretation, the German "*probeweise*" is taken in the sense of "*auf die Probe stellen* (put to a test)," and the "situation" that is put together is a possible situation in the world that is pictured by the sentence.[37]

In contrast, "*by way of* experiment" concerns not the purpose of the sentence but the very process of constructing it. It takes experimentation, trial and error, or a kind of tinkering to fit the parts together such that they add up to a sentence. This translation picks up on the "*probieren* (trying out)" in "*probeweise*"; and it underscores that the sentence itself is a constructed "situation," namely a configuration of names (*TLP* 3.14, 3.143). The builder of sentences is thus likened to an engineer who must know, for example, in what sentences a given name can occur, how it can combine with other names, and so on. This tinkerer is concerned to get the sentence right; how it will fare in the world is a separate question altogether. And every correctly put together sentence is a situation, even a world unto itself, and that it pictures a situation in the world is, literally, coincidental.

The engineering analogy suggests yet another interpretation of *TLP* 4.031. Builders of sentences are creative and playful inventors of worlds, they rehearse possibilities, possible sentences along with possible worlds. This analogy to art exploits the fact that, in German, a theatrical rehearsal is a "*Probe*" (and that rehearsing is "*proben*"). In rehearsals things are tried out, tentative results are produced which are then subject to scrutiny and criticism – and this dimension, too, resonates in "*probeweise*."

"In the sentence a situation is as it were put together experimentally (*probeweise*)" – this remark records an idea that occurred to Wittgenstein while he was conducting his thought experiment concerning the relation of language and world (always under the hypothetical

---

[37] In his correspondence with translator C. K. Ogden, Wittgenstein never mentions this remark. Are we to assume, therefore, that Wittgenstein thought the translation "for the sake of experiment" adequate?

assumption that language is powerful enough to express thoughts about this relation). His *Einfall* is presented as an isolated mental event, it stands by and for itself. If it were seamlessly worked into a flow of discursive reasoning, we might not have paused to note how it refers to science, engineering, and art all at the same time. Indeed, one of these three aspects might have been singled out from the start, thus assuming dominance and rendering our questions moot. The aphoristic character of the remark comes to bear when the reader is challenged to trace out its articulation or *Klärung*, having to confront its multiple meanings and working them back into the larger context. Is it the point, perhaps, of the suggested internal relation between facts in the world and sentences as facts, that a well-invented and structurally sound sentence is always already a candidate for truth and falsity in the world? Or is the point that a successful experiment upon the combination of words inevitably results in a probe or *Probe*, an instrument or a test of what is or is not really the case? Or yet again, is the point that a playful invention within and constrained by language (the ways in which names can and cannot be combined) is an extension of our senses – a sensor – that helps us determine reality?[38] These interpretive suggestions lend consistency to *TLP* 4.031 and its wider context; but they require a reader who plays along, who has become caught up in the thought experiment, and who supplies what Wittgenstein did not spell out.[39]

This "triple look" at *TLP* 4.031 considered only the meaning of "*probeweise*" or "experimentally." Two options present themselves now. The first option is to dwell a little longer and take a reflexive turn. If in a sentence a situation is put together experimentally, then what about this sentence? Does it advance a (scientific) hypothesis about the relation of language and world? Does it fail to create a situation

---

[38] This, of course, is what is stated in the second half of *TLP* 4.031; see note 34 above. Compare *NB*, April 3, 1915: "The sentence is a measure of the world."

[39] Critiquing and extending Diamond and Conant's program, Ostrow 2002 recommends a similar approach in respect to the notions of "sense" and "nonsense," suggesting that the piecemeal activity of seeking out nonsense amounts to the discovery of the "liberating word." Ostrow 2002, p. 16 quotes from Wittgenstein's *Philosophical Remarks* (*PR*), p. 2: "Philosophy unties the knots in our thinking, which we have tangled up in an absurd way; but to do that it must make movements that are just as complicated as the knots. Although the *result* of philosophy is simple, its methods for arriving there cannot be so."

and to become a world unto itself and is it therefore, strictly speaking, not a soundly constructed sentence at all but mere nonsense? At the very end of the *Tractatus*, Wittgenstein invites us to revisit *TLP* 4.031 with these questions in mind, that is, to take a fourth look. In the *reductio*-argument he has put together a situation experimentally and conducts an experiment on our illusion that sentences like *TLP* 4.031 can express thoughts about the relation of mind and world. Now we see that *TLP* 4.031 is itself an experiment to express such a thought – one that results in failure.[40]

The second option is to move on in the text and to briefly consider the next remark (*TLP* 4.0311), another isolated and systematically ambiguous *Einfall* or idea, one that puts a different twist on the reflection that preceded it.

"One name stands for one thing, another for another thing and among them they are connected, so the whole presents – like a living picture – the state of affairs." As we begin to articulate or clarify this idea, our first question might pick up on another artful ambiguity. What does the "among them" refer to, we might ask – among each name and its corresponding thing, among the names, or among the things? The first of these three possibilities can be ruled out very quickly. The name *stands for* a thing and that is no "connection" at all but an arbitrary co-ordination. To add that name and thing are connected would be confusing or redundant; also it would not give us the last part of the remark, namely that the whole sentence presents the state of affairs. This leaves us with the second and third possibilities, and the point here is that, once again, we do not have to choose between them. Indeed, the remark works best when we do not fix the meaning of "among them": there is a connection among the names (the sentence) and a connection among the things (the state of affairs), and since the names are co-ordinated with the words, the whole sentence presents a state of affairs.

So far so good, but now arises a host of problems. Wittgenstein did not write "the whole sentence" but only "the whole," which would seem to include the whole of names and things, their co-ordination

---

[40] The fourth section of the conclusion will point out that this experiment – the sentence *TLP* 4.031 – *makes sense* by showing us that it does not *have sense*.

to each other, their relations among each other. This makes it difficult to simply oppose sentence and state of affairs. Instead, the state of affairs is presented by a whole in which names are co-ordinated with things while at the same time, as signs, names *are* things. We thus encounter again that a sentence *and* a state of affairs present a state of affairs because sentences *are* states of affairs. So, on the one hand the picture stands in a distant picturing relationship to what is pictured, on the other hand the picture immediately participates in what is pictured – it is of the same kind.[41] At the same time, the picture is no ordinary picture, it is a "living picture (*lebendes Bild*)." This living picture does not "represent (*darstellen*)" the state of affairs but "presents (*vorstellen*)" it.[42]

Our previous discussion of the sentence that rehearses a situation helps us to once again recognize a playful ambiguity here. Wittgenstein first reminds us of his geometrical conception of representation by means of co-ordination and projection, a kind of mapping. He also reminds us that it is not we who represent states of affairs, but that states of affairs present states of affairs.[43] And as in a game of charades – the game of creating a living picture or *tableau vivant*[44] – certain elements (names, things, postures, or other signs) can haphazardly fall into a certain configuration and this configuration becomes a state of affairs that can then picture another state of affairs. Here, then, one state of affairs performs another when we take the German words "*vorstellen*" (to present) and "*Vorstellung* (performance)" in their theatrical meaning. The term "presents" thus assumes the same double meaning as when, in a game of charades,

---

[41] This, then, reminds us of chapter 1 and its discussion of the internal relation between object and representation, mind and world.

[42] In the remark preceding it (second part of *TLP* 4.031), for example, Wittgenstein uses "represent (*darstellen*)." Though he did make changes to the *Notebooks* version of *TLP* 4.0311 (replacing "represents" by "stands for"), he left the final clause unaltered.

[43] One of the next remarks in the original contexts of the *Notebooks* reads as follows: "Thus the sentence represents the state of affairs so to speak on its own accord (*auf eigene Faust*)." Dated November 5, 1914, this entry suggests that the sentence has a will of its own, that it does the representing quite by itself, by its own devices (Anscombe translates "off its own bat"). One can also take it as a miniaturized *reductio*-argument which shows that the question of volition simply drops out of the business of representation altogether. Representing does not involve doing, instead, representations arise spontaneously when certain structural relations obtain. This remark from the *Notebooks* was not included in later versions.

[44] Pears and McGuinness's edition of the *Tractatus* and Anscombe's translation of the *Notebooks* use "*tableau vivant*" for "*lebendes Bild*."

we have to guess what a certain person is presenting – she performs a posture and that posture represents or pictures something.[45]

In our interpretation of *TLP* 4.031 we confronted the possibilities of science, engineering, and art, and now we encounter in *TLP* 4.0311 two interpretations, one in terms of projective geometry, the other in terms of theatre or play. Again, our participation in the thought experiment allows us to reconcile and contextualize these interpretations – they need not be at odds with one another. This time, however, the allusion to art and aesthetics does not serve the celebration of a creative playfulness that lets us create sentences as small worlds unto their own. Instead, it brings out a lack of authenticity where one thing masquerades for another. The *tableau vivant* or living picture is not alive (it is "*lebend*" but not "*lebendig*"). Also, the notion that pictures (not authors, speakers) do the representing anticipates some of Wittgenstein's final remarks of the *Tractatus*: when the problem of representation is solved, life and experience have dropped out of sight (*TLP* 6.431, 6.52, 6.521); and once we appreciate the radical contingency of the world as it is and happens to be, we have to realize that what is of value to us cannot be expressed *in* that world (*TLP* 6.41). Since our values or our will can do nothing to alter the fundamental contingency of the world, any attempt to do so will be a source of unhappiness – it tempts us to force what cannot be forced and blinds us to reality. And the only way to achieve happiness – impossibly difficult at that – is just to live "in agreement with the world" as it is and happens to be (*TLP* 6.43).[46]

To be sure, the detailed interpretation of just two examples does not establish that every remark of Wittgenstein's inaugurates a thought experiment.[47] But as it happens, these two examples return us to

---

[45] We are familiar with that ambiguity also when we speak in the medical context of "presenting symptoms" – symptoms that present themselves, that are presented by the patient, and that represent a disease.

[46] Compare *NB*, June 11 and July 5, 1916; also Ishiguro 1981, and Diamond 2000.

[47] The pool of examples will be expanded throughout this book as other close readings join in. Take *TLP* 4.014 for another example: "The gramophone record, the musical thought, the score, the waves of sound, all stand to one another in that pictorial internal relation, which holds between language and the world. To all of them the logical plan is common. (Like the two youths in the fairy tale, their two horses, and their lilies. They are all in a certain sense one.)" This remark conveys a seemingly spontaneous insight (*Einfall*), inaugurates a process of clarification (*Klärung*), and ultimately eludes into a state of suspense. Encountering the last two parenthetical sentences, one may wish to know more about the fairy tale in question.

Georg Christoph Lichtenberg and his experimental method of philosophy. His *Einfälle* are what occur to him, they are records of a mental game of charades where a somewhat haphazard process can forge legitimate connections that can then produce creative insights into the world. But this very method of discovery also unsettles, unmoors him. It places him in a world of contingency and possibility in which all connections are as they are and happen to be, while his inventive mind has already connected them differently.

I wonder how many ideas there are hovering scattered in my head of which many pairs, if brought together, could prompt the greatest discoveries . . . and so one must bring things together deliberately, one must *experiment* with ideas. –

One is never happier than when a strong feeling tells us that we are living in *this* world *only*. My unhappiness is that I exist never in *this* but in any number of possible chains of connection which my imagination creates with support from my *conscience*.[48]

CRITICISM AGAINST SKEPTICISM

Aphoristic thought experiments belong to the critical tradition in philosophy not just because they engage the reader in critical thinking, allowing them to think themselves the thoughts expressed in the book. They belong to this tradition also in that the critique of metaphysics and language serves as their background or point of departure – the author and the reader of aphorisms no longer live in a unique,

---

While the definite article points to Goethe's *Märchen*, which revolves around a lily and a youth who are in many ways one, Jim Klagge points out that Wittgenstein is referring to the Grimm brothers' "Golden Children" – in which the two youths, two horses, and two lilies mirror each other and yet, in a fairy-tale sense, are "literally" one. The added reference to fairy tales suggests that the comparison between music and language is more than a mere analogy. Instead, it invokes a parallelism between music, language, and the world which are yet "in a certain sense one." Wittgenstein made this Schopenhauerian point far more explicitly in his notebooks, "perfectly aware how unclear all these sentences are" (*NB*, August 2, 1916). While suggesting more than a mere analogy, Wittgenstein withholds spelling out what more there is to the matter.

[48] Lichtenberg 1968/71, K 308 (pp. 53f. in Lichtenberg 1969) and J 948. Lichtenberg's description of greatest happiness corresponds to Wittgenstein's experience of feeling "absolutely safe" as described in LE, p. 41; cf. Malcolm 1984, p. 58. Short of finding this safety, both authors dwell in the sphere of wonder and possibility, the world of the thought experiment (see John 1988 and, for Lichtenberg, Schöne 1982).

rationally justified world but in any number of possible chains of connection. To understand why the aphoristic thought experiment is Wittgenstein's method of choice, one needs to appreciate that this choice is by no means unprecedented. On the contrary, Wittgenstein employs the popular idiom of an ill-defined and far-reaching critique of language to present his own, carefully delimited critique.

Somewhat along the lines of Gerhard Neumann (quoted on page 103 above), Franz Mautner and J. P. Stern offer definitions of the aphorism that align it more closely with philosophy than with literature. The aphorism is what inaugurates a movement or procedure of thought, namely an experiment that begins with a succinct record of what and how something really occurred. This experiment prompts attempts to articulate its insight since even its most concise formulation surrounds the aphorism with a field of linguistic tension.[49] Having concluded that the aphorism inaugurates a figure or movement of thought, they ask about the conditions that gave rise to such a method of thinking and writing, and find that those conditions make the aphorism "symbolical of the age, from Lichtenberg's day [the late eighteenth century] to ours, during which it has flourished." Stern elaborates:

The romantic stress on individual experience, the atomization of thought and feelings, the absence of commonly accepted religious beliefs, metaphysical presuppositions and moral standards, and the disintegration of a common culture – all these represent a mode of thought and feeling explored in many books and essays in the wake of Friedrich Schlegel, Leopardi, Baudelaire, Schopenhauer, and Nietzsche. The parallel between this modern consciousness and the aphorism is striking. In both cases fragments are endowed with values once resident in the whole: it is by virtue of an immanent, that is, self-conscious integration that they cease to be fragments, and no longer by virtue

[49] See Mautner 1976 and Stern 1959. Stern's book is of particular importance since he reflects Wittgenstein's relation to Lichtenberg throughout. His literary definition of the aphorism (p. 216) touches on many of the features that were highlighted in this chapter: "The aphorism, we have found, is a strange and surprisingly complex configuration of words. Its charm hides in an antithesis, perfectly integrated, issuing from a double look at a word or an idea. It conceals its autobiographical source, yet displays its process of generation . . . It is something of an experiment in words and ideas, yet it commits aphorist and reader alike to an irretrievable occasion in experience . . . It strikes us as both remarkably philosophical and remarkably literary . . . It and its definition involve us in a great many second thoughts about distinctions which common sense thought firmly established. And it gives one insight while suggesting many – indeed we find it difficult to tell how many, since it is always a little more than their occasion and a little less than their cause."

of a belief in a transcendent whole . . . Both modern self-consciousness and its symbol, the aphorism, are attempts at creating autonomous, self-centered, and "windowless" microcosms whose communication with the world and with each other is difficult in the extreme.[50]

Franz Mautner adds that in the philosophy especially of Kant, modern self-consciousness assigns center-stage in science and philosophy to "the *Einfall*, the unproven and unprovable hypothesis or 'inner intuition.'"[51] A systematic treatise is an appropriate medium for a general system of reason that dogmatically secures the agreement of language and world, representations and their objects. The aphorism becomes appropriate when criticism must accompany reason in all its endeavors, that is, every time it ventures out to make a claim on reality. The writers of aphorisms share a distrust of the lengthy treatise with its conceit of drawing things together:

Fiction has more letters than fact. (Karl Kraus)

An aphorism is a link in a chain of thoughts; it demands that the readers reconstruct this chain with their own means: this is demanding a lot. An aphorism is an audacity. (Friedrich Nietzsche)

There can hardly be a stranger commodity in the world than books. Printed by people who don't understand them, sold by people who don't understand them, bound, criticized and read by people who don't understand them, and now even written by people who don't understand them. (Lichtenberg)[52]

---

[50] Stern 1959, pp. 221f. In line with their epistemological characterization of the aphorism, Stern, Neumann, Mautner (see the following note), or Grenzmann (1976, pp. 196f.) end up taking Schlegel's romantic fragment as an example of the aphoristic method of writing and thinking. This undercuts Manfred Frank's attempt to oppose the two: "Wittgenstein's texts are no aphorisms but belong to the genre of the fragment." According to Frank, aphorisms are self-sufficient while romantic fragments intend an elusive whole and do so in a series where one fragment limits the other and where this process of ironic mutual negation indirectly represents the whole in its unrepresentability (Frank 1992, pp. 101–103). However, though the aphorism is usually taken to isolate an *Einfall* or idea, the four theorists of the aphoristic method emphatically reject that self-sufficiency is one of its defining features. Instead, they recognize that aphorisms frequently play off each other and are often carefully sequenced by their authors (least so by Lichtenberg and most conscientiously by Wittgenstein).

[51] "The first German aphorisms that self-consciously meant to represent a new literary genre – those of Friedrich Schlegel – were written just at the time when the *Einfall*, the unproven and unprovable hypothesis or 'inner intuition,' assumed center-stage in science and philosophy, and when there was a demand for the unity of art, science and philosophy" (Mautner 1976, p. 39, see pp. 406–410 regarding Schlegel and the romantic fragment).

[52] In German, Kraus's nearly untranslatable aphorism reads "*Schein hat mehr Buchstaben als Sein*" (1955, p. 267). Nietzsche's "*Sentenz*" was translated as "aphorism," a term that he himself would come to prefer (quoted on p. 54 of Mautner 1976; cf. pp. 406f.). Lichtenberg, 1968/71, K 172 (p. 176 in Lichtenberg 1990).

But more characteristic even than the distrust of treatises and books is the distrust of what occurs to the writer of aphorisms, that is, distrust of the *Einfälle* or ideas themselves. Their very source at the heart of subjectivity renders them suspect:

Shake an aphorism and out falls a lie and left over is banality. (Arthur Schnitzler)

To write an aphorism if one can is often difficult. It is much easier to write an aphorism if one cannot. (Karl Kraus)

Aside from the good & genuine my book the Tractatus Log.-Phil. also contains kitsch, that is, passages with which I filled in the gaps and so-to-speak in my own style. How much of the books consists of such passages I don't know & it is difficult to fairly evaluate now. (Ludwig Wittgenstein)[53]

Banality and commonplace, subjectivity and vanity, clever didacticism and willful paradoxicality – all these threaten the aphorism. And especially for *fin de siècle* writings and especially in Wittgenstein's Vienna, they turned it into a formidable proving-ground. In order to write good aphorisms, everyone agreed, one has to acquire the art of writing artlessly. The dangerous temptation to cultivate aphoristic writing as a literary style undermines its ability to function critically. Wittgenstein addresses this danger when he notes in the *Tractatus*: "All philosophy is 'critique of language.' (Though not in the sense of Mauthner.) Russell's achievement is to have shown that the apparent logical form of the sentence need not be its real one" (*TLP* 4.0031). With this remark Wittgenstein distances himself from an ardent proponent of the aphoristic method who produced three volumes of *Contributions to a Critique of Language* (1901–1902). Wittgenstein does so by enlisting Bertrand Russell for a cause which the British philosopher furthered unwittingly and only by implication.[54]

Not to be confused with Franz Mautner, quoted above, Fritz Mauthner (1849–1923) set out "to save his world from the tyranny of language."[55] He eagerly took credit for what has been termed the

---

[53] Schnitzler was quoted by Gray 1987, p. 82 in a discussion of how aphorisms about aphorisms display the ambivalence of their authors. According to Gray, Karl Kraus's remark (1955, p. 132) expresses that "true aphorisms 'occur' to one when one least expects them" (Gray 1987, p. 85). Wittgenstein's observation appears in MT, diary pp. 30f. (dated May 16, 1930). Also, compare Mautner 1976, p. 52, where he quotes R. M. Meyer's verdict about the aphorism, that "banality is its unforgivable fault."

[54] However, compare the remark in Janik and Toulmin 1973, p. 121.

[55] Mauthner 1901/02, vol. I, p. 1.

Sprachkrise or crisis of language in *fin de siècle* Vienna, suggesting, for example, that he influenced its most celebrated manifestation, Hugo von Hofmannsthal's "Letter of Lord Chandos."[56] In that letter, the fictional Lord Chandos addresses himself to the real Francis Bacon, who has been credited as the inventor of the scientific aphorism and who served as patron saint for Mauthner's critique of language.[57] In his letter, Chandos despairs of the power of language to communicate truth. Leaving behind him his experience of the fullness and joys of life, Chandos becomes aware of the metaphorical, abstracted character of words that "crumbled in my mouth like mouldy fungi":

> Single words floated round me; they congealed into eyes which stared at me and into which I was forced to stare back – whirlpools which gave me vertigo and, reeling incessantly, led into the void . . .
>
> [T]he language in which I might be able not only to write but to think is neither Latin nor English, neither Italian nor Spanish but a language none of whose words is known to me, a language in which inanimate things speak to me and wherein I may one day have to justify myself before an unknown judge.[58]

Unlike Wittgenstein, Mauthner and Hofmannsthal focus on words, not sentences, and on the inability of words to capture the essence of things. Where Wittgenstein allows that descriptive sentences are composed of elements and are therefore just like the facts that they describe, Mauthner's and Hofmannsthal's crisis of language encompasses the descriptive language of science. Since "with the words of language and philosophy human beings can never move beyond a pictorial representation of the world," Mauthner writes, "language never coincides with nature, even where real or approximate laws have been found: in mathematics, in mechanics."[59] Having learned

---

[56] For a careful assessment of this claim, see Gray 1986, pp. 335 and 337f.

[57] See the entry on "Bacon's Doctrine of Idols" in the second, expanded edition of Mauthner's highly idiosyncratic dictionary of philosophy, Mauthner 1923, vol. I, pp. 127–145. (The first edition appeared in 1910.)

[58] Hofmannsthal 1952, pp. 134f. and 140f.

[59] Mauthner 1923, vol. I, pp. xi (introduction, section I) and p. 396 ("Encyclopaedia," section III). According to Gershon Weiler, "Mauthner demands a complete adequacy between things described and the terms of description" (1970, p. 93). Mauthner reiterates the abyss of language and nature (unbridgeable within language) in 1923, vol. I, pp. 429 ("Development"), 506 ("Form," section III), and 617 ("Goethe's Wisdom"); vol. II, pp. 107 ("Hypothesis") and 406f. ("Nature"); vol. III, pp. 106f. ("Schopenhauer [Will]"), 240f. ("Substance [*Stoff*]") and 513f. ("Chance").

from Ernst Mach that concepts serve to economically organize our sensations, Mauthner concludes that they cannot be true to nature. Failing to "coincide" with nature and experience, language conveys no truth whatsoever. The aphorism must therefore serve as a last refuge from a predicament that was described by Richard Gray:

> Subscribing to the characteristic world-view of this period, Mauthner conceives of reality as a chaos of non-related fragments. Only fragmentary forms of thought and expression – the *aperçu*, the aphorism – are commensurate with such a reality. Not only do these fragments imitate the fragmentariness of reality, but they make no claim to permanentness, to closure and finality; they resist being frozen into concepts.[60]

Mauthner's diagnosis of a crisis as well as his endorsement of the aphorism are based on a preconception of what it takes to achieve "adequacy to nature." He declares, for example, that "relations in nature are not associations, least of all human associations." This declaration is taken to imply that the language of philosophy and science cannot convey any truth. At the same time it confidently asserts a metaphysical view of how relations in nature differ from relations in language. Franz Deubzer points out that Mauthner's decisive divorce of language from world leads to a mystical identification of speaking and thinking – a suicide of language or thought would be necessary to liberate the human being because, on Mauthner's view, they entrap each other.[61]

In contrast, Wittgenstein's "critique of language" begins by working out that language can and does convey truth precisely because it aims for nothing more than representations of the world. Since names stand in for things in sentences, they are neither metaphors nor abstractions from the world. The words by themselves do not picture anything, only sentences do. There is no loss of reality to

---

[60] Gray 1986, p. 337. The scientific worldview of reality as a chaos of nonrelated fragments derives from Ernst Mach. His relation to Mauthner is explored in Arens 1984 and Weiler 1970. See Spicker 1997, p. 315: "The effect of Lichtenberg-admirer Ernst Mach on aphoristic writing in Austria, especially on his student Hofmannsthal, his temporary friend Schnitzler, on Musil [who wrote his dissertation on Mach] and Wittgenstein ought to be elucidated more clearly."

[61] See Deubzer 1980, pp. 28 and 77f. Concerning the "suicide of language or thought," see Janik and Toulmin 1973, pp. 121–132, especially 131. Like Haller in his chapter on Mauthner (Haller 1990), Janik and Toulmin tend to overlook just how profoundly Mauthner and Wittgenstein are at odds.

bemoan in language, since language itself is a configuration of signs just as the world consists of configurations of things. While concepts cannot be true or false, and while it makes no sense to demand that they coincide with nature, pictures can be true of nature by agreeing or disagreeing with a given state of affairs. They are true of nature also in that they are of a piece with it; they are facts like other facts.[62] With this, however, Wittgenstein reaches a limit of language: how sentences represent cannot itself be represented (*TLP* 2.174, 3.332, 4.12). Where Mauthner justifies his global and undifferentiated skepticism with metaphysical claims about the relation of language and world, Wittgenstein critically delimits language from within and thereby exposes Mauthner's claims as meaningless. Finally, Wittgenstein opposes Mauthner's mystical identification of language and thought. He considers sentences as thoughts only to the extent and just as long as the hypothesis concerning the unlimited power of language allows him to do so.[63]

Mauthner recruited the aphorism for his radically skeptical "critique of language." Wittgenstein reclaimed the "critique of language" for a critical tradition that, following Kant, saw criticism as a middle course between skepticism and dogmatism. Thereby he also reclaimed the critical function of aphoristic writing. Karl Kraus and Wittgenstein did not write aphorisms because indefinite and

---

[62] This conclusion regarding the recovery from the crisis of language of a describable reality echoes the antiskeptical reading of the *Tractatus* by Friedlander 2001. We arrive at this conclusion in radically different ways, however. While I suggest that Wittgenstein arrives at it through a critique of metaphysics, Friedlander resurrects a metaphysical, if not mystical Wittgenstein.

[63] Gershon Weiler identifies the difference between Mauthner and Wittgenstein, but wishes to maintain that they nevertheless mean the same by "critique of language." For both, he argues, this critique is "an inquiry into the limits of what can be and what cannot be said." According to Weiler, they differ in method: Wittgenstein "disagrees with Mauthner in his assessment of natural science, since he holds that propositions of natural science are what language is primarily suited for expressing . . . In Mauthner's view propositions of science cannot be certainly true and so the poetic use of language has the distinct advantage of not claiming to express truth at all" (1970, p. 301). Weiler's curious distinction between meaning and method overlooks, however, that Wittgenstein's "critique" mitigates Mauthner's and Hofmannsthal's skepticism. Wittgenstein's (and Kant's) "critical philosophy" is opposed to skepticism and dogmatism, and the limits it sets are constitutive of scientific truth. All that remains by way of similarity between Mauthner and Wittgenstein is their (interestingly different) appeal to a ladder metaphor at the end of the *Tractatus* and in the opening of Mauthner 1901/02.

fragmented thoughts are true to an indefinite, fragmented world.[64] In the tradition of Lichtenberg, in the world of modern physics and philosophy the aphorism is not simply a symptom or sign of the alienation of modern consciousness. Instead, it resists this alienation by taking the subjective occurrence of an idea as the starting point for a process of articulation only through which the concreteness of reality can be recovered.[65]

CRITICAL ANALYSIS OF LANGUAGE AND WORLD

Wittgenstein's skepticism regarding the limits of what can be expressed in speech is readily apparent. It tends to overshadow the positive result of his critique, namely that he imposes a limit also on the globalized skepticism of Mauthner and Hofmannsthal. This anti-skeptical aspect of Wittgenstein's "critique of language" can be elucidated by briefly considering the second part of *TLP* 4.0031: "Russell's achievement is to have shown that the apparent logical form of the sentence need not be its real one."

The achievement referred to is Russell's critique of definite descriptions. Apparently, the sentence "The present king of France is bald" has the same logical form as "Nicholas Rescher is bald." Since the expressions "The present king of France" and "Nicholas Rescher" both appear to stand for a person, both sentences seem to say of some person that he is bald. Russell has shown, however, that a name can stand for its bearer only when there really is someone or something that bears that name (Nicholas Rescher, for example). Definite descriptions ("the present king of France") do not stand for anything and require a different kind of analysis. The apparent logical form of "the present king of France is bald" is therefore not its real one. Though Wittgenstein does not in the end agree with Russell's proposed analysis of names and definite descriptions,[66] in *TLP* 4.0031 he favors Russell's exemplary critique of language over Mauthner's confusedly metaphysical and skeptical one.

---

[64] Deubzer 1980, pp. 54–62 elaborates this for Karl Kraus.

[65] For Lichtenberg, see Gockel 1973.

[66] For a good introduction to these matters, see Anscombe 1971, chapters 2ff. Compare above, chapter 1, pp. 33–41.

Russell's critique of language emphasizes the compositional character of language and world. Indeed, the purpose of logical analysis is to identify the elements out of which sentences are composed. By taking "the present king of France" to be a name, we disguise the various elements that are combined in it where this combination of elements amounts to a substantive claim about the world: "Present-day France is a monarchy, the current monarch is a king."

The first sentences of the *Tractatus* commit author and reader to Russell's and not to Mauthner's or Hofmannsthal's world.

1 The world is all that is the case.
1.1 The world is the totality of facts, not of things.
1.11 The world is determined by the facts and them being *all* the facts.

Since the world is composed of discrete elements, the analysis of language needs only to decompose language into its discrete elements to show that language can be co-ordinated with the world. Analysis thus establishes the possibility of language to convey truth about the world. It uncovers a conception of the world that is implicit in language. As Wittgenstein makes clear on various occasions, this conception differs profoundly from such conceptions as, for example, that of Hofmannsthal's Lord Chandos. In his happy days and "in a state of continuous intoxication," Chandos

conceived the whole of existence as one great unit: the spiritual and physical worlds seemed to form no contrast . . . and in all expressions of Nature I felt myself . . . The one was like the other: neither was superior to the other, whether in dreamlike celestial quality or in physical intensity – and thus it prevailed through the whole expanse of life in all directions; everywhere I was in the centre of it.[67]

When Mauthner and Hofmannsthal suggest that language cannot be true to the world, what they mean by "world" is not a describable totality of facts but rather a world of lived experience, a world that is in flux, where things past, present, and future are interrelated and cannot be isolated. Wittgenstein warns in *Philosophical Remarks* against the conceit of wanting to express the world, *so* conceived: "What belongs

---

[67] Hofmannsthal 1952, p. 132.

to the essence of the world cannot be expressed by language. For this reason, it cannot *say* that all is in flux. Language can only say those things we can also imagine otherwise."[68] In order to imagine how something could also be otherwise, we have to individuate or isolate it first. We have to take those things one at a time: "One thing can be the case or not be the case and everything else remain the same" (*TLP* 1.2). The opening remark of the *Tractatus* does not merely conceptualize the world as something analyzable and describable, it also inaugurates the corresponding method of thinking about the world.

At first sight, "1   The world is all that is the case" is very puzzling. A footnote – the only one in the *Tractatus* – underscores what the reader might have expected: the numbering designates it as a remark of enormous weight. Since we seem to be confronted with a system of sentences we might suspect that it is something like a first premise in a rationalist deduction. Descartes, for example, begins his physics with statements such as "Matter is extended." Should we consider "The world is all that is the case" along similar lines, as a self-evident axiom? Or else, does the sentence present an arbitrary definition? Is there any way at all to take it as a sentence about the world, for example, as making the substantive claim that the world is finite rather than infinite?[69] These questions inaugurate an activity of imagining how one could possibly disagree with this remark. If it is an incontestable axiom, disagreement ought to be impossible. If it is a stipulative definition, one can choose a different convention without substantial disagreement. If it is an empirical claim, the facts of the matter should settle any dispute.

As we have seen, Mauthner and Hofmannsthal are disagreeing with Wittgenstein's opening remark when they consider the world an intrinsically unstructured web of lived experience, its center everywhere, its periphery nowhere – and yet there appears to be no fact to the matter; the question cannot be decided by an appeal to science. Mauthner, Hofmannsthal, and Wittgenstein just seem to lay

[68] *PR* §54. David Stern 1995, chapter 6 discusses the problem of the flow or flux of life. Compare *PO*, p. 189.
[69] One of the first readers to raise these questions was a rather perplexed Gottlob Frege (1989, pp. 19f.).

claim to the world in different ways, they posit the world differently. Wittgenstein posits it as a finite knowable structure, the one we soberly consider from a distance with our descriptive sentences. Accordingly, he takes the aphoristic method as one that challenges the reader to integrate isolated remarks within a conception of reality. Mauthner and Hofmannsthal posit the world as a chaotic and unthinkable wealth of sensations that envelop us. Accordingly, they take the aphoristic method as a means of reproducing a wealth of disconnected fragments.

The aphorism that opens the *Tractatus* thus establishes the aphoristic method along with a conception of the world. In both regards it differs from Mauthner and responds constructively to the "crisis of language" of *fin de siècle* Vienna. The subjective occurrence of an idea serves as the starting point for a process of articulation, and this process recruits the concreteness of reality for the idea.[70] For example, through this idea that the world is such that it yields to a process of analysis and articulation (*TLP* 1), the world is claimed to be knowable. In piecemeal fashion, the world can now be recovered through the production of this knowledge. The resulting sciences describe the world as a composite of separate facts, and so the apparent posit of *TLP* 1 is vindicated or has become realized.

Beginning with the opening remark of the *Tractatus*, Wittgenstein's aphorisms self-consciously exemplify a way of writing and thinking. Each provides the precise record of a mental event, and by its compactness each retains the character of an event or of an *Einfall* that invades a space of reflection and possibility. Like those of Lichtenberg, Wittgenstein's aphorisms serve heuristic purposes; they alluringly submit an illuminating but tentative insight that stands ready to be scrutinized. They draw on the circumstance that, as Lichtenberg put it, "the metaphor is much wiser than its author," or that,

---

[70] Wittgenstein's exchange with Frege shows in which sense *TLP* 1 represents the subjective occurrence of an idea. Frege had challenged him to spell out the difference between "the world is all that is the case" and "the world is the totality of facts." Wittgenstein responded: "The meaning of these two sentences are one and the same but not the conceptions (*Vorstellungen*) that *I* associated with them when I wrote them down." Frege takes this to agree with his own distinction between sense and reference, commenting on the underlined "*I*": "In this, too, I see a sign of agreement. The actual meaning of the sentence is the same for all; however, the conceptions someone associates with the sentence are his alone; he is their bearer. No one can have the conceptions of another." See Frege 1989, p. 22.

to quote Wittgenstein, "one often makes a remark and sees only later *how* it is true."[71] Their aphorisms are vestiges of and prompts for thought experiments. They challenge their readers to reenact a movement of thought, inviting them to actually undergo a certain experience.

[71] Lichtenberg 1968/71, F 369 (p. 87 in Lichtenberg 1990) and *NB*, October 10, 1914.

CHAPTER 4

Tense and mood

The previous two chapters have adopted very different perspectives on the *Tractatus*. Chapter 2 took the global view by reconstructing its overarching philosophical thought experiment, the *reductio ad absurdum*. Chapter 3 treated each remark as a thought experiment on its own, the aphorism, as a miniature of the whole.[1] And while chapter 2 focused on the logic of Wittgenstein's argument, chapter 3 looked at its "strictly philosophical and simultaneously literary" form of presentation.[2] As they stand, each perspective represents one of the two aspects that were identified by Wittgenstein as making up the value of his book:

> If this work has a value it consists in two things. First [chapter 3] that in it thoughts are expressed, and this value will be the greater the better the thoughts are expressed. The more the nail has been hit on the head . . .
>   On the other hand [chapter 2] the *truth* of the thoughts communicated here seems to me unassailable and definitive. I am therefore of the opinion that the problems have in essentials been finally solved. And if I am not mistaken in this, then the value of this work secondly consists in that it shows how little has been achieved when these problems are solved. (*TLP* preface)

Are we really to believe, however, that these two aspects are quite unrelated to one another, or might there exist between them a kind of interdependence? Wittgenstein suggests the latter by writing of a single value that consists in two things. The last two chapters have offered a clue as to where one might look for such a relationship of

---

[1] "Every sentence I write always intends the whole already, that is, again and again the same thing & it is as though they were only views of one object seen from different angles." Wittgenstein wrote this in November 1930 (*CV*, p. 9).
[2] See LvF (quoted more extensively on p. 48 above).

mutual support. The overarching *reductio*-argument and the individual aphorisms were both characterized as thought experiments. This chapter will show that this is more than a superficial similarity. It will explore the hypothetical character of all experiments with ideas, of *reductio*-arguments and aphorisms. The *reductio*-argument begins with a hypothesis and proceeds upon its assumption until that hypothesis leads to contradiction, at which point it is rejected. And the aphorism begins with the occurrence of an idea or *Einfall*, and it is the tentative, hypothetical character of this *Einfall* which prompts a subsequent movement of thought or clarification that may issue in an appreciation, qualification, or abandonment of the hypothesis.

By focusing on the experimental or hypothetical character of the *Tractatus* – overall and in each of its parts – this chapter brings together matters of argument or logic and matters of language or writing: a hypothesis, after all, is characterized not just by the rôle it plays in arguments and experiments, it is also characterized linguistically as a "what if" statement in the (overt or implied) subjunctive mood. In both respects, hypotheses are a particular kind of sentence, and curiously enough, the *Tractatus*, with its seemingly complete classification of sentences, disregards hypotheses almost entirely. This chapter will also explore, therefore, Wittgenstein's almost perfect silence about the sentences in which the *Tractatus* is written. As we have seen, he states that these express thoughts, that they are nonsensical, that their author can be understood, and that they can help us to see the world rightly. But he does not show that all of this may indeed apply to a hypothetical manner of speaking. Indeed, as he develops his thoughts on what can and cannot be said, Wittgenstein never addresses what, if anything, a hypothesis says.[3]

An apparent digression will prepare the ground for this discussion. Continuing where the last chapter left off, it shows that, aside from the hypothetical mode of speaking, the *Tractatus* disregards another prominent grammatical feature or dimension of language. Wittgenstein shows that the precondition for the truthful linguistic representation of the world is the perfect match between

---

[3] The terms "hypothetical" or "hypothesis" occur four times in the *Tractatus*, of these only *TLP* 5.5351 and 6.36311 can be related to our question.

compositional language and a world composed of facts. As he recon-
structs and elaborates this precondition, Wittgenstein brackets from
consideration richer considerations of a world in flux, a world of
experience, and to this end he also restricts the range of relevant
grammatical features of language.

CAUGHT IN THE PRESENT

We generally think of the arts as being concerned with the world of
experience, a world in flux. One might therefore be surprised to learn
that throughout the twentieth century and continuing today, many
artists have found themselves attracted to the *Tractatus*, responding to
its austere presentation of language and world. This is true not only of
writers and painters,[4] but also of artists who cannot isolate particular
images or pictures but whose work progresses in the medium of time,
namely composers and filmmakers. There are the musical treatments
of Arne Nordheim, Tibor Szemzo, and M. A. Numminen and at least
two films, Derek Jarman's *Wittgenstein* and *Wittgenstein Tractatus* by
Péter Forgásc.[5] A film of the *Tractatus* – what could that be, and how
might it advance our discussion?

   Produced for Hungarian television in 1992, the film by Péter
Forgásc consists of seven segments, each about 4 minutes long, and
each devoted to one of the seven main propositions and, by virtue of
the broadcast schedule, to the seven days of the week, the seven days
of creation.[6] Due to their brevity and similarity of structure, these
are seven invocations (Forgásc also calls them prayers or meditations)

---

[4] Much has been written about Wittgenstein's influence on the arts, see, for example, Schmidt-
Dengler *et al.* 1990. A considerable number of responses to Wittgenstein by visual artists are
collected in Kosuth 1989. Among novels, the best ones refer to Wittgenstein without quoting
or representing him: Bernhard 1989 and Markson 1988. Wittgenstein appears as a character,
more or less literally, in Murdoch 1954, Kerr 1993, and Duffy 1987. See also Bernhard 1982.

[5] Nordheim 1986, Szemzo 1992, Numminen 1989, Eagleton and Jarman 1993, and Forgásc 1992
(with the musical score by Szemzo 1992).

[6] This analogy was noted and is, indeed, central to the interpretation by Eli Friedlander:
"Consider a work that is divided into seven parts, that opens with the world as such, appearing
out of nothing, and that ends with the withdrawal and silence of the creator, after all that
could be done has been done" (2001, p. 15). Friedlander continues by posing a question that
tempts us to forget Wittgenstein's critical and antimetaphysical stance: "But if that description
fits Wittgenstein's *Tractatus*, should the book then be understood as addressing the question
of the emergence of Being out of Nothing, or should this feature be dismissed as a mere
coincidence, or at best as a joke in bad taste on the part of Wittgenstein, who thereby relates
his text to the Scriptures?"

of Wittgenstein's picture theory by a maker of moving pictures. One might also say that they put the picture theory to a special kind of test: the litany of statements from the *Tractatus* (complemented only by a few passages from *Culture and Value*) runs up against historical time as it unfolds on film; they run up against a world in flux.

As in all of Forgács's films, the pictures we see in *Wittgenstein Tractatus* come from his archive of European home movies, primarily from the 1930s and 1940s. What we see are records of actual events, and while we see them, the grainy, scratchy quality of the film stock is a constant reminder that we are seeing memorable, yet banal, and often happy moments in the lives of people who have by now died, many of them perishing in concentration camps, on the battlefield, in their cities and homes.[7] In the fifth segment, for example, we see what looks like the film of an amateur anthropologist who visits a gypsy village and entices the villagers to dance for the camera. Forgács slightly enhances the initial awkwardness of this encounter by beginning with a slow succession of stills of a man standing in the doorway of his hut and of women shyly, graciously turning away from the camera's gaze. All the while, the following words run across the screen and are spoken by the narrator: "Everything we see could also be otherwise. Everything we can describe at all could also be otherwise" (*TLP* 5.634). These words are repeated a minute or so later when the film has sped up, when a man has taken the lead to dance, coaxing the women to burst into an exuberant romp.

Everything we see could also be different? This is surely not true for Péter Forgács, who works with found footage, with pictures that, once recorded, can no longer be otherwise. And surely it is not true for those gypsies who, like the Jews, were subject to Nazi persecution and extermination – they cannot undo their history.

Wittgenstein wrote that "[I]n the world everything is as it is and happens as it is" and "all happening and being-so is accidental" – it has no force of necessity, thus need not be so (*TLP* 6.41). Forgács and his film *Wittgenstein Tractatus* raise pressing questions: do Wittgenstein's statements apply to the past, or does the *Tractatus* consider only

---

[7] Many of Forgács's films carefully reconstruct these biographies. In *The Maelstrom*, for example, we see the home movies of a Jewish family in the Netherlands, their happy lives throughout the thirties, as well as their moments of joyful togetherness under Nazi occupation. Its final images show them packing their suitcases on the eve of their deportation.

present moments when it accounts for the true scientific description of the world in terms of an agreement between pictures and all that *is* the case? When reflecting on the limitations of the *Tractatus* in later years, Wittgenstein characterized his earlier approach in just these terms:

> The approach that leads us down into a canyon, as it were, from which there is no escape into the open countryside, is taking the present as the only reality. This present, constantly flowing or, rather, constantly changing, cannot be grasped. It disappears before we can think of grasping it. Bewitched, we remain stuck in this canyon in a vortex of thoughts. The mistake must be that we try to grasp the fleeing present by scientific methods.[8]

With its focus on descriptive language and the sentences of natural science (*TLP* 4.11, 6.53), with its interest in the determination of the world as we find it at any given moment (the totality of facts and currently obtaining states of affairs), the *Tractatus* does not consider any sentences other than those in the present tense.[9]

As for Forgásc's film, by confronting Wittgenstein's eternal present with images of the past, it shows us that everything we see could have been different, that there is no necessity to what was as it was and happened as it happened – and that is the tragedy of the dead. It also shows us that everything we now see in the past can no longer be otherwise, no matter how haphazard we judge it – and that is the tragedy of the living. But the medium of film also recovers a present for these moments past: in a naïve and curiously cheerful way these

---

[8] Page 1 of manuscript 107, dated September 1, 1929, quoted on p. 150 of David Stern 1995. On the other hand, Wittgenstein also notes: "When one says that 'everything flows,' we feel that we are hindered in pinning down the actual, the actual reality" (*PO*, p. 189). Stern shows that Wittgenstein's later philosophy struggles with precisely this dilemma. As he reconsiders the relation of language and experience, Wittgenstein no longer speaks of "actual reality" as a present state of things, but considers the world as a common referent to various kinds of practices where both the world and these practices share a natural history.

[9] Compare *PG*, part I, appendix 5: "It appears to me that the present, as it occurs in the sentence 'the sky is blue' (if this sentence isn't meant as a hypothesis), is not a form of time, so that the present in *this* sense is atemporal." To the extent that the totality of given facts *is a world*, it is timeless. That a particular totality of facts does not last but is always superseded by another one does not touch upon the atemporal nature of propositions. Instead, it refers to "the nature of the reality we encounter" in which it so happens "that every fact of experience can be brought into a relationship with what is shown by a clock." See also *PR* remark 54: "If someone says, only the *present experience* has reality, then the word 'present' must be redundant here, as the word 'I' is in other contexts."

dancing gypsies are still there, dancing happily on the screen, no matter what their place in history.[10]

Wittgenstein's silence about the past and about sentences in the past tense is not merely a failure to engage in the philosophy of history. It is also a failure to deal with questions of meaning and truth for sentences in the past and future tense.[11] Forgásc's pictures *are* true because they *were* true. On Wittgenstein's account, however, a sentence is true only if it pictures a state of affairs that actually obtains. The sentence "The gypsies were dancing" fails this test, as does "The gypsies will be dancing." Do these statements refer to states of affairs at all or do they refer to a time at which a corresponding statement in the present tense is true or false?[12] The *Tractatus* offers no answer to questions like these. Instead, it denies that there is a "passage of time" (*TLP* 6.3611).[13] It postulates "the present as the only reality" and this postulate serves as "a norm of representation" which underwrites a knowable world in which descriptive sentences can agree with how things are.[14] By the same token: "That

[10] In this particular segment, Forgásc also makes another point. The camera itself, its presence, and its coaxing changes what we see. Everything we see can be different: first they are shy, now they dance. Wittgenstein frequently refers to film and the cinema when he reflects back on the *Tractatus* and its inability to capture that "words only have meaning in the flow of life" (*LWPP: Last Writings on the Philosophy of Psychology*, I, §913). If all is in flux, does that mean that we confront a quick succession of individual pictures, a quick succession of states of affairs? When we are in the cinema, what we see on the screen may indeed be isolated present events, one picture at a time, but on the roll of film, every picture has a neighbor and is not isolated. See *PO*, pp. 190, 101f., also 336 and 356f.

[11] Compare above note 29 in chapter 2.

[12] The filmmaker and documentarian Péter Forgásc faces yet another problem concerning the "truth" of his images. Appropriately enough he devotes the first segment of his film to this problem, quoting from *CV*, p. 44: "How hard I find it to see *what is right in front of my eyes!*" His task is to see human suffering at moments of apparent happiness, the moments, that is, when home movies are made. The first segment shows persons emerging like ghosts from overexposed footage, it shows pictures being put together like a jigsaw puzzle, images unfolding, damaged and scratched. And when a likeness of Wittgenstein appears, a close-up of a famous photograph that has him peering in, sternly from above, the narrator makes a small, but decisive intervention in the text that signals his difficulty of applying the *Tractarian* picture theory to the pictures at hand. He reads: "The world is everything. That is the case."

[13] Wittgenstein owes this conception to Heinrich Hertz. According to Hertz, physics refers processes in time to timeless structures that can refer to the states of a clock: There is a logical and mathematical, reversible rather than temporal let alone historical relation between a structure at one state of the clock and a structure at another state of the clock. See Hertz 1956, §424.

[14] See the quote above, p. 130. In *On Certainty* (*OC*), §321 (cf. §§400–402) Wittgenstein notes that the introduction of postulates that serve as norms of representation is "all too reminiscent of the *Tractatus*."

the sun will rise tomorrow, is a hypothesis; and what this means is: we don't *know* whether it will rise" (*TLP* 6.36311). What makes a statement about the future into a hypothesis is that, within the framework of the *Tractatus*, we cannot specify its truth-conditions, in other words, it has no determinate meaning and marks only what we do not know.

Some interpreters of Wittgenstein have seen his remark about the hypothetical character of an inductive inference as a gesture toward David Hume. Hume, after all, made famous the question whether we can know that the sun will rise tomorrow. Max Black, for example, therefore places *TLP* 6.36311 in the company of 5.1361, with its Humean critique of causality.[15] However, Wittgenstein does not arrive at his comment about hypotheses by way of a reflection on cause and effect relationships and whether something can ever be known to be the cause of something else. There is neither an epistemological nor an ontological concern here with whether one event or set of events can harbor within it the realization of another. Instead, Wittgenstein's comment occurs in the context of remarks about Heinrich Hertz and the ability of science to consider the world as a dynamic system that is presently given and that circumscribes what can and cannot be the case, irrespective of time: "What can be described at all, that can happen, too, and whatever the causal law is supposed to exclude, cannot be described either" (*TLP* 6.362). Natural science need not concern itself with the future, and when it does so, it leaves its position of knowing what is and assumes a position of ignorance about what will be (*TLP* 6.363 and 6.3631). Wittgenstein thus arrives straightforwardly at the remark about a hypothetical future and does not take a metaphysical detour through the problem of causes and substances. For the *Tractatus*, the world that we can know, that we can speak about truthfully, is the world as it is, the world at present.[16] Its future and past are mere hypotheses – to say that the sun will rise tomorrow

[15] Black 1964, pp. 365f. and 243f.
[16] Downplaying the Humean dimension of Wittgenstein's critique of causality and nonlogical necessity, Anscombe 1965, p. 14 boldly associates *TLP* 6.35311 with *TLP* 6.431: "So why does [Wittgenstein] say we do not know that the sun will rise? Not, I think, because the facts may falsify the prediction, but because there may not be any more facts: as in death the world does not change, but stops." This association is suggested by Wittgenstein's conception of a world that is "my world" at any given present time (*TLP* 5.641). Compare Anscombe 1971, pp. 12 and 80, and note 9, above.

has no truth-conditions, no meaning in a world that is all that *is* the case.[17]

HYPOTHESES IN THE SUBJUNCTIVE MOOD

By maintaining silence about sentences in the past and future tense, the *Tractatus* is systematically incomplete. Rejecting a global skepticism about the power of language and specifying the limits of language through a critique from within, Wittgenstein works out what language can do, what it is good at. Though it cannot express any sense whatsoever, facts *are* expressible in speech. Facts, of course, are states of affairs that do obtain, and the totality of facts is the world. A state of affairs that does not obtain now but that did obtain, will obtain, or might obtain is no fact at all.

Not all hypotheses are predictive statements about the future. Thought experiments, *reductio*-arguments, aphoristic thinking and writing also involve hypotheses, and as we will see in the following, all these hypothetical procedures favor the subjunctive mood. And so, aside from tense, there is grammatical mood for the *Tractatus* to be silent about.[18] Indeed, my interpretation implies that, despite first appearances, the entire *Tractatus* is written in the subjunctive mood

---

[17] To be sure one might be able to extend Wittgenstein's account or substitute another account for it, one in which predictions and retrodictions, sentences with "will" or "was" have truth-conditions. It is significant, however, that this problem did not arise for the author of the *Tractatus*, that he does not address it, and need not consider it a problem at all. Here is why. An attempt to spell out truth-conditions for a sentence with "will" in it might go as follows: the sentence in the future tense "the sun will rise tomorrow" is true if and only if tomorrow we can truthfully say in the present tense that "the sun is rising." On this account, what we do not know but can only hypothesize about the future will be known once the future has become the present. We can only pretend to give truth-conditions for a sentence in the future tense, but really we are postponing the matter until the time when we can substitute for it a sentence in the present tense, one with truth-conditions. Thus, the sentence with "will" really has no truth-conditions now and really represents no knowledge. It merely stands in for the time when we will be able to determine truth or falsity and when we will have knowledge. The inability to specify truth-conditions for sentences in the past and future tense is therefore no defect of Wittgenstein's account. Instead, it marks an important epistemological distinction, one that needs to be marked.

[18] Stenius 1960, pp. 157–176 (in a chapter on "Descriptive Content and Mood") shows that the *Tractatus* explicates the language game for sentences in the indicative mood: "the attributes 'true' or 'false' are reserved to *sentences* in the *indicative*" (p. 167). He attempts to amend Wittgenstein's account for statements in the imperative and interrogative moods by restricting the scope of his picture theory: rather than providing a criterion of sense, it "explains how we understand the descriptive content of a sentence-radical" (p. 167). Stenius thus appreciates that, as it stands, the *Tractatus* is concerned only with indicative sentences in the

and thus employs expressions that are not considered in its survey of language. Obviously, this claim needs to be backed up by further evidence and argument.

This argument begins in the next section by considering the literary and philosophical significance of the subjunctive mood – how it makes possible the thought experiments of the *Tractatus*. The section that follows establishes why the method adopted by Wittgenstein is just right for his critique of philosophy. We can then determine where subjunctive expressions fit within the classification offered by the *Tractatus* and, finally, how a work written in the subjunctive mood is nonsensical and can yet promote understanding.

"THIS GREAT ENGINE TO OPEN NEW TRACKS OF ENQUIRY"

Since the subjunctive mood is used ever more rarely and since many of its verbal constructions are becoming extinct in English, Laurence Sterne's whimsical 1761 treatment of "a white bear" serves as a welcome reminder of its possibilities.

A white Bear! Very well. Have I ever seen one? Might I ever have seen one? Am I ever to see one? Ought I ever to have seen one? Or can I ever see one?

Would I had seen a white bear! (for how can I imagine it?) If I should see a white bear, what should I say? If I should never see a white bear, what then?

If I never have, can, must or shall see a white bear alive; have I ever seen the skin of one? Did I ever see one painted? – described? Have I ever dreamed of one? Did my father, mother, uncle, aunt, brothers or sisters, ever see a white bear? What would they give? How would they behave? How would the white bear have behaved? Is he wild? Tame? Terrible? Rough? Smooth?
– Is the white bear worth seeing? –
– Is there no sin in it? –
Is it better than a *Black One?* [19]

present tense, but he does not take this to be an essential feature (and he therefore does not take *TLP* 4.022 to define "sentence"). Again, I would recommend a more literal approach to the *Tractatus*, especially in light of the fact that Wittgenstein continued to use "sentence" far more narrowly than we are colloquially inclined to do (as we will see, for example, he did not consider hypotheses "sentences").

[19] See Sterne 1940, volume v, chapter 43. Just one prominent example of the difficulty of sustaining the subjunctive mood in English is Norman Kemp Smith's translation of Kant's *Critique of Pure Reason*. Kant wrote a chapter on noumena and phenomena entirely in the subjunctive mood ("if one could talk of the things in themselves, what might one say about them?"). In order to avoid tedium and repetition, the translation reverts, for the most part,

If this is the wild and playful side of the subjunctive mood, Wittgenstein's Vienna represented its tentative and dubious side. In the first chapter of his *Analysis of Sensations*, Ernst Mach ridicules the man who says "it seems to me that you have given me a beating," while Allan Janik and Stephen Toulmin describe Viennese society as being so delicate and unstable that a more direct tone might easily bring it down.[20]

Before turning to the formal aspects of the subjunctive mood in the context of the *Tractatus*, I will consider its strictly philosophical and simultaneously literary significance. As with writing aphorisms, Wittgenstein's use of the subjunctive is not primarily a matter of art and aesthetics, but concerns the method and conduct of thought. This was true even of Tristram Shandy's father when he "danced his white-bear backwards and forwards through half a dozen pages" and justified his grammatical extravaganza as an impulse for philosophical experimentation with ideas:

the use of the *Auxiliaries* is, at once to set the soul a going by herself upon the materials as they are brought her; and by the versatility of this great engine, round which they are twisted, to open new tracks of enquiry, and make every idea engender millions . . . The verbs auxiliary we are concerned in here, continued my father, are, *am*; *was*; *have*; *do*; *did*; *make*; *made*; *suffer*; *shall*; *should*; *will*; *would*; *can*; *could*; *owe*; *ought*; *used*; or *is wont*. – And these varied with tenses, *present*, *past*, *future*, and conjugated with the verb *see*, – or with these questions added to them; – *Is it? Was it? Will it be? Would it be? May*

to the indicative mood – inadvertently fostering the widespread misunderstanding that this is the point where Kant's critical philosophy breaks down and where it treats noumena as existent see (A 249).

[20] Mach refers to scene 8 of Molière's comedy *The Forced Marriage* in which a skeptical philosopher insists that one should never put matters positively: "that's why you may not say, I have received a beating, but: it appears to me as if I had received a beating from you" (Mach 1914, p. 37). Janik and Toulmin quote Emperor Franz Joseph: "My realm resembles a worm-eaten house. If one part is removed, one cannot tell how much will fall." Therefore, civil servants who were opposed to his policies remained in office, and therefore, perhaps, Franz Joseph never adopted telephone, automobile, typewriter, electric light and modern plumbing (see Janik and Toulmin 1973, pp. 37f. and 41f.). Along with Kraus and Loos, Wittgenstein sought a more direct tone and set out to subvert this "Austrian delicacy." According to Engelmann, against the backdrop of subjunctive embellishment, euphemism, and ornament, they insisted on the "difference between an urn and a chamber-pot" (1967, pp. 122–132, especially p. 129). Compare one of Wittgenstein's letters in which he anxiously inquires about the fate of his manuscript: "And now, only *one* more request: Make it short and sweet with me. Give me a quick 'no' rather than an oh so slow one; that is Austrian delicacy which my nerves are not quite strong enough to endure at the moment" (LvF, p. 95).

it be? Might it be? And these again put negatively . . . Or hypothetically, –
If it was; If it was not? What would follow? – If the *French* should beat the
English? If the *Sun* should go out of the *Zodiac?* . . . *Tristram* . . . shall be
made to conjugate every word in the dictionary, backwards and forwards
the same way; – every word, *Yorick,* by this means, you see, is converted into
a thesis or an hypothesis . . . every one of which leads the mind on again,
into fresh tracks of enquiries and doubtings. – The force of this engine . . .
is incredible in opening a child's head.[21]

"Or hypothetically, – *If it was; If it was not?* What would follow?"
This is the question also of *reductio*-arguments, evidently in the subjunctive mood. "If this hypothesis were true," these arguments say,
"what would follow from it?" This mode of questioning allows us to
entertain the hypothesis without endorsing it; we adopt it tentatively
for the sake of a thought experiment that tests its mettle. Only as we
arrive at the conclusion can we return from the subjunctive to the
indicative mood: "If we *were to* adopt this hypothesis, we *would* end
up contradicting ourselves, and therefore, the hypothesis *is* false or
incoherent and *must* be rejected."

Also, to say "if we were to adopt this hypothesis, we might run
into a contradiction" is different from saying "if we were to drop this
stone, it would fall to the ground." In the latter case, we are considering a so-called irreal or counterfactual conditional. In that case
we know that when the stone is dropped, it will fall to the ground –
no subjunctive here! – and all we do is talk about a case where the initial
condition (dropping the stone) is not fulfilled but might be. In contrast, the hypothesis of a thought experiment or *reductio ad absurdum*
invites us to think with a sense of possibility, to play things through
under the assumption that the hypothesis, no matter how unlikely, is
potentially true. Or we might set out to conduct a *reductio*-argument
and discover that the hypothesis contradicts a long-held belief of
ours – and then decide not to reject the hypothesis but to question instead that long-held belief.[22] A statement of the sort "if this

---

[21] Sterne 1940, volume v, chapters 42 and 43, and volume vi, chapter 2. This passage was
quoted by Schöne 1982, pp. 65f. *Tristram Shandy* was one of Lichtenberg's and Wittgenstein's
favorite books. For a similar list of questions, seriously put, see Lichtenberg 1968/71, C 300
through C 342. As for Wittgenstein, Drury recollects Wittgenstein as saying: "A book I
like greatly is Sterne's *Tristram Shandy*. That is one of my favourite books" (in Rhees 1984,
pp. 133f.).

[22] How such processes work is subject of the philosophical literature on belief-revision (compare
the work of Isaac Levi, Henry Kyburg, or Keith Lehrer).

hypothesis were true, where might we go from here" is therefore a so-called potential conditional or *conjunctivus potentialis*. It invites us to inhabit for a while the subjunctive sphere of possibility.

Aphoristic writing often invokes such potential conditionals. For example, take this philosophical thought experiment by Lichtenberg: "I have often wished that there might be a language in which it would be impossible ever to say a falsehood, or where at least every breach of truth would be a breach of grammar."[23] Like a *reductio*-argument, this thought experiment proceeds hypothetically, it begins with a "what if" in the subjunctive mood. In contrast to an irreal or counterfactual conditional, there are no initial conditions here which are not in fact, but might well be satisfiable. Instead, there is no expectation that there could ever be such a language. To entertain this possibility is to conduct a thought experiment about the limits of language that remains confined within the subjunctive sphere.

Albrecht Schöne has actually undertaken the task of counting occurrences of the various varieties of subjunctive construction. He has found that the subjunctive was far more frequently employed in the eighteenth and nineteenth centuries than it is today, and he found that Lichtenberg's frequency of usage, especially of the potential conditional was way ahead even of his contemporaries.[24] Schöne takes the actual employment and mastery of the subjunctive as an expression of a "hypothetical-experimental" style of writing and thinking, a style that does not require explicitly subjunctive constructions, since in many cases a suppressed subjunctive can be inferred from context, from method of hypothesis or mode of qualification.[25] Indeed, all or most of the aphorisms by Lichtenberg, Novalis, and Schlegel, and arguably also those by Schopenhauer, Nietzsche, and Kraus originate in the suppressed subjunctive "If I thought this possible, what might occur to me?" Wittgenstein, for example, could have premised every remark of the *Tractatus* by writing something like

---

[23] Quoted from an unpublished lecture note in Schöne 1982 p. 33, also in Magin 1913, pp. 41f. and Stern 1959, pp. 163f. Since this remark cannot be found in any standard editions of Lichtenberg's aphorisms, it is quite unlikely that Wittgenstein encountered it. And yet, one might say that in the *Tractatus* Wittgenstein pursues a scaled-down version of Lichtenberg's vision, establishing that every breach of logic would be a breach of grammar. See *TLP* 5.4731 asserting that "language itself prevents all logical errors."

[24] See Schöne 1982, pp. 17–21.

[25] Inversely, not all formally "subjunctive expressions" count as genuine subjunctives – especially where they use the subjunctive to express what will be the case, once a certain condition is fulfilled (compare Schöne 1982, pp. 27–29, 89–101).

"If any sense whatsoever were expressible in speech and I wanted to express thoughts about the relation of language and world, it would first occur to me that the world is all that is the case." Instead, all of his remarks in the *Tractatus* can be said to be elliptical, giving us only the last part of the cumbersome construction – what and how it really did occur to him under the conditions of the thought experiment. Insofar as they presuppose hypothetically that it is possible to speak about the relation of language and world, his remarks therefore involve an implied subjunctive. Only while exploring this possibility can a thought occur to him which – as a real occurrence – he records in the indicative mood: "The gramophone record, the musical thought, the score, the soundwaves all stand in the same internal relation to one another as that which obtains between language and world. To all of them the logical structure is in common" (*TLP* 4.014). Here, the implied subjunctive allows Wittgenstein's imagination to venture further than the consideration of language itself. Going beyond even the musical metaphor, a parenthetical afterthought draws the reader into the speculative world of a romantic fairy tale, wedding the idea of internal relations and of common logical plan to the poetic ideal of unity in difference: "(Just as in the fairy tale the two youths, their two horses and their lilies. They are all in a certain sense One.)"

If remarks like this one testify to Wittgenstein's ability to experiment aphoristically with ideas, there are many others that more explicitly display his fondness and remarkable mastery of the subjunctive mood. Here is just one of numerous examples from the *Tractatus*: "If this weren't so, how could we apply logic? One might say: if there were a logic, even if there were no world, how then could there be a logic, since there is a world" (*TLP* 5.5521).[26] A sampling from *Culture and Value* underscores how Wittgenstein uses expressions in the subjunctive mood to provoke the imaginative activity of the aphoristic thought experiment. Again and again he posits or invents a world in which objects appear in new and different states of affairs, while

---

[26] See the subjunctive constructions of 2.0121, 2.0211f., 3.031, 3.05, 3.328, 3.3411, 4.0411, 4.12, 4.2211, 5.123, 5.46, 5.47, 5.535, 5.541, 5.555, 5.61, 6.1223, 6.36, 6.374, 6.53. Like many of these examples, *TLP* 5.552 and 5.5521 state in the indicative mood how *it is* within the parameters of the thought experiment and go on to show how it would be, if it were not so. That is, an explicitly subjunctive condition is grafted upon an implicit one.

names appear in new and different configurations.[27] Wittgenstein's subjunctive formulations thus disengage us from the world as we find it and thereby create a vantage point from which we can reflect it (Lichtenberg: "If everyone inhabited his own planet, what would philosophy then be?"):[28]

If anyone should think he has solved the problem of life . . .

If someone is merely ahead of his time . . . (it will catch up with him one day.)

(If the hem of his clothes hadn't caught in the machine?)

If it is said on occasion that (*someone's*) philosophy is a matter of temperament . . .

If one wanted to characterize the essence of Mendelssohn's music . . .

If I say A. has beautiful eyes . . .

If you use a trick in logic . . . (whom can you be tricking but yourself?)

If someone prophesies that the generation to come will take up these problems & solve them . . .

If you offer a sacrifice & then are conceited about it . . .

If, for example, certain metaphors are established as dogmas of thought *for the people* . . .

If I realized how mean & petty I am . . .

If this stone doesn't want to budge, if it is wedged in . . . (first, move other stones around it.)

If you already *have* someone's love . . .

If in life we are surrounded by death . . .

If there is anything in the Freudian theory of dream interpretation . . .

If people did not sometimes commit stupidities . . . (nothing intelligent at all would ever happen.)

If I had written a *good* sentence, & it happened to be two rhyming lines . . . (this would be a mistake.)

---

[27] Compare above, pp. 113–114. Such inventions run counter to the grammar of descriptive sentences that is elaborated within the *Tractatus*. "If I know an object, I also know all the possibilities of its occurrence in states of affairs . . . A new possibility cannot be found subsequently" (*TLP* 2.0123). Many aphorisms "find new possibilities." However, they do not thereby contradict *TLP* 2.0123 or alter our knowledge of the object. By envisioning a different world, they reflect the meaning and contingency of this one (see chapter 5). The following remark by Lichtenberg, for example, tells us something about the grammar of "sex" in our ordinary usage: "If not even the sexes could be told by the clothing, but we would have to guess even the sex, a new world of love would arise" (Lichtenberg 1968/71, F 320).

[28] Lichtenberg 1968/71, C 142 (p. 44 in Lichtenberg 1990). Goff 1969 therefore highlights that Wittgenstein's language resists confinement "to a single form of attention": "Aphoristic language brings about a shift from the commonplace to the extra-ordinary by cutting off fixed, ready-made meanings and by pointing reflexively to the context and direction of linguistic use" (pp. 65 and 68).

If it is true, as I believe, that Mahler's music is worthless . . .
If God really does *choose* those who are saved . . .
If nightdreams have a similar function as daydreams . . .
If someone can believe in God with complete certainty . . . (why not in the soul of others?)
If a false thought is only expressed boldly & clearly . . . (a great deal has been gained already.)
If you cannot unravel a tangle . . .
If Christianity is the truth . . . (then all the philosophy about it is false.)
If the believer in God looks around & asks "Where does everything I see come from?"[29]

Add to this: If any sense whatsoever were expressible in speech . . . (how would objectivity and truth be possible?)

NOT FALSE BUT NONSENSICAL

The considerations thus far should have rendered plausible the notion that the sentences of the *Tractatus*, elliptically or explicitly, inhabit the subjunctive mood. Moving beyond mere plausibility, a next step of the argument will relate the ubiquity of subjunctive expressions to Wittgenstein's critical method.

Mautner had characterized the aphorism as an interplay of *Einfall* and *Klärung*, that is, between the occurring idea and its articulation or clarification. Schöne elaborates this pair of terms by presenting Lichtenberg's aphorisms as an interplay between the "hypothetical-experimental" production of a thought and its "critical-skeptical" reflection.[30] Like Mautner, he identifies the aphorism not with aesthetic or formal features, but as a movement of thought. Schöne goes beyond Mautner by emphasizing that the subjunctive mood creates the linguistic space of possibility in which such movements of thought can occur. Also, having identified Lichtenberg's fondness for subjunctive constructions, Mautner and Schöne both refer to Lichtenberg's

---

[29] Among all the remarks beginning with "if" clauses in *Culture and Value*, these are the ones that introduce a thought experiment. The earliest one is from 1930 and the last from 1950; see *CV*, pp. 6, 11, 14, 17, 27, 28 (two times), 29, 30, 32, 37, 44, 48, 50, 51, 57, 66, 76, 83 (three times), 85, 86, 89, 96.

[30] Schöne 1982, pp. 129–145. Note that Schöne joins company with the literary theorist Franz Mautner, not with the skeptical critic of language Fritz Mauthner.

"sense of possibility," one that places him in close proximity to Robert Musil.[31]

Like Lichtenberg and Wittgenstein, Musil wrote philosophy in a literary manner with a background in science and engineering. He was author not only of a dissertation on the philosophy of Ernst Mach, but also from 1930 until 1952 of a monumental novel about Wittgenstein's Vienna through the eyes of a *Man Without Qualities* – an unfinished novel that eventually becomes a series of aphorisms. Ulrich is the "man without qualities" precisely because, in addition to the five sensory senses, he has "a sense of possibility."[32] Ulrich was to have written already during his student days an essay in which he claimed "that God probably prefers talking of the world in the *conjunctivus potentialis* (*hic dixerit quispiam* = someone might object here . . .), for God makes the world and thinks all the while that it could just as well be different."[33]

Engineers and scientists manipulate the world as it is, in the present and in the indicative mood. Like the *demiurge*, they are the first to realize that their creations render the world contingent and without necessity. They realize that along with how they remake the world and how it was made in the first place, there are many ways of how it could be. Effortlessly they move from the indicative ("everything we see") to the subjunctive mood ("could also be different").[34]

In this spirit, Musil's *Man Without Qualities* introduces its readers to the comically contingent and highly uncertain last days of the Austria-Hungarian Empire by opening the novel matter-of-factly:

There was a depression over the Atlantic. It was traveling eastwards, towards an area of high pressure over Russia, and still showed no tendency to move northwards around it. The isotherms and isotheres were fulfilling their functions. The atmospheric temperature was in proper relation to the average annual temperature, the temperature of the coldest as well as of the hottest

---

[31] Schöne (ibid., p. 162) discusses the proximity of his and Mautner's views on Lichtenberg; cf. Mautner 1968, pp. 17 and 40. See Nordmann 1986 for a critique of Schöne's account concerning the relation of Lichtenberg's aphoristic method to experimental physics.

[32] See Schöne 1982, pp. 149f., Mautner 1968, p. 40. On the relation between Wittgenstein and Musil, see Döring 1999, Gray 1986, Janik and Toulmin 1973.

[33] Musil 1980, p. 15.

[34] Compare chapter 1, note 59 above, which cites various places where Kant, Hertz, and Lichtenberg use the very same phrase.

month, and the a-periodic monthly variation in temperature . . . In short, to use an expression that describes the facts pretty satisfactorily, even though it is somewhat old-fashioned: it was a fine August day in the year 1913.[35]

Musil here describes the world as he found it – as does the most famous of Wittgenstein's thought experiments within the *Tractatus*:

If I wrote a book "The world as I found it," there would also have to be reported in it about my body and stated which members are subject to my will and which not etc., for this is a method of isolating the subject, or rather to show, that in an important sense there is no subject: For, of it alone the book could say *nothing*. – (*TLP* 5.631)

Not only is this thought experiment conducted in the subjunctive mood, it also designates this form of experimentation as a method for a critique from within that can specify the limits of knowledge and language. Indeed, this remark anticipates the proposal in *TLP* 6.53 that "the right method of philosophy *would really be*" to use nothing but the descriptive sentences of the natural sciences. If someone would actually write the proposed book (a book very different from the *Tractatus*), the sentences occurring in it would be ordinary assertive sentences in the indicative mood, very much like the beginning of Musil's novel. The right method of philosophy would really be not to speak in the subjunctive mood at all. But since the right method would have "nothing to do with philosophy" anymore (*TLP* 6.53), a thought experiment in the subjunctive mood may just be the only suitable way of engaging philosophy.[36]

In the language of science, in the language of the right method, all sentences are either true or false. Indeed, that is what recommends the language of science. In contrast, "Most sentences and questions that have been written about philosophical matters are not false but non-sensical" (*TLP* 4.003). The greatest philosophical misunderstanding

---

[35] Musil 1980, p. 3. There is evidence that Wittgenstein knew this novel (Joachim Schulte, personal communication).

[36] The previous chapter (especially the second section) has already shown that the experimental character of his *reductio*-argument protects Wittgenstein from having to say anything at all: "To understand Wittgenstein is merely to understand that he conducted a thought experiment in the course of which an attempt to express philosophical thoughts ran up against the limits of language and thus resulted in failure." While this indicates why Wittgenstein's chosen method is a very good alternative and even a close analogue to "the right method," the current reflection on the subjunctive mood indicates why, for Wittgenstein, it may be the only viable alternative, one that he must choose if he wants to engage philosophy at all.

is therefore philosophy's misunderstanding of itself, the belief particularly of "uncritical" philosophers that philosophy makes claims, presents theses, is engaged in the business of truth and falsity, that it is a "higher" science. But if critical philosophy simply tried to prove these claims or theses false, it would be committing the same mistake: an opinion that is judged false could have been true, and to judge it false thereby grants it the status of being a quasiscientific statement, just one that happens to be false. Critical philosophy must therefore do more and show that philosophical sentences "are not false but nonsensical." Elizabeth Anscombe has characterized this challenge in general terms, describing Wittgenstein's method almost exactly:

> [W]hat a philosopher declares to be philosophically false is supposed not to be possible or even really conceivable; the false ideas which he conceives himself to be attacking must be presented as chimaeras, as not really thinkable thoughts at all. Or, as Wittgenstein put it: An *impossible* thought is an impossible *thought* (*TLP* 5.61) – and that is why it is not possible to say what it is that cannot be thought; it can only be forms of words or suggestions of the imagination that are attacked. Aristotle rejecting separate forms, Hume rejecting substance, exemplify the difficulty: if you want to argue that something is a philosophical illusion, you cannot treat it as a false hypothesis. Even if for the purposes of argument you bring it into contempt by treating it as an hypothesis, what you infer from it is not a contradiction but an incoherence.[37]

For the purposes of argument, Wittgenstein brings our unqualified faith in the expressive powers of language into contempt by treating it as the hypothesis of a *reductio*-argument. By establishing that this hypothesis leads him into the failure to express any sense whatsoever (to express matters of value, for example), he arrives at the conclusion that "there is indeed the inexpressible in speech." In the context of the *reductio*-argument, whether he inferred a contradiction from his hypothesis or discovered its incoherence amounts to the same: the hypothesis is not inaccurate or false, it is not even a proper sentence that could be accurate or inaccurate, true or false.[38]

Expressions in the subjunctive mood are just that – nonsensical because they are and can be neither true nor false. And yet, when they serve as hypotheses in the context of a thought experiment, they

---

[37] Anscombe 1971, p. 163.
[38] Remember that along with the hypothesis itself, its corollary has run into trouble.

take the guise of a statement that could be true or false. And only as we try to decide their truth or falsity do we discover that they were nonsensical to start with and remain irredeemably so ("Any number can be divided by zero," "The author of this book died before it was written").

To substantiate the claim that subjunctive expressions are neither true nor false, we will have to see what the *Tractatus* does or does not say about such expressions, and in particular, why on its account of sense and nonsense we have to consider them nonsensical. This will finally answer the question whether the *Tractatus* as a whole is self-defeating.

NONSENSE, SENSE, AND SENSELESSNESS

According to the *Tractatus*, subjunctive expressions are not sentences, properly speaking.

The sentence *shows* its sense.
The sentence *shows* how things stand, *if* it is true.
And it *says, that* they do so stand. (*TLP* 4.022)

The first part of this definition treats the sentence as a picture: "What a picture represents is its sense" (*TLP* 2.221). The model of a traffic accident in court or a picture shows how things might stand. A sentence is such a picture (*TLP* 4.021, 4.031, 4.1211). But when we take the sentence and write it down or utter it, we do not just state its sense, we assert it: "This is, indeed, how things stand." Once asserted and if it is accurate, the sentence says that things stand just as it shows them to be standing: "Every sentence must already *have* a sense; assertion cannot give it one, for its sense is precisely what it asserts. And the same applies to denial, etc." (*TLP* 4.064). So, when we write or speak an ordinary sentence in the indicative mood, we express its sense and assert or deny it.[39]

[39] Here I am taking 4.022 to define what a sentence is: every sentence must show how things stand, if it is true, *and* must say that they do so stand. It is notoriously difficult to agree on what Wittgenstein means by "sentence." Some critics (Max Black, for example) want to distinguish between "proposition" and "sentence" where Wittgenstein uses only the one word "*Satz*" (for example, Black 1964, pp. 98f.). But then again, Wittgenstein also talks of "*Satzzeichen* (propositional sign)" and "*Elementarsatz* (elementary sentence)," raising the question in

In contrast to the sentence as defined in *TLP* 4.022, (i) the subjunctive sentence *shows* its sense; (ii) the subjunctive sentence *shows* how things would stand, *if* it could be asserted and judged true; and (iii) it does not *say that* they do so stand. Expressions in the subjunctive mood assert or deny nothing at all, they say nothing and are therefore not properly sentences. Yet, I will argue, they show what they do not, perhaps cannot, say – and this makes them nonsensical but not therefore senseless.

To be sure, the *Tractatus* does not entertain the question whether it is possible for subjunctive or nonsensical expressions to show something without saying anything. Can nonsensical expressions show, for instance, that the world is all that is the case, that the limits of language are the limits of the world, or that there is indeed the inexpressible? A passage from Wittgenstein's *Notebooks* presses the issue: "Why shouldn't there be a mode of expression with which I can speak *about* language . . .? Let's assume that music provides such a mode: then it is at least characteristic for *science* that in it occur *no* musical themes."[40] If music were a way of speaking about language, it would not be *about* language in the sense in which science is *about* how things are. Can music, for instance, show that there is indeed the inexpressible in speech? Can music "speak" beyond the limits of language and thus transcend the world (*TLP* 5.6), perhaps speak of something higher? And if we may assume that music can do this, could not a form of nonscientific, nonsensical language, perhaps expressions in the subjunctive mood, accomplish the same?

Such questions take us far afield (and into chapter 5 below). Let us therefore begin more soberly with what Wittgenstein means by "nonsense," whether expressions in the subjunctive mood fit the bill, and

which sense these are "sentences." Another difficulty concerns the relation of projection and assertion. In *TLP* 3.13 he appears to deny that the sentence contains its sense: it is what pertains to projection but not what is projected. Other statements suggest the opposite, namely that the sentence need not be asserted at all in order to be a sentence with sense. I think I can bypass these difficulties since I am here concerned with the difference between sentences, tautologies and contradictions, and nonsense, that is, with the difference between expressions that say something and those that do not. Along with *TLP* 4.022, I therefore take *TLP* 6.1264 and 4.461 as a definition of "sentence" for this context: "The significant sentence asserts something and its proof shows that it is so" (*TLP* 6.1264). Compare *NB*, pp. 33 and 37.

[40] *NB*, p. 52.

finally, whether there might be nonsensical expressions that are not senseless. In most contexts we do not distinguish between "senseless" and "nonsensical." So we might be tempted to answer quickly here: nonsense is lack of sense, and nonsensical expressions are obviously senseless. For once, however, Wittgenstein wants us to make a subtle distinction: "Frege says: Every properly formed sentence must also have sense; and I say: Every possible sentence is properly formed, and if it has no sense, this can only be because we have assigned no *meaning* to some of its parts" (*TLP* 5.4733). As opposed to Frege, Wittgenstein identifies two very distinct ways in which a sentence can go wrong. First, it can be an impossible sentence, not properly formed, one that does not really belong to our language.[41] But secondly, even a properly formed sentence can lack sense because we have failed to specify just what we mean by certain words or expressions.

For Wittgenstein, a sentence is properly formed and logically permissible just as soon as it is grammatical – "language itself prevents all logical errors" (*TLP* 5.4731). But some constructions are ungrammatical – and those Wittgenstein calls nonsensical. This accords with colloquial usage in that some of our favorite examples of "nonsense" have the nursery rhyme quality of outrageous nonsentences: "The watch is squatting on the table," "I am putting this handshake into a hole," or "He thought he saw an Argument \ That proved he was the Pope: \ He looked again, and found it was \ A Bar of Mottled Soap."[42]

When Wittgenstein equates nonsense with the violation of grammar, what he has in mind is the grammar of the language that can produce true sentences which are in agreement with the world. Since our

[41] This agrees with Frege's conception of nonsense. Fregean nonsense occurs when a sentence fails to meet a syntactic criterion "even if the natural language sentence string has all the appearance of being syntactically well-formed." Accordingly, Wittgenstein's movements of thought demonstrate for apparently well-formed sentences like "A is an object" or "The world is all that is the case" that they "are nonetheless syntactic gibberish" (cf. Williams 2004, pp. 10–15). To be sure, Wittgenstein does not apply a simple criterion of grammaticality such as Russell's bipolarity, that is, the need that every sentence should be either true or false. If bipolarity were a criterion of meaningfulness versus nonsense, the sentences of logic would also fail the test and would have to be considered nonsensical. That is why Wittgenstein introduces the distinction between senseless and nonsensical expressions. And that is why the judgment of nonsensicality issues from a failure to assign determinate meaning along the lines of the descriptive sentences of science.

[42] The first of these is from *NB*, p. 70, the second adapted from p. 108, and the last from Lewis Carroll's "Sylvie and Bruno" (Carroll 1936, p. 701).

everyday language "dresses up the thought" such that it is "humanly impossible to immediately discern from it the logic of language" (*TLP* 4.002), the *Tractatus* took on the task to articulate the grammar of a descriptive language, the language of natural science. It tells us how names are to be arranged in sentences so that the sentences can picture states of affairs.

> In everyday language . . . the word "is" is used as copula, as sign of equality, as the expression of existence . . .
> Thus arise easily the most fundamental confusions (of which all of philosophy is full).
> In order to avoid these errors, we must employ a sign-language that excludes them . . . That is, a sign-language that satisfies *logical* grammar – logical syntax. (*TLP* 3.323–3.325)

As opposed to everyday language, a language that does nothing but picture states of affairs is such a sign language and thus avoids confusion. It permits as a grammatical use of "is" the sentence "Mercury is the planet closest to earth" and excludes constructions such as "God is because he must be." The latter construction is nonsensical because it violates the logical syntax of the descriptive language: it takes a word that is used to connect subject and predicate and somehow tries to predicate *it*, thereby creating a mystical state or property of "being." A similar consideration applies to expressions in the subjunctive mood: since they do not assert anything, they do not meet the two criteria for grammatical sentences and are therefore nonsensical (*TLP* 4.022). For the same reason hypotheses do not qualify as "sentences" either. Wittgenstein made this explicit in later discussions of the views of the *Tractatus*: "A hypothesis differs from a sentence in virtue of its grammar. It is a different grammatical structure."[43]

When he compared his view to Frege's, Wittgenstein also noted that it is possible for a perfectly grammatical sense to lack sense, to be senseless. The sentence may be well formed and therefore not at all

---

[43] *Wittgenstein and the Vienna Circle* (*WVC*), pp. 210f.; see pp. 159–162 and p. 99: "A hypothesis is not a sentence, but a law for constructing sentences." Wittgenstein elucidates this in *PG*, part I, appendix 6, p. 222: "It's clear that reality – I mean immediate experience – will sometimes give an hypothesis the answer yes, and sometimes the answer no . . .; and it's clear that these affirmations and denials can be given expression. The hypothesis, if *that* face of it is laid against reality, becomes a sentence." See also *WA2*, p. 174.

nonsensical, but it may still fail to picture a state of affairs. Wittgenstein's example for sentences that are senseless but not nonsensical are the propositions of logic.[44] "The moon is visible or it is not visible" is a well-formed sentence, no less grammatical than "The moon is visible or it is hidden behind a cloud." And yet, the first of these sentences is senseless, while the second has sense and is significant. It is always true as a matter of logic that "The moon is visible or it is not visible" – we cannot imagine any state of affairs that would make this sentence false.[45] This sentence therefore has no truth-conditions, its truth does not depend on anything since it is always true. In contrast, "the moon is visible or it is hidden behind a cloud" has truth-conditions. It is false on a bright summer day at noon. When it is true, things stand in such a way that the moon is either visible or else hidden behind a cloud. That things stand in such a way is its sense which the sentence shows and which is expressed when it is asserted.

We have now defined nonsense as any construction that violates the grammar of descriptive, scientific language. Well-formed sentences that satisfy logical syntax are the opposite of nonsense.[46] And it appears that we have also specified the difference between sentences that are *sinnvoll* (full of sense or significant, that is, something that signifies) and *sinnlos* (senseless): "in order to say, whether 'p' is true (or false), I must have determined under which conditions I call 'p'

---

[44] See Black 1964, pp. 160f. and *TLP* 4.461 to 4.464 for the discussion of logical propositions as senseless but not nonsensical. In the discussion of his difference with Frege in *TLP* 5.4733, Wittgenstein cites as another example the statement "Socrates is identical." As it stands, it is nonsensical (the grammar of "identical" does not permit it to be treated as a property or quality; *TLP* 5.473) as well as senseless (we have not assigned a meaning to the word "identical" that would allow us to treat it as a property). If we gave a different meaning to the word "identical," the otherwise grammatical sentence "Socrates is identical" might end up being a perfectly ordinary descriptive sentence.

[45] "(I know, for example, nothing about the weather when I know that it rains or doesn't rain)" Wittgenstein comments in *TLP* 4.461.

[46] This account does not deny Ian Proops's assertion that "we cannot think of nonsense as resulting from the inappropriate combination of meaningful parts. If we have nonsense, it is not because we have meaning-bearing parts that fail to gel, but because we fail to find any meaning-bearing elements in the first place" (2000, p. 73). However, I would insist against Proops that one cannot sensibly talk of "meaningful parts" or "meaning-bearing elements" in sentences that are not put together appropriately: the same sequence of letters can function as a name in a construction that heeds how this name can occur in sentences, but it does not serve as a meaning-bearing element in an ungrammatical construction. This dependence of meaning on grammaticality is borne out by Wittgenstein's treatment of "Socrates is identical" as senseless (*TLP* 5.4733: "identical" bears no meaning) and nonsensical (*TLP* 5.473: this is not a grammatical sequence of words), see note 44 above.

true, and thereby I determine the sense of that sentence" (*TLP* 4.063).
A sentence has sense if it has specified truth-conditions and otherwise it is senseless. As we will see, while this defines what it means
for a sentence to be significant or to have sense, in other contexts
Wittgenstein uses the word "sense" differently.

Armed with these distinctions between well-formed and nonsensical, between significant and senseless sentences, we can now generate
a simple grid for Wittgenstein's rather straightforward classification
of sentences.

	Sinnvoll, significant, has or makes sense	*Sinnlos*, senseless, lacks sense
Well-formed, grammatical, satisfies logical syntax	I	II
Nonsensical, ungrammatical, violates logical syntax	??	III

We are familiar by now with the distinction between the first two types
of sentences: "The sentence shows what it says, tautology and contradiction that they say nothing" (*TLP* 4.461). Well-formed, significant
sentences constitute type I, whereas type II consists of well-formed
sentences that lack truth-conditions and are therefore senseless. While
logical propositions, tautologies, and contradictions are a paradigm
example, also belonging to this second class are grammatical sentences
where so far we have failed to assign meaning to some of their words.[47]
So, by way of summary, we can say that

[47] James Conant and Cora Diamond therefore emphasize that sentences do not have a priori
features according to which, by necessity, they are to be classified in a certain way. It is
important to the conception of Wittgenstein's early philosophy that we pay attention to our
illusions, imaginatively take nonsense for sense, try to assign meaning – which is precisely
what we are asked to do regarding the hypotheses of his experiment. Only our failure
will persuade us that some sentence belongs irredeemably into one class or another. Many
initially senseless expressions can be given meaning by appropriately operationalizing terms.
Compare *TLP* 5.4733 (see note 44 above) but also Wittgenstein's procedure in *LE*, p. 38,
where he explores to what extent the notion of goodness can be operationalized (it *can* be –
not the notion of absolute goodness, however).

I comprises the sentences that show what they say, that represent or picture states of affairs in the indicative mood, that have sense – paradigmatically these are the sentences of natural science.

II comprises statements that show that they say nothing, statements that are senseless but not nonsensical – paradigmatically these are the propositions of logic (tautologies, contradictions).

Tautologies and contradictions show that they say nothing. When we try to determine their sense by determining under which conditions we would call them true, we find that tautologies leave room for reality to be as it may, and we find that contradictions give reality no chance at all. In both cases, their truth or falsity is already fixed and they do not say anything or lay claim on the world in any way (*TLP* 4.463).[48]

Some of the expressions of group III lay claim to the world, they pretend to be saying something and do not even realize that they are in the same group with openly nonsensical and senseless nursery rhymes. The confused metaphysical sentences of philosophy are Wittgenstein's paradigm examples. They are nonsensical *and* senseless (*TLP* 5.473 *and* 5.4733, 4.003 or 3.323 *and* 6.53). They create a nonsentence by taking the copula "is" as a predicate, and they fail to assign a meaning to "is" or "being" as a predicate or property. They ask "whether the good is more or less identical than the beautiful" (*TLP* 4.003).

III comprises expressions that fail to show anything, that claim to say something when there is no sense to be asserted; these expressions are senseless and nonsensical, they flaunt or misunderstand the logic of language as do, for example, nonsense poems and all those philosophical statements in the indicative mood that purport to represent something as do the sentences in I, but to which correspond no matters of fact: "yellow tables chairs," "the slithy toves gimble," "this book is tired," or "He thought he saw a Rattlesnake \ That questioned him in Greek: \ He looked again, and found it was \ The Middle of Next Week."[49]

[48] *L32–35*, pp. 136f. reiterates this distinction between I and II.
[49] See *ibid.*, p. 137 for the first two (Wittgenstein derived the second from Lewis Carroll's "Jabberwocky"), *L30–32*, p. 3 for the third. The fourth example comes from Lewis Carroll's "Sylvie and Bruno" (1936, p. 330; cf. p. 153).

Most commentaries on the *Tractatus* agree that it distinguishes between these three types of expressions in speech.[50] Our grid creates four slots, however, raising the question whether there could be a fourth group, and whether subjunctive expressions belong into this group.

If there were such a fourth category of expressions, these would be nonsensical or ungrammatical – in that respect, expressions in the subjunctive mood do qualify – and yet be *sinnvoll*, that is, they would somehow be significant. According to the discussion so far, there cannot be such a thing. It was noted above that "a sentence has sense if it has specified truth-conditions and otherwise it is senseless." This suggests that we can determine sense or senselessness only when we can presume that the expression is already well formed and not nonsensical. The problem is exemplified by sentences such as "The desk penholders the book" or "The length of this room is 39,598,465,234 angstrom (that is, roughly 12 feet)." Even though we could assign meaning to all the parts of these expressions, they are nonsensical – when we talk about some objects being on the desk, we cannot describe this as an activity of the desk, and when we measure rooms we have to use an appropriate measure (meters and centimeters, inches and feet, but not measures of atomic distance). This use of "desk" is ungrammatical, it violates how the word can occur in possible sentences (*TLP* 3.203, 2.0123, 3.3ff.).[51] Similarly, one violates the grammar of "measuring in angstrom" when applying this to the length of a room.[52] But with nonsensical sentences like these, we would not bother to emphasize that they are nevertheless not senseless since we can assign meaning to all their parts. Indeed, we would not even go about determining the

---

[50] It should be noted that Wittgenstein also discusses "completely generalized propositions" of science, propositions that organize and unify the presentation of scientific facts (*TLP* 5.526, 5.5261). There has been little discussion of these propositions – even though they do not appear to fit into Wittgenstein's classification and even though they do reappear in *PI*.

[51] This example for "nonsense" appears at the end of the third manuscript of the "Notes on Logic" that are included in *NB*.

[52] See p. 150 above and *PO*, p. 449; cf. *PI* 513. Measuring in angstrom is not just impractical. As opposed to measurement in meters or feet, it could not yield a precise measurement: due to the nature of the measuring devices and the object measured, different measurements would not agree with one another. Comparison to the same state of affairs can render the measurement true at one time, false at another. Compare note 45 above.

sense of expressions that do not qualify as possible sentences in the first place. As long as "sense" is defined exclusively as a property of well-formed sentences, namely that they have truth-conditions, our fourth slot will have to remain empty.

But is Wittgenstein really limited to this one sense of "sense"?[53] The next chapter will explore this question more thoroughly. For now, however, just two clues may suffice to indicate at least the possibility that the fourth slot need not remain empty. Both are closely associated with our discussion so far and the text of the *Tractatus* itself.

The reconstruction of Wittgenstein's *reductio*-argument established that its conclusion "there is indeed the inexpressible in speech" is tantamount to "we cannot express any sense whatsoever in speech." This would suggest that some "sense" is inexpressible in speech, and this sense would obviously be distinct from the "sense of a significant sentence."

The second clue is provided by the "frame" of the *Tractatus*, that is, by the preface that anticipates the final remark (*TLP* 7) and contains implicit instructions to the reader, and by the two penultimate remarks (*TLP* 6.53 and 6.54) that reflect on what has been achieved. In 6.54 Wittgenstein tells us that his sentences are nonsensical, while in the preface he speaks of "the sense of the book."[54] Taken together, the two remarks amount to the claim that even the nonsensical sentences of the *Tractatus* can convey the sense of the book – not, however, in virtue of being significant sentences that have sense. Indeed, we could not understand Wittgenstein and finally recognize that his sentences are nonsensical if the nonsensical sentences could not convey some sense (*TLP* 6.54).

[53] Compare Diamond 2000, p. 164: "There is the distinction between sentences with sense and those of logic and mathematics; there is a distinction between all those and sentences containing one or more symbols without meaning, nonsensical sentences. Ethical sentences are not a subcategory of the latter but a non-category."

[54] "One could put the entire sense of the book (*den ganzen Sinn des Buches*) roughly into the words: What can be said at all, can be said clearly; and whereof one cannot talk, about that one must remain silent." The *Tractatus* uses "sense" also when speaking of the sense (in English one would say: meaning) of life and of the world; and though Wittgenstein normally holds that only sentences have sense and not words (they have reference or meaning only in the context of a sentence), he also refers to "punishment and reward in the ordinary sense" (*TLP* 6.41, 6.422, 6.521).

Very tentatively, then, let us acknowledge the possibility of a fourth group of expressions.

IV comprises expressions that show what they do not say, these expressions are nonsensical but not senseless; while they do not claim to say anything and do not have sense, they are not caught up in a misunderstanding of the logic of language; their expression can make sense, albeit not in a propositional or semantic manner; for the time being, the paradigmatic examples are subjunctive expressions and thus the nonsensical remarks of the *Tractatus* itself.

Revisiting the grid, we note that the *Tractatus* remains silent about the distinction between III and IV, likewise about extrapropositional or nonlinguistic sense, about sentences in the subjunctive mood, and thereby about the character of its own nonsensical, yet not senseless sentences.

	Sinnvoll, significant, has or makes sense	*Sinnlos*, senseless, lacks sense
Well-formed, grammatical, satisfies logical syntax	I The sentences of natural science (6.53), saying that things stand as shown (4.022), 4.461 and 6.1264	II Expressions that show that they say nothing (tautologies, contradictions, 4.461), see 4.4611 and 5.525
Nonsensical, ungrammatical, violates logical syntax	IV Expressions of "any sense whatsoever" that is inexpressible in speech: "the sense of this book," "the sense of the world" (Preface, 6.41), see 6.422, 6.521	III Misunderstandings of the logic of language, professing to express in speech what is inexpressible in speech, see 4.003, 3.323 *and* 6.53; 5.473 *and* 5.4733

It looks as if we have now made room for a very peculiar kind of expression – it is to be an expression of sense that is not an expression in speech. Chapter 5 will demonstrate that this is not such a peculiar thing, after all.[55] For the time being, however, we can see already where the exploration of this kind of expression may lead: assertive propositions in the indicative mood say something by claiming to be a picture of a state of affairs, and they are senseless and/or nonsensical if they fail to determine a picture (I, II, III). In contrast, nonsensical expressions in the subjunctive mood make no such claim, they do not partake in the linguistic business of picturing (IV). Sentences, questions or problems, answers, even the senseless as well as nonsensical metaphysical doctrines of philosophy gravitate toward assertions in the indicative mood, straining to say something. In contrast, the subjunctive mood of possibility is a form of silence about the world. And Wittgenstein's nonsensical demand that "whereof one cannot speak, thereof one must remain silent" (*TLP* 7) entreats the philosopher to take residence in the experimental realm of the aphorism, suspended from the world in the subjunctive mood, eluding the pervasive self-misunderstanding of metaphysics, ethics, and aesthetics that there are facts to its matters.

THE LANGUAGE OF THE *TRACTATUS*

"Whereof one cannot speak, about that one must be silent." Thus concludes the *Tractatus* (*TLP* 7). Thirty years later, Wittgenstein noted: "Don't *by any means* shy away from talking nonsense! It's just that you must listen closely to your nonsense."[56]

If we followed the only strictly correct method (*TLP* 6.53), we would maintain silence about that whereof we cannot speak. We

---

[55] This, in particular, will distinguish the current proposal from suggestive, but ultimately arcane proposals by previous authors. Following Hadot 1959, p. 478, Favrholdt suggests that there are four uses of language, among them the "absurd," the "representing," and the "indicative" use (where "indicative" means something like "showing" or "pointing" and is not opposed to "subjunctive"). According to Hadot, the latter part of the *Tractatus* uses language indicatively (1959, p. 482), according to Favrholdt it uses language absurdly (1964, p. 141). Both suggest that the propositions of the *Tractatus* are nonsensical in a nonvicious manner.

[56] *CV*, p. 64 (dated March 5, 1947). See *WVC*, p. 69 for an earlier instance (December 30, 1929): "What, you swine, you don't want to talk nonsense? Go ahead and talk nonsense, it doesn't matter!" Wittgenstein was referring to Saint Augustine's "what saith any man when he speaks of Thee? Yet woe to him that speaketh not, since mute are even the most eloquent" (1991, p. 3). Compare the final quote of chapter 2, p. 90 above.

would not utter anything but scientific or descriptive sentences, and if someone tried to talk philosophy with us, all we could say, again and again, is "What do you mean?" But there is another method of maintaining silence, of not saying anything when we cannot speak about something. This one is less than strictly correct because it involves us in the production of nonsense.[57] But as long as we know that we are talking nonsense by speaking in the subjunctive mood, and as long as we therefore do not even pretend to be saying something where we cannot, this method of thought experimentation allows us at least to engage philosophy. Attending carefully, listening closely to our nonsensical hypotheses, trying imaginatively to take nonsense for sense, treating our hypotheses as if they might be true or false, we find that all our attempts fail. The subjunctive hypotheses never make the transition to verified or falsified statements in the indicative mood. The *reductio*-argument shows that they were irredeemably nonsensical from beginning to end.[58]

So much for Wittgenstein's method. We can take his description literally and will not find it self-defeating.

---

[57] See the beginning of chapter 3, pp. 92f. above, where it was shown that Wittgenstein's preface announces the necessity of doing so: nonsense will have to be spoken in order to draw limits to the expression of thought in speech.

[58] Here emerges once again the previously mentioned point of close contact with the work of Cora Diamond and James Conant (see the last section of chapter 2). Diamond remarks in 2000, p. 157 that Wittgenstein demands from his readers "a kind of imaginative activity, an exercise of the capacity to enter into the taking of nonsense for sense." In relation to the author – the utterer of nonsense – this exercise puts us neither inside (we are not mistaking nonsense for sense) nor on the outside (we are not just seeing someone produce gibberish). The notion of the thought experiment elaborates this imaginative activity, and for expressions in the subjunctive mood it holds systematically that they are neither inside (they do not say anything) nor outside (they provoke the imaginative activity of taking nonsense for sense). Conant tells a very similar story with a somewhat different vocabulary (2000, pp. 194, 196, 213f.). Diamond's "imaginative activity" is Conant's attempt to recognize the symbol in the sign. The nonsensical sentences of the *Tractatus* are mere signs, and the readers' real experience of failure to recognize symbols in these signs reveals to them that the apparently substantial nonsense of the *Tractatus* is really mere nonsense. A problem in Diamond's and Conant's approach surfaces when Juliet Floyd states a paradoxical consequence of their approach, namely that "for Wittgenstein there is thinking without thoughts" (1998, p. 85). Following Wittgenstein, Floyd denies that the *Tractatus* could accomplish such a thing as drawing limits to thought. However, she does take it to accomplish the identification of thought with what is expressible in speech. The paradox evaporates for Floyd, Conant, and Diamond as soon as one explicitly allows that there may be thoughts that cannot be expressed in speech.

6.54 My sentences serve as elucidations in the following way: anyone who understands me eventually recognizes them as nonsensical, having climbed through them – on them – beyond them. (One must, so to speak, throw away the ladder after one has climbed up on it.)

One must overcome these sentences and then see the world right.

Wittgenstein's sentences serve as elucidations in that they invite us to enact his thought experiment. By trying to make sense of the hypothesis and its corollary, by trying to formulate sentences that express thoughts about the relation of language and world, we learn to understand him and the failure he experienced. We thus recognize that the sentences that prompted the thought experiment but failed to say anything about the world as it is, lie beyond the limits of meaningful scientific language and are simply nonsense. Having used them for the thought experiment, we can now throw them away, discarding them as we would any hypothetical premise of a successful *reductio*-argument. Having discarded them, we no longer need to talk nonsense and engage in the futile effort of turning it into significant sentences. Instead, we can now follow the strictly correct method of philosophy and stay away from philosophy altogether. No longer trying to express in speech what cannot be so expressed, we use speech to express facts and nothing else. Having overcome the flawed aspiration to express in speech any sense whatsoever, we now see the world right.

This, then, is one way of putting how the *Tractatus* is perfectly consistent even as we take literally that its sentences are nonsensical: one remains silent when speaking nonsense knowingly. Our subjunctive expressions are not saying anything nor laying claim on what is inexpressible in speech.[59] Since they refrain from assertion and thus from saying anything, these expressions do not distort matters of value or turn them into something akin to a contingent fact.

There is another way of noting the achievement of consistency. Interpreters of Wittgenstein have generally assumed that Wittgenstein's difficulty derives from a problem of self-referentiality:

---

[59] Statements in the subjunctive mood do not say anything about anything. Therefore they cannot serve as metalinguistic statements, they do not constitute a language of their own that says something about the descriptive language of science. This distinguishes the current proposal from Bernstein 1966, pp. 236f., which exempts Wittgenstein's "ladder language" as a type of metalanguage.

now that we have reached the end of the *Tractatus*, how are we to apply its message to itself? It was in response to this problem of self-referentiality that Wittgenstein was to take the desperate measure of claiming that yes, indeed, the *Tractatus* applies to its own sentences and that they, too, are nonsensical.

According to the interpretation developed here, there is no problem of self-referentiality. Wittgenstein never reflects upon the language in which the *Tractatus* is written and does not somehow apply the work to itself. Instead, it is just as the preface lays it out. The book determines the limits of language from within. However, the only available strategy that does so requires that one speaks on the other side of that limit. Within the limits of language one produces sentences that have sense, and what is on the other side of the limit is simply nonsense. So, nonsense was used to set up the thought experiment that allowed for the limits of language to be drawn from within. Nonsense was not used, however, to reflect on itself. Instead, on the hypotheses that got the thought experiment started, it should have been possible to reflect on the relation between significant sentences and the world. There was a promise or hope that we might be able to convert our nonsensical hypotheses into significant sentences. Our success would then exemplify that what we wanted to express in language, can indeed be so expressed. This, however, proved illusory. We found this out by attending to significant sentences. Finding that they are unfit, simply not made to say anything about themselves (*TLP* 3.332), we also found out that all sentences about the sense of sentences are equally unfit and simply, irredeemably nonsensical.

While *TLP* 6.54, the preface, and to some extent 6.53 reflect on the *Tractatus*, on the course of the thought experiment, on the experiences of those who reenacted it (they finally recognize its sentences to be nonsensical), there is no deep problem of self-referentiality in this, no puzzling variant of the liar's paradox. On most accounts, the paradox of the self-referential statement "this sentence is false" spell deep philosophical trouble.[60] In contrast, when Wittgenstein's remark 6.54 suggests that "this remark is nonsensical," this underscores simply

---

[60] Whether the liar's paradox spells trouble for Wittgenstein is quite another matter. In the *Tractatus* he rules it out along the lines of *TLP* 3.332. For his later views, see *LFM*, pp. 206–209, and *Remarks on the Foundations of Mathematics* (*RFM*), part I, appendix III, 12.

that it does not achieve what a simple description of fact can achieve. The closing remarks of the *Tractatus* do not assert that such remarks cannot mean anything to the reader. They tell us instead that they convey sense not in virtue of a sense that is contained in them and expressed by them. Of course, how they do this remains a mystery – for now.

CHAPTER 5

The senses of sense

In the years between completion and publication of the *Tractatus* Wittgenstein insisted that he could not change a word of it.[1] He had conducted his thought experiment in earnest, after all, recording faithfully "what – and how it has – really occurred" to him. He had seriously pursued his hypotheses and under their guidance attacked the problem of clarifying the relation of language and world: if it *were* possible to solve these problems, his solution *could well have been* "unassailable and definitive."[2] But alas, since this solution undercuts the very hypotheses that underwrote and induced the experiment, it has to be abandoned and the value of his book therefore consists partly "in that it shows how little has been achieved when these problems are solved." And so, though his sentences turn out to be nonsensical, he considered them by no means arbitrary, and nor should we.[3]

---

[1] This is apparent in his correspondence with Russell, Frege, the prospective publisher von Ficker, and his translator C. K. Ogden.

[2] It is therefore, after all, that generations of philosophers were able to engage the *Tractatus* critically, debating its views on language and logic. As with any *reductio*-argument, there are particular steps to be attended to. We can ask, for example, whether within the hypothetical framework of the thought experiment Wittgenstein correctly arrived at the penultimate conclusion that all sentences are of equal value (*TLP* 6.4).

[3] It is striking to see how readily some of his most astute interpreters correct or dismiss his formulations. This is also true of those who aim for literal faithfulness to the text (including, occasionally, Black 1964, pp. 297, 303, 363). Resolute approaches seek literal interpretations of *TLP* 6.54 and its nonsensicality claim but also engender a style of "dialectical" reading, which affords the interpreter considerable latitude. Here are two examples where no textual is cited for rather strong claims. Friedlander 2001, pp. 24f. determines that what we want to express in speech are not, first and foremost, our thoughts or what we have in mind: "From the outset we must remember that Wittgenstein thinks of the *Tractatus* as a problem of expression . . . And what needs expression, we must keep in mind, is the world" (see also note 10 of the conclusion below). Floyd 1998 seeks to determine where Wittgenstein is ironic and where we need to take him at face value: "These remarks from the Preface appear to commit Wittgenstein to the existence of thoughts, to there being a sharp distinction between

My interpretation began innocently enough with a rather ortho-
dox treatment of Wittgenstein's views. It did not reject or even qualify
what, already in 1959, Elizabeth Anscombe called "the best-known
thesis of the *Tractatus*," namely that "'metaphysical' statements are
nonsensical, and that the only sayable things are propositions of natural science."[4] And yet, for all my attempts to stick closely to the text,
I am now referring not just to what Wittgenstein wrote but also to
what he did not write about – to the language in which the *Tractatus*
itself was written, to statements in past and future tense and the subjunctive mood, to expressions that are nonsensical but not senseless,
to thought and any sense whatsoever that is inexpressible in speech
but nevertheless expressed by the *Tractatus*. I have implied that, in
spite of his silence about all these aspects of language and meaning,
Wittgenstein recognized them.[5] Indeed, only this recognition was to
have allowed him to claim, literally and sincerely, that his sentences
are nonsensical and yet can help us see the world rightly.

This chapter shoulders the remaining burden of proof. In particular, it will defend as quite natural the assumption that a great

---

thoughts and their expression. But he is not so committed. He is not claiming that thoughts
exist and are expressed in the *Tractatus* – much less 'unassailable' and 'definitive' ones."

[4] Anscombe 1971, p. 150.

[5] The attribution to Wittgenstein of a distinction that he did not explicitly make raises questions
of interpretive parsimony. This chapter provides an extended argument for the "naturalness"
of the distinction, its consistency with Wittgenstein's own words, and its capacity to solve long-
standing interpretive puzzles. It is also worthwhile to compare it to similar attributions by other
commentators. I distinguish two senses of "sense" in order to make room for sentences that are
nonsensical and yet make sense. This, in turn, allows me to address the "enormous difficulty of
expression" that motivated the *Tractatus* and that confronts Wittgenstein and his readers alike.
James Conant distinguishes two senses of "show" in order to allow for the distinction between
elucidatory and constative propositions (2002, p. 382). Constative propositions correspond to
the sentences that have sense and are used to speak descriptively about the world. Elucidatory
propositions, however, are used by no one but Frege and Wittgenstein, they are sentences "in
which an apparently constative use of language is revealed as illusory." Conant and I have
in common that we explicate a distinction that, at best, is only implicit in the *Tractatus*. In
terms of textual evidence, I have tried to show that my proposal fares considerably better
than Conant's (see, for example, note 48 in chapter 2). Most importantly, perhaps, Conant's
distinction proves esoteric in that it addresses how twentieth-century analytic philosophy
reflects and critiques itself. My suggestion of two senses of "sense," in contrast, is of immediate
significance to the general problem of expression. Also it relates the *Tractatus* to Wittgenstein's
lifelong intellectual pursuit. A similar argument can be made in regard to Cora Diamond's
introduction of a "transitional language" and later of a transitional state in 1988, pp. 9f. and
2000, p. 157.

many expressions are nonsensical and yet not senseless. This assumption appears odd only from the inside of Wittgenstein's thought experiment and from the vantage point of analytic philosophy in the tradition of Frege and Russell. This tradition is interested in knowledge and belief, words and ideas, thoughts and representations, and within this theoretical framework it is hard to make out how a nonsensical aphorism differs from metaphysical nonsense. But against this tradition stands Wittgenstein's conception of philosophy as a critical activity. And considered in the light of practice, we can appreciate how nonsensical aphorisms can engage us in a manner that makes sense – while metaphysical nonsense does not.

After Wittgenstein's thought experiment was reconstructed (*reductio ad absurdum*), the chapters that followed investigated its literary analogue (the aphorism) and its linguistic or grammatical character (the subjunctive mood). This chapter turns finally to thought experimentation as an activity, that is, as a critical intervention.

LOGICAL ANALYSIS AND A STANDARD OF CLARITY

Various interpretations of the *Tractatus* took their cue from Wittgenstein's use of the term "elementary sentence," and especially his claim that "it is apparent that in the analysis of sentences we must come upon elementary sentences which consist of names in immediate combination" – where the names are "simple signs" that correspond to simple objects (*TLP* 4.221 and 3.201, 2.02). This approach suggests that Wittgenstein pursued a chemical conception of analysis: our sentences have sense just to the extent that we can precisely specify the conditions under which they are true or false. Our ordinary language is full of ambiguities but the completely analyzed sentence is unambiguous: there is only one complete analysis of each sentence and it takes us all the way down to the simple names that stand in for simple objects (*TLP* 3.323, 4.002, 3.325, 3.25, 3.251).[6] Accordingly, whether or not a sentence has sense is an objective matter, depending not so much on our ability to assign definite meaning to our terms

---

[6] See Griffin 1964, Graßhoff 1997 and 1998, Lampert 2000 and 2003; for a critique of this approach, see Nordmann 2003.

but on the result of a successful analysis where imprecise designations give way to precise characterizations of simple objects in their physical states.

In recent years this static conception of the *Tractatus* has given way to readings that foreground Wittgenstein's method. Nonsense is discovered not by a failure of analysis (which is always incomplete in practice) but by Wittgenstein and his readers undergoing a certain experience of failure. In this conception, one might ask, is there any rôle left for logical analysis, to simple objects and an image of objective determinacy of meaning? If the static conception attributes to Wittgenstein a dogmatic "theory of nonsense," some proponents of the alternative reading skeptically deny that Wittgenstein has any "theory of nonsense" at all. The notion of the thought experiment as critical intervention finds a middle ground between these dogmatic and skeptical positions.

Peter Sullivan articulates the notion that Wittgenstein has no "theory of nonsense" and along the way insists on a conception of nonsense that directly contradicts the one defended here:

Taken straight, as it were, nonsense is simply, and open-endedly, a failure to make sense. When, however, there is in play some specialized or theoretically developed conception of what it is to make sense, it is natural to parse "nonsense" as non-*sense*, and so to mean (or to seek to mean) by it, determinately, a failure to achieve whatever on that specialized conception counts as making sense. It is essential to what I called a fully honest acceptance that the system itself is nonsense that, in this acceptance, "nonsense" must be taken straight, and cannot be understood in the second of these ways.[7]

We might question Sullivan's appeal to honesty by asking why we *have* to take it straight. After all, Wittgenstein never wrote that his book was nonsense and made no sense. What he did write was that his sentences are nonsensical (*TLP* 6.54), that they can have no sense because they are ungrammatical. Now, is the reason why they have no sense that their analysis objectively fails to lead us to simple names and simple objects? Is the reason that our attempts to assign meaning to all of their parts must fail? Or is the reason, finally, that these

---

[7] Sullivan 2004, p. 38. To be sure, if one posits one "system" all one has is the all-or-nothing alternative of accepting or rejecting it altogether.

sentences cannot make sense even in the context, for example, of a thought experiment? There are many reasons for rejecting the first of these options. Indeed, Wittgenstein did not take the procedure of clarification "to depend on anything more than the logical capacities that are part of speaking and thinking": it does not depend on an analysis that is somehow prior to or independent of our ability to mean something definite by what we say.[8] Instead, analysis is nothing but clarification. When I express myself ambiguously, someone may ask me whether I mean to exclude this or to assert that and nothing else. This back and forth fixes the precise conditions under which the sentence – as I mean it – will be true or false. This form of analysis is tantamount to a "clarification of thoughts on particular occasions."[9] In the course of this clarification, we establish that the objects for which the names in our sentence stand, function like simple objects.

Whether or not a sentence has meaning therefore does not depend on a fixed taxonomy of sentences. And yet, our attempts to specify the meaning of our sentences are guided by an idea or ideal of what it is for a sentence to have sense. And this ideal is embodied by the descriptive sentences of sciences. These serve as exemplars of analyzable sentences for which the conditions of their truth and falsity can be specified with clarity and precision. Only those sentences can have sense that can be assimilated to the model provided by science. Perhaps, there are no limits to our imaginative ability to assign meaning in such a way that any string of words comes out as a description of a state of affairs. But this very idea of "successfully" assigning meaning implies a limit of language and a conception of when a sentence has sense and when it is non*sense*: it is nonsense when it violates the grammar of sentences that picture states of affairs.

In the words of Thomas Ricketts, the *Tractatus* is thus an attempt "to think through at the most general level" what conception of a describable reality is presupposed by the successful formulation of sentences that have sense. He continues:

---

[8] Conant and Diamond 2004, p. 64; cf. Ricketts 1996, p. 75. Among those reasons is our previous discussion of *TLP* 5.4733, which indicates that the sentence "Socrates is identical" could be perfectly meaningful as long as we choose to assign some definite adjectival meaning to the word "identical." Wittgenstein's antimetaphysical, critical orientation provides another reason; for further reasons see Nordmann 2003.

[9] Hutto 2003, p. 77; this conception of analysis is also endorsed by Ostrow 2002.

When we throw away the ladder, we give up the attempts to state what this conception of representation and truth demands of language and the world, give up trying to operate at an illusory level of generality, without however rejecting the conception of truth as agreement with reality. Rather, we understand what this conception comes to, when we appreciate how what can be said can be said clearly, when we appreciate the standard of clarity set by the general form of sentences.[10]

Whenever we try to use sentences to express something other than facts, we experience at a level of concreteness that our attempt must fail to meet the standard of clarity set by those sentences that are true or false in virtue of their agreement or disagreement with reality, namely the descriptive sentences of science. We thus discover nonsense because our attempt to use sentences differently fails to yield sentences that have sense. This does not preclude, however, that these sentences and our failure might somehow make sense.

MAKING SENSE

The previous section rejected Sullivan's claim that "nonsense is simply, and open-endedly, a failure to make sense." For all we know, a sentence is nonsensical if it cannot *have* sense, that is, if it cannot be made to look like good scientific sentences and if it cannot be analyzed or clarified. But it is for this chapter and the following sections to show how such nonsensical sentences can nevertheless *make* sense.

We can embark on this project by criticizing another strong but unpersuasive claim about Wittgenstein's conception of "nonsense." Summarizing recent interpretations of the *Tractatus*, Hilary Putnam casts doubt on the possibility of "deep" or "substantial" nonsense that somehow manages to be "about" the higher or to express ineffable truths. His doubt, like that of Sullivan, applies to my proposal that there might be a kind of nonsense that is not senseless: "But why should one *not* say that there is such a thing as 'deep' nonsense? Well,

---

[10] Ricketts 1996, p. 94. Note that Ricketts begins by moving Wittgenstein in the proximity of Kant. Though Wittgenstein's transcendental reconstruction of successful scientific language cannot lead to a theory of language and world in its own right, it does not therefore abandon the standard of clarity that is set by this language. And of course, this ideal standard of clarity can inform our conceptions of sense and nonsense even if, upon closer scrutiny, science itself does not meet this standard. To suggest the abandonment of the ideal would be to throw the baby out with the bathwater – see chapter 2, note 61 (but compare Ricketts 1996, p. 99).

for one thing, notice that the *Tractatus* explicitly maintains that what cannot be *said* cannot be *thought*."[11]

Putnam's point fails to persuade for two reasons. First, as we saw before, it can be disputed whether Wittgenstein ever actually maintained that what cannot be said cannot be thought.[12] More importantly, Putnam takes what the *Tractatus* "explicitly maintains" – a doctrine supposedly established in the course of the thought experiment – to tell us where the experiment leaves us. In particular, this is the message we are to take away from it: since the sentences of the *Tractatus* are nonsensical, we should reject the work entirely and, on the authority of the rejected work, we should reject along with it the very possibility of thoughts that are not expressible in speech.[13]

In contrast, I propose that to reject the sentences of the *Tractatus* means that we should *also* reject its hypothesis and its corollaries. The notion that thoughts should be identified with sentences is one such corollary: if it were true that any sense whatsoever (that includes all our thoughts) is expressible in speech, then we could obviously say what we think. However, once this assumption is rejected, the issue is left open and there may well be thoughts that cannot be expressed. In other words, Frege's (and Mauthner's) supposition that thinking is a kind of speaking belongs to the experimental set-up of Wittgenstein's investigation – it holds just as long as that investigation lasts.[14]

We should therefore find another way to describe where Wittgenstein's experiment leaves us. Having rejected that any sense whatsoever is expressible in speech, we look around us and take note of what is left. There is on the one hand the language of science and its sentences that express facts. There are on the other hand our various attempts to express thought and sense that is inexpressible in speech.

---

[11] Putnam 1998, p. 110.

[12] See pp. 82f. above for a critical discussion of the passages that have been cited as support for this claim (preface, *TLP* 3, 4.114f., 5.61). Here, I only repeat what I argue there, namely that this view holds only within the context of the thought experiment, that it cannot be exported from it, and indeed, that it is reduced to absurdity by the *Tractatus*.

[13] Perhaps unfairly, Ostrow 2002, p. 8 and Williams 2004, p. 19 criticize Conant and Diamond on similar grounds. See note 61 in chapter 2, above.

[14] Compare the previously quoted diary entry of May 9, 1930: "One often thinks – and I myself *often* make this mistake – that everything one thinks can be written down. In reality one can only write down – that is, without doing something that is stupid & inappropriate – what arises in us in the form of writing" (MT, diary p. 27).

Since the language suitable for describing the world is foreclosed to these attempts, we try other avenues of making ourselves understood, of imaginatively latching on to each other's meanings, of falling in with each other. Do we in each instance or in general know that there is a sense, that there are thoughts to be latched on to? It is part of our predicament that we do not know this – but we cannot rule it out either.[15]

Just as the identification of thought and sentence belongs to the hypothetical set-up of Wittgenstein's thought experiment, so does his restriction through the hypothesis of the *reductio*-argument to just one kind of sense, namely the sense of a significant sentence. His argument concerns the limits of what can be expressed in speech, and the notion of "expression in speech" restricts him to the kind of sense that a sentence can have or possess: "I can only mention the objects. Signs stand in for them. I can only speak *of* them, *express them in speech* I cannot" (*TLP* 3.221).[16] In order for something to be expressed in speech, it must be somehow put into words and thus be contained in the sentence. Signs, names, and (Wittgenstein's crucial discovery) facts can be expressed in speech, and thereby the sense of a significant sentence. Significant sentences *have* a sense, this is their character or property and it is objectively determined by their truth-conditions (by our assignment of determinate meaning). If a sentence lacks this character and if it is therefore senseless, we would also call it void of content.

What, then, would be that other kind of sense, the kind that is left out from consideration when one focuses on what can be expressed in speech? The *Tractatus* invokes this other notion a few times only. It mentions the "sense of the book" (along with the non-sense of its sentences; *TLP* preface), the "sense of life and world"

---

[15] Accordingly, Wittgenstein and Kant agree that questions of true or false knowledge can only be settled in a scientific language, that is, one in which the determination of truth requires the determination that "this is how it is." Compare *NB*, p. 52 (May 27, 1915): "What cannot be expressed, that we do not express –. And how can we *ask* whether *that* is expressible which cannot be *expressed*?" This remark can be read narrowly (where "to express" means "to express in speech") or widely (where "to express" means "to express in any way whatsoever") and describes the same predicament on both readings.

[16] Compare the discussion of this on pp. 50–52, above (reminder: "express in speech" is the translation of "*aussprechen*," which Wittgenstein equates with "*in Sprache oder Schrift ausdrücken*").

(in English, one would normally speak here of the meaning of life; *TLP* 6.521, 6.41), also "punishment and reward in the ordinary sense" (*TLP* 6.521).[17]

However, even in the midst of interpreting the *Tractatus* one can be tripped up by Wittgenstein's wider conception of "sense." This happened to Max Black when he questioned Wittgenstein's use of "senseless" in *TLP* 5.132: "Laws of inference which – as in Frege and Russell – are to justify the inferences, are senseless, and would be redundant." Black notes: "(*sinnlos*): one might have expected 'nonsensical' (*unsinnig*) here." It is easy to see why Black is puzzled. The laws of inference proposed by Russell and Frege are to help out logic. But logic, according to Wittgenstein, requires no such help and takes care of itself.[18] Black notices that the proposed laws of inference are therefore not like tautologies or contradictions, which are senseless but not nonsensical. Instead, they are more like bad philosophy – so why doesn't Wittgenstein call them nonsensical? The answer is disarmingly simple. He calls them senseless because they are not required, because "they would be redundant" or superfluous – they are pointless, have no purpose, and we can associate no sense or meaning with them.[19] Here, then, is a first difference between the two kinds of sense. Particular sentences are significant if they have sense, void of content if they do not have sense. Wittgenstein's book, in contrast, either makes sense or it is pointless.[20]

We encounter the wider notion of "sense" again when Frege asks Wittgenstein in a letter whether there is any difference in meaning between "the world is all that is the case" (*TLP* 1) and "the world

---

[17] See note 54 of the previous chapter (*TLP* 6.41, 6.422, 6.521). The German word in all these cases is "*Sinn*."

[18] See the discussion on pp. 35ff., above.

[19] Just like "sense," the German word "*Sinn*" can refer to the meaning of a sentence and of an artwork, to the point or purpose of an action, and to our five or six senses (including the "sense of possibility"). With respect to *TLP* 4.461, Erik Stenius noted yet another relevant sense of the German word: "In order to correspond to the German word *Sinn* the word 'sense' must be understood here not only in its meaning of linguistic 'sense' but also in the meaning of 'direction,' given to it in mathematics . . . Sentences resemble arrows in that the sense (*Sinn*) of a sentence is *directed* in contradistinction to the meaning (*Bedeutung*) of a name" (1960, p. 171).

[20] And so we see that this "*sinnlos*" did not just trip up Max Black but also the translators, Pears and McGuinness. Instead of translating in *TLP* 5.132 "have no sense," they should have used "make no sense" or – Ogden's choice – the neutral formulation "are senseless."

is the totality of facts" (*TLP* 1.1). Wittgenstein acknowledged in his
response that they have the same sense (namely, none) but that there
is a difference in "the ideas that *I* associated with them when I wrote
them."[21] This suggests that it depends on the ideas we associate with
it whether something that does not have sense can nevertheless make
sense.[22]

With this notion of association and with Wittgenstein's underlined "*I*" arises another distinction between the two notions of
sense. The *Tractatus* associates the sense of a sentence with its factual
character: the significant sentence is a configuration of names and that
configuration is a fact that can model other facts because these are
also configurations of objects. Wittgenstein highlights this intimate
relation between facts in language (the sense of sentences) and facts
in nature (states of affairs) when, for example, he uses the odd formulation that the sentence "a is f" shows "that the object a occurs
in its sense" (*TLP* 4.1211). Accordingly, the determination of sense
is a mechanical procedure, no more or less difficult than determining what is the case. This is, of course, how significant sentences
can be true and false, and why they alone can give us true and
"objective" knowledge of the world. The procedure works without
reference to a particular human subject who uses "a is f" to show
something.

An example from Wittgenstein's later writing establishes the contrast to the case where it matters "what ideas *I* associate" with something. It exemplifies that making sense through the association of
ideas is not grounded in the factual character of a sentence or, in this
case, of an action:

Recall that after Schubert's death his brother cut some of Schubert's scores
into small pieces and gave such pieces, consisting of a few bars, to his favorite
pupils. This act, as a sign of piety, is *just as* understandable to us as the

[21] On September 16, 1999 Frege quotes this from a letter he had received from Wittgenstein (1989, p. 22).
[22] Wittgenstein later explores how associations make sense by somehow "fitting": "What is closely associated with one another, *brought into* association, that seems to fit each other" (*PI*, part II, section vi, p. 183). *RFM*, part I, remark 171 asks how one can tell whether an association has a point and answers: "Often we can say: 'This one corresponds to a gesture, this one doesn't.'"

different one of keeping the scores untouched, accessible to no one. And if Schubert's brother had burned the scores, that too would be understandable as a sign of piety.[23]

To complicate matters one might add that if Schubert's brother had burned the scores, that would also be understandable as a sign of spite. Though feelings of piety and spite are not expressible in speech, these feelings are nevertheless attached to words, rituals, and more or less symbolic actions. However, they are not expressed *in* those words or actions, and this is why the same feeling – if one can speak of sameness here – can attach to very different actions, while very different feelings can be attached to the same action. What is expressed through speech or action must therefore be judged very differently from the sense that is expressed in speech by a significant sentence.

We can understand the action of Schubert's brother as an act of piety, but we cannot know as a matter of fact that this is what it is. Indeed, as much as we might want to have knowledge in matters of value, meaning, and feeling, too, we would not want to do so at the price of treating them like mere matters of fact. By distinguishing sentences that have sense from activities that make sense, we therefore mark a difference which, according to Wittgenstein, we wanted to preserve all along: it is the difference between understanding something as a contingent fact like all others, and understanding something as meaningful.[24] We have already encountered this distinction in Wittgenstein's "Lecture on Ethics." There he took as one of his examples what it means to understand something as a miracle ("the scientific way of looking at a fact is not the way to look at it as a miracle").[25] He elaborates this in his diary:

The transformation of water into wine is astounding at best & we would gaze in amazement at the one who could do it, but no more . . . It must be the marvelous that gives this action content & meaning. And by that I don't mean the extraordinary or the unprecedented but the spirit in which it is done and for which the transformation of water into wine is only a symbol (as it were) a gesture. A gesture which (of course) can only be made by the

[23] This is from the "Remarks on Frazer's *Golden Bough*" in *PO*, p. 127.
[24] I use the term "meaningful" very loosely here, as we do in everyday language. For a fact to be meaningful it has an air of noncontingence.
[25] LE, p. 43; cf. pp. 55–57, above.

one who can do this extraordinary thing. The miracle must be understood as gesture, as expression if it is to speak to us. I could also say: It is a miracle only when *he* does it who does it in a marvelous spirit. Without this spirit it is only an extraordinarily strange fact. I must as it were know the person already before I can say that it is a miracle. I must read the whole of it already in the right spirit in order to sense the miracle in it.[26]

"For imagine whatever fact you may, it is in itself not miraculous," Wittgenstein remarks in the "Lecture on Ethics." One might add that whatever fact we imagine, it is also not in itself pious, spiteful, or in any other way meaningful. The imaginative activity of making sense thus steps in where matters of meaning have no foothold in the facts that compose the world: "The sense of the world must lie outside the world. In the world everything is as it is and happens as it happens. *In* it there is no value" (*TLP* 6.41).

The sense of significant sentences lies inside the world. Wittgenstein calls this "inside" because it stands in an internal relation to the world, but also because the world in question is Arthur Schopenhauer's world as representation, a world that traps us like a hall of mirrors. The limits of significant language are the limits of that world – by way of their internal relatedness world, thought, and language mirror each other completely (*TLP* 4.26, 5.524, 5.6). The sense of the world, in contrast, must lie outside this knowable world of representation. This "outside" need not be a mystical realm of the "higher." It is Schopenhauer's world as will, the world of music and action, a world in which gestures convey and assign meaning, in which we are invested as makers of sense.

It was a bit misleading, therefore, to write in the previous chapter that the subjunctive statement shows its sense: as a nonsensical, ungrammatical construction it does not have a sense to show but can only make or yield sense.[27] More accurately, perhaps, I should have

---

[26] MT, diary pp. 82–84; cf. pp. 132f. and 150f.

[27] See p. 144 above. Why, one might ask, does the subjunctive "if we were to drop this stone, it would fall to the ground" not have a sense to show just like the corresponding sentence in the indicative mood? As discussed in chapter 4, p. 136, this expression of an irreal or counterfactual conditional is not for our present purposes considered a genuinely subjunctive expression precisely because it might as well have been formulated as a factual indicative in the present tense ("once I drop this stone, it falls to the ground"). The subjunctive does not do any work here. In the present tense, the sentence would function as the description of a contingent state of affairs, one that does not, but might actually obtain. A genuine statement

written that we prompt it to show what it cannot say. As I elaborate this puzzling formulation, we encounter once again the close connection between the aphorism's procedure of thought and the formal structure of the *reductio ad absurdum* – and this time, we encounter it as Wittgenstein describes it in his own words.

Some of the preceding examples have placed subjunctive expressions that make sense in the company of actions (what Schubert's brother did), gestures (doing and reading something in a certain spirit), and lives (of those who perform those gestures). Indeed, not statements in the subjunctive mood, but music, actions, performances, gestures, and lives serve as paradigms for expressions that are nonsensical and yet not senseless: statements in the subjunctive mood are but one instance of this paradigm.

Someone ought to cry foul here. If by "nonsensical" Wittgenstein means the same as "ungrammatical," it is trivial that gestures, actions, and lives are nonsensical – they are not even sentences, so how could they ever be "grammatical"? Indeed, little would be gained by calling them nonsensical, were it not that many gestures and actions are performed in the medium of language, and were it not that, according to the *Tractatus*, statements in the subjunctive mood – including those of the *Tractatus* itself – are not even "sentences" either. Moreover, Wittgenstein was struck throughout his life by the fact that gestures as well as many written or spoken expressions make sense in the context of life and action and yet do not have sense within a linguistic grammar. His investigation in the *Tractatus* of the limits of language explored just this boundary. A few examples from his later writing can make this point, before we turn to an example that concerned him during the writing of the *Tractatus*.

Noting in 1937 that he never had a general concept of sentence and language, Wittgenstein remarks that though he recognized "this and that as signs (Sraffa)", he nevertheless "couldn't provide a grammar

in the subjunctive mood "shows how things would stand, if it could be asserted and judged true" only with the help of an imaginative activity that may require us to imagine a different grammar, too. See chapter 4, pp. 137f. and note 27, also the previous and following discussion of the word "desk" in "the desk penholders the book."

for them." The reference to Piero Sraffa tells us what "this and that sign" refers to here. In one of their discussions, Sraffa famously gave Wittgenstein the finger, asking him what the grammar of that gesture was.[28] Only Sraffa's gesture may have persuaded Wittgenstein that he could not provide a grammar even for a codified, conventional sign such as that insulting finger. But much earlier than that he was already aware that many concepts, and the thoughts associated with them, required a very different "mode of verification" than do significant sentences. "I must as it were know the person already before I can say that it is a miracle," he wrote above. His diaries elaborate this further: "here, too, it holds that the meaning of the sentence 'this one is an apostle' lies in the mode of its verification. To describe an apostle is to describe a life . . . Believing in an apostle means to relate toward him in such & such a way – relate actively." In the case of the miracle, the fact of its occurrence is not in itself miraculous. What holds for the action of transforming water into wine also holds for the words produced by the apostle. They are meaningful as the words of an apostle not because they are true or false but in that he says them.[29]

A thought experiment in the subjunctive mood underscores this identification of gestures with written expressions that are nonsensical and yet make sense:

One could conceive a world where the religious people are distinguished from the irreligious ones only in that the former were walking with their gaze turned upwards while the others looked straight ahead . . . What I mean is that in this case religiosity would not seem to be expressed in words at all & these gestures would still say as much & as little as the words of our religious writings.[30]

While writing the *Tractatus*, Wittgenstein was for a few months engaged in another thought experiment that involved not the analogy of language to gestures but of language to music. He returned to this relation throughout his life, but only a few months into this

[28] MS 157b, p. 10 quoted in David Stern 1995, p. 107. For two versions of the anecdote regarding Sraffa, see Malcolm 1984, pp. 57f.; a third variant was invented by Derek Jarman and Terry Eagleton in their film *Wittgenstein* (1993). Here, all three versions are mixed together.
[29] MT, diary p. 73f. Compare *Zettel*, remark 164, and *LCA*, p. 11: "In order to get clear about aesthetic words you have to describe ways of living."
[30] MT, diary p. 61; cf. also pp. 172f. and 190.

particular thought experiment he realized that he was dealing with an unbridgeable difference between significant sentences and what is meaningful but nonsensical. The experiment began with a remark on February 7, 1915: "Musical themes are in a certain sense sentences. Knowledge of the nature of logic will therefore lead to knowledge of the nature of music."[31] One month, but only two remarks later, he expanded on this: "Melody is a kind of tautology, it is complete in itself; it satisfies itself."[32] On April 5 he notes: "The sentence is no jumble of words" and continues this remark a week later: "Nor is a melody a jumble of tones, as all unmusical people believe."[33] A few months pass until he proposes to consider how movements or actions become objectified and thinglike "as for example: a melody, a spoken sentence."[34]

All of these remarks insist on a commonality between a sentence and a melody. But even though a melody can be considered a complex thing just like a spoken sentence, it resists analysis. Our sentences are significant to the extent that we can assign a determinate meaning to each of their components. We may need to be pressed, but we trust that in principle, at least, we can mean something definite and our sentences can have clear truth-conditions. This cannot be achieved for a melody, and this difference highlights a specificity of descriptive language. Descriptive language is unique precisely because its "complex signs" can be analyzed. This feature also

---

[31] *NB*, February 7, 1915. In the course of these reflections, Wittgenstein would also remark that "the older a word is, the deeper it reaches" (March 5). This may have been prompted by the deep reach of the word "*Satz*," which means "sentence" but also designates the "movement" for example of a sonata. Wittgenstein included "The musical theme is a sentence/movement (*Satz*)" in *PT* 3.16021. It is one of thirty-one remarks of the *Prototractatus* that were not incorporated in the *Tractatus*.

[32] On February 15, halfway between these first two remarks on music and logic, Wittgenstein included this coded remark in the notebook: "Worked a little bit yesterday. Not a day goes by these days when I don't think of logic – if only in passing – and this is a good sign. I have all kinds of presentiments (*Ich ahne alles Mögliche*)! – Last night at Captain Scholz's where music was played (until 12pm). Very pleasant" (SD, p. 55). The day after the remark on melody and tautology, he notes: "Humankind always had the presentiment that there must be a sphere of questions in which the answers are – a priori – arranged symmetrically and unified into a complete regular structure" (*NB*, March 5, 1915; cf. *TLP* 5.4541).

[33] *NB*, April 5 and 11, 1915; cf. *TLP* 3.141 but also an entry dated June 5, 1932 in MS 114, quoted by Albers 2000, pp. 168f. So far, the analogy between music and language helps Wittgenstein explore in which way language or a sentence "is articulated" (*TLP* 3.141 and *NB*, January 29, 1915 – immediately preceding the first remark on musical themes).

[34] *NB*, May 19, 1915.

distinguishes significant sentences from the ways in which music is meaningful:

> But is *language* the *only* language?
> Why shouldn't there be a mode of expression with which I can speak *about* language so that it can appear to me in co-ordination with something else?
> Let's assume that music provides such a mode: then it is at least characteristic for *science* that *no* musical themes occur in it.
> I myself am here only writing down *sentences*. And why?
> *How* is language unique?[35]

This remark has begun answering its own question. Since the significant sentences of science stand in a strictly internal relation to thought and world, the language of science cannot be co-ordinated with something else. Like gestures, actions, ceremonies, or lives, music becomes meaningful through the spirit in which it is composed, performed, or heard. More than any other art, according to Schopenhauer, it does not become objectified in the world of representation, but is an expression of the will, that is, co-ordinated with "something else."[36]

Having thus arrived at the question of how the language of science and representation is unique, Wittgenstein drops the analogy between music and logic, and from now on takes music as a form of expression that, though nonsensical, can be understood (like the *Tractatus* itself).

> The musical phrase is a gesture for me. It insinuates itself into my life. I make it my own.
> ... I can listen again and again to a piece of music that I know (completely) by heart; & it could even be played by a music box. Its gestures would remain

---

[35] Ibid., May 29, 1915. The intervening steps do not explicitly refer to music, though the comparison of language to music appears to remain in the background throughout (*NB*, May 20, 24, 27 and 28, 1915): "A complex is a thing, after all!" – "Even though perception provides us no acquaintance with simple objects; the complex ones we *know* from perception, we know through perception that they are complex. – And that in the end they must consist of simple things?" – "Is there no realm outside the *facts*?" – "'Composite sign' and 'sentence' are *synonymous*. Is it a tautology to say: *Language* consists of *sentences*? It seems, *yes*."

[36] See Schopenhauer 1966; cf. Janik 1966 and Janik and Toulmin 1973, pp. 150–157, 175. In the *Notebooks*, Wittgenstein refers to Schopenhauer only once: "The world of representation is neither good nor evil, but the willing subject. I am aware of the complete unclarity of all these sentences" (August 2, 1916). Compare three remarks about art in general: "Art is expression. The good artwork is expression perfected. The artwork is the object seen from the point of view of eternity" (*NB*, September 19, 1916).

the same for me even though I always know what will come. Yes, I can even be surprised again and again. (In a certain sense.)[37]

Now, if music takes on meaning because of the thoughts, feelings, and – in particular – movements we associate with it, this should also hold for poetry and nonsensical nursery rhymes, including statements like "The desk penholders the book," "I am putting this handshake into a hole," or "The idea of perfection in an imperfect being proves the existence of a perfect creator." One might argue that these are gestures, too. They playfully celebrate illogic, defy conventional grammar, or reach for elusive, transcendent truths by means of language. While none of these gestures or expressions have sense, with just a little effort we can make sense of them. For example, if it has not been done yet, we can easily imagine Nick Park, Jan Swankmajer, or Walt Disney creating a world in which the desk takes on the precarious balancing act of penholdering a book (we can see the desk bend, stretch, tiptoe around the room). Similarly, we can make sense of the statement that "The idea of perfection in an imperfect being proves the existence of a perfect creator." We might do so by first of all pointing out its uncritical presupposition that philosophy is a science in its own right, that such matters as the existence of God are its subject matter, that it speaks *about* such matters, that it can provide a proof that somehow adds to our knowledge of the world. We can then strip it of this pretense to have sense, to belong to a ("higher") science, and to produce knowledge. The statement now appears as a "document of a tendency in the human mind" which we can still respect deeply. Without ridiculing it, we make sense of it as the "desire to say something about the absolute," to reach for something transcendent, and to appropriate within language what lies beyond its limits. However, such desire "can be no science" and cannot produce significant sentences. "This running against the wall of our cage" is therefore a quixotic human gesture in the medium of philosophy; it is at once profound and pathetic.[38]

---

[37] *CV*, pp. 83f.; cf. 79–81 and the overview in Albers 2000, pp. 143, 161, 166, 157, 176. For the later Wittgenstein, music is an expression of feeling that cannot be described but understood, though it cannot be said *what* was understood. *PI* remark 527 contrasts music and picturing (and the picture theory of language) in order to illustrate how his now modified view of language assimilates it more closely to music. See also *PI* 536.

[38] I have been quoting from the last sentences of LE, p. 44; see pp. 45f. above. More often than not, this is how the history of philosophy is taught.

I *The significant sentence (of natural science)* (i) has sense (contrast: senseless = void of content) (ii) its sense is specified through the determination of truth-conditions (iii) expresses a fact by, literally, putting it into words (the resulting configuration of words *is* the fact) (iv) their common logical structure establishes contingent internal relations between fact, sentence, thought	**II** *Tautology, contradiction (logic)* (i) well formed but void of content (ii) does not determine the world one way or the other (has no truth-conditions; is always true or always false) (iii) says nothing (iv) indicates dimensions of the logical space in which internal relations are represented: the tautology includes everything and excludes nothing; the contradiction excludes everything and includes nothing
IV *The meaningful expression (of art and critical philosophy)* (i) makes sense (contrast: senseless = pointless) (ii) "we prompt it to show what it cannot say" (iii) expresses a feeling, thought, value, etc. through speech, gesture, music, the life we lead, action, ceremony, performance (iv) one cannot say or know what is expressed; its sense is no internal property but associated from outside the world of representation	**III** *The confused statement (of ethics, metaphysics, theology)* (i) pointless or futile (ii) an attempt to say something, it unwittingly ends up being gibberish (iii) it typically pretends but fails to be a significant sentence (iv) can be considered a document of the tendency in the human mind to run against the wall of its cage

The two senses of "sense" thus distinguish the significant sentences of science from meaningful yet nonsensical gestures in music, philosophy, and the lives we lead (categories I and IV). It is the practice of critical philosophy that distinguishes between irredeemably metaphysical nonsense and admittedly nonsensical but nevertheless meaningful expressions (that is, between categories III and IV).[39]

Having cleared up the confusion that surrounds the desire to say something about the absolute, two options present themselves. We can abandon the attempt to say something about the absolute and try a variant of ethics, aesthetics, or metaphysics that is not concerned with matters of value at all but which operationally defines all its terms by referring them to observable events in the world. This would be an attempt to transform the confused statements of category III into the significant sentences of I.[40] Alternatively, we can accept that we are speaking nonsense and not in any way "about" absolute value. Instead of seeking to add to the imaginary stock of "philosophical knowledge," we can produce a document of our attempt to run up against the limits of our cage.[41] Neither option, to be sure, satisfies the original desire, which remains unexpressed in language.

REVEALING GESTURES

Wittgenstein identifies certain nonsensical expressions with gestures that are meaningful nevertheless. Such nonsensical expressions are more akin to musical phrases than to the significant sentences of

---

[39] The boundaries between the categories are therefore not fixed. Our imaginative ability to make sense may fail and leave statements in category III or it may transmute them into another kind of statement. By the same token, significant sentences (category I) can become meaningful beyond their having sense. We can treat them also as gestures of contentment or resignation, for example. These can therefore inhabit categories I and IV at once (the next section provides two examples of this). Compare Diamond 2000 and its emphasis on the imaginative activity of "taking nonsense for sense." I am proposing that this activity can be understood as "attempting to make sense" where sentences do not obviously have sense.

[40] Wittgenstein suggests this strategy in LE, p. 38. We can say, for example, that a person is "good" just as long as she does not break the law, somewhat as we can define that a "good" tennis player is one who ranks among the top 10 percent of all tennis players, etc.

[41] Metaphysical nonsense thus belongs to category III only as long as it stubbornly mistakes itself for a kind of science with a subject matter of its own about which it formulates true or false hypotheses. In category IV, that same metaphysical nonsense can be taken as a kind of music or poetry. Compare *PI* remarks 528 and 529, or Rudolf Carnap's famous suggestion that "metaphysicians are musicians without musical ability" (Carnap 1959, p. 80). To the extent that it is not confused about its own status, nonsense poetry, with its willful violations of grammar, performs a playful gesture. Confused metaphysical statements are therefore actually in worse shape than deliberate gibberish.

science. By thus admitting two senses of "sense," Wittgenstein raises another question. In the case of the significant sentence, we know exactly what it means for it to have sense – it is a picture of a state of affairs.

> I want to say "What the picture says to me is itself." That is, that it says something to me consists in its own structure, in *its* forms and colors. (What would it mean if one said "What the musical theme says to me is itself?")
>
> . . . How does one *lead* someone to an understanding of a poem, or of a theme? The answer to this says how sense is here explained.[42]

To answer the question what it means for something nonsensical to make sense, we first of all require examples of how expressions can show what they do not say. We can then go on to inquire how we can prompt them to show what they cannot say. Fortunately, Wittgenstein provides a considerable variety of such examples.

The most famous examples figure centrally in the *Tractatus*. "The sentence shows its sense" but does not say what this sense is. All the sentence says is that things are as the sentence shows them to be (*TLP* 4.021).[43] Thus, even a significant sentence that has sense shows what it does not say. In this case, "what the picture says to me is itself." In other words, if I know grammar and have given meaning to each part of the sentence, its (internal) relation to the world is immediately

---

[42] *PI* remarks 523 and 533. This contrast between (painted) pictures and music is prepared by a return specifically to the picture theory of language in remark 520.

[43] Compare *TLP* 4.121: "The sentence cannot represent logical form, it is mirrored in the sentence. What is mirrored in language, language cannot represent. What expresses *itself* in speech, *we* cannot express through it. The sentence *shows* the logical form of reality. It exhibits it." For the first time in the course of this investigation it is not clear whether I can take Wittgenstein quite literally here. I find it puzzling that he writes "express through" instead of "express in." *TLP* 4.121 would pose no problem if Wittgenstein had written: "What expresses *itself* in speech, *we* cannot express in it or represent through it." This would leave room for the wider notion "expressing with, through, or by means of language," and this differentiated notion of "expression" would admit of nonsensical expressions that one can make sense of. On the reading proposed here, 4.121 should therefore not be taken to equate, in general, "language cannot represent and we cannot express in language" with the generalization "we cannot express through speech." It is possible, of course, that Wittgenstein here equates these only in regard to logical form. One might say that *any* attempt to express logical form must fail – it has no sense, nor could we make sense of such expressions. The resulting statements would lack truth-conditions *and* are pointless to start with. They are senseless according to both conceptions of sense.

evident – I can simply see it.[44] Wittgenstein illustrates this immediacy for the case of the significant sentence:

> The truth-conditions determine the degrees of freedom that are left to the facts by the sentence.
>
> (The sentence, the picture, the model are in a negative sense like a solid body which restricts the freedom of movement of the others; in a positive sense they are like the space bounded by solid substance into which a body can fit.) (*TLP* 4.463)

In his *Notebooks*, Wittgenstein illustrates his spatial analogy with a schematic drawing . On the right we see a solid body that corresponds, for example, to assertions and their conjunction: If A and B is the case, reality has plenty of room to maneuver as long as it does not contradict A or B. The sentence "A and B is the case" thus serves as a negative constraint. Indeed, there are only two facts that could jointly prove this sentence false, namely not-A and not-B (whereas the facts A, B, C, D, etc. and the statements "A or B," "A and not-C," and so on are all consistent with this sentence). On the left we have an empty space bounded by solid substance: It shows the positive sense of "A and B is the case." The sentence positively determines reality because it demands that the world leave room for A and B to both be the case, that it must accommodate both these facts. To say that A or B is the case, that C, not-C, D, or not-D, and so on are the case, misses the point of this sentence, which is to fix reality in a certain way. Wittgenstein's comment on this drawing underscores that it makes immediately visible how significant sentences determine reality bit by bit: "This conception is *very* clear and ought to lead to the solution."[45]

Wittgenstein achieves the same clarity of conception for the senseless propositions of logic. While the significant sentence shows (but does not say) what it says, tautology and contradiction show that they say nothing (*TLP* 4.461). Wittgenstein adduces a mental diagram to illustrate this. The diagram also serves as a contrast to significant sentences and their negative and positive ways of determining reality:

---

[44] To be sure, this immediate visibility is often shrouded by the disguises of everyday language (*TLP* 4.002); compare Black 1964, p. 192.

[45] *NB*, November 14, 1914.

tautology is an absolutely negative constraint, that is, it does not constrain at all. Every sentence is consistent with it. Contradiction is an absolutely positive constraint, that is, it does not admit anything at all. No sentence is consistent with it:[46] "Tautology leaves reality the entire – infinite – logical space; contradiction fills the entire logical space and leaves not a point to reality. Neither of them can therefore determine reality in any way" (*TLP* 4.463).

To be sure, there is also quite another way of immediately seeing what the sentence shows. Since "in the sentence a state of affairs is as it were put together experimentally" (*TLP* 4.031), we can recognize a possible state of affairs in the world just by looking at the sentence. "So the sentence 'fa' shows that the object a occurs in its sense, two sentences 'fa' and 'ga' that in both of them there is mention of the same object" (*TLP* 4.1211). This illustrates not only how a significant sentence shows its sense. We can also use the two significant sentences "fa" and "gb" to make sense of the nonsensical expression "there are 2 things."[47] Indeed, we can even use two nonsensical expressions "fa" and "gb" to make sense of the nonsensical expression "there are 2 things."

Wittgenstein makes this point in an emphatic letter to Bertrand Russell. To say, for example, that object *a* stands adjacent to object *b* "doesn't say that there are two things, it says something quite different; *but whether it's true or false*, it SHOWS what you want to *express* by saying: 'there are 2 things.'" The significant sentence shows this simply "by there being two names which have different meanings."[48] But if a significant sentence can show this, so can the nonsensical expression "*a* is more beautiful than *b*" – it does not say that there are two things, it says nothing at all; *but though it is nonsensical*, it SHOWS what you want to *express* by saying: "there are 2 things." Both the significant sentence and the nonsensical expression can therefore show what they cannot and could not say. Wittgenstein thus used the example of a

---

[46] Wittgenstein duly notes that from a contradiction everything follows: "Shouldn't the contradiction therefore be the sentence that says the most?" And yet, it cannot form a consistent conjunct with any of the sentences that are entailed by it; it therefore "vanishes . . . outside all propositions" (*NB*, June 3, 1915).

[47] The expression "there are two things" does not connect anything with anything and produces no picture of a state of affairs. "Things" is not used as a name that picks out a particular object; and "to be" is here used as a predicate rather than as a connective.

[48] Wittgenstein to Russell (August 19, 1919) in *CL*, p. 126.

sentence like "object *a* stands adjacent to object *b*" to make sense of "there are 2 things," that is, to make sense of an ungrammatical expression that does not have sense of its own since it fails to picture a state of affairs.[49]

When Wittgenstein writes that a sentence shows its sense, he means that the sense "shows itself."[50] The sentence "object *a* stands adjacent to object *b*" pictures a state of affairs and "what the picture says to me is itself," that is, the relation of "*a*" and "*b*" in the sentence mirrors the relation of the two objects in the state of affairs, and this is the sense of the sentence. However, if we appeal to this sentence in order to make sense of "there are 2 things," we are as it were prompting the sentence to show us something besides its sense, something that is implicit and usually goes unnoticed – just as, usually, "there are 2 things" goes without saying. Since we have already likened metaphysical statements like "there are 2 things" to musical phrases, we can now take up Wittgenstein's question: "What would it mean if one said 'What the musical theme says to me is itself?'"[51] It would seem that we have to prompt the metaphysical statement and the musical theme to show what they do not say, that is, to show something other than a "content," which would be like the sense of a significant sentence.

Now, one might object that no attempt should ever be undertaken to make sense of "there are 2 things." That there are two things must always go without saying, it is a matter that takes care of itself while we speak of more than one object in sentences that have two names that stand in for different things. But this objection would not hold for the next example, in which significant sentences are used to make sense of a life and to value it. As with the life of the apostle, making sense here "means to relate toward him in such & such a way – relate actively." In a letter of 1917 to Paul Engelmann, Wittgenstein referred to a poem by Ludwig Uhland which shows what it could not have said by restricting itself to simple descriptive sentences. According to

---

[49] We have been considering how sentences show what they do not say. The case of "there are two things" dramatically exemplifies Wittgenstein's more general claim "What *can* be shown, *cannot* be said" (*TLP* 4.1212); compare Wittgenstein's "Notes dictated to Moore" in *NB*, p. 111.

[50] Black 1964, p. 190.   [51] *PI* remark 523.

Engelmann, the poem "gives in 28 lines the picture of a life."[52] It does so without attempting to express in speech the horrors of war, the loss of youth, or the imminence of death. Instead it merely describes a soldier who brings a sprig of a plant home from a crusade, plants and nurtures it. Sitting under the tree many years later he is reminded of "days of old and the far-off land." Wittgenstein commented: "And this is how it is: if one does not attempt to express the inexpressible in speech, *nothing* gets lost. But what is inexpressible in speech

[52] Engelmann 1967, pp. 83f., which includes Alexander Pratt's 1848 translation of "Count Eberhard's Hawthorn" by Ludwig Uhland (1787–1862):

> Count Eberhard Rustle-Beard,
> From Württemberg's fair land,
> On holy errand steer'd
> To Palestina's strand.
>
> The while he slowly rode
> Along a woodland way;
> He cut from the hawthorn bush
> A little fresh green spray.
>
> Then in his iron helm
> The little sprig he plac'd;
> And bore it in the wars,
> And over the ocean waste.
>
> And when he reach'd his home,
> He plac'd it in the earth;
> Where little leaves and buds
> The gentle Spring call'd forth.
>
> He went each year to it,
> The Count so brave and true;
> And overjoy'd was he
> To witness how it grew.
>
> The Count was worn with age
> The sprig became a tree;
> 'Neath which the old man oft
> Would sit in reverie.
>
> The branching arch so high,
> Whose whisper is so bland,
> Reminds him of the past
> And Palestina's strand.

Whatever the merits and meaning of this poem, it may have had additional sentimental significance for Wittgenstein and Engelmann. The hawthorn may also have symbolized their wartime friendship, which was just beginning to blossom when this letter was written on April 19, 1917.

is – inexpressibly – *included* in what is expressed."[53] Uhland's poem does not say that this is a contented, resigned, or serene life, it says many quite different things; *but though it is fiction*, it sнows what one might want to *express* by saying: "there is a wistful tenderness even in a war-torn world." Once again, it shows this only as we relate to it actively. We prompt it to show this by taking significant sentences to make sense of a nonsensical one that best remains unspoken.[54]

Engelmann notes that Wittgenstein's enthusiasm for Uhland's poem was "aroused by what is banal (in the highest sense of that word)." He provides a second literary example where the author hints at the sublime while telling an overtly banal tale about a musical genius. In the case of "Mozart's Journey to Prague," however, its author Eduard Mörike does not restrict himself to significant sentences. When he arrives at the sublime moment at the story's center, he advances poetic nonsense. In the story, Mozart is discovered to be the inadvertent thief of a precious pomegranate. He makes good by performing on the piano selections of his new opera *Don Giovanni*, including the dramatic first appearance of the dead *commendatore*:

On a whim he extinguished the candles of the two candelabras that were standing on each side of him, and through the dead quiet of the room rang that terrible chorale "Your laughter will be silenced before morning." As from remote galaxies sounds tumble out of silver trombones, ice-cold, piercing to the core and soul, downwards through blue night.

According to Engelmann, Wittgenstein was "enraptured" by this story – "and in it especially by the passages describing musical effects in words: 'As from remote galaxies . . .' he would recite with a shudder of awe."[55] But in the quoted passage, Mörike is most definitely not *describing* a musical effect. If Wittgenstein appreciates this passage,

[53] "Und es ist so: Wenn man sich nicht bemüht das Unaussprechliche auszusprechen, so geht *nichts* verloren. Sondern das Unaussprechliche ist, – unaussprechlich – in dem Ausgesprochenen *enthalten!*" Engelmann 1967, pp. 6f.; cf. 83f., also p. 50, above for the translation of "*aussprechen* (express in speech)." Numerous other poems employ a similar strategy, most famously, perhaps, Jacques Prévert's "Déjeuner du matin."

[54] Here and with the sentence "*a* stands adjacent to *b*" we have two examples of significant sentences (category I) that through our activity of making sense also belong to category IV (see note 39, above).

[55] Engelmann 1967, p. 86; see Mörike 1976. Engelmann commented: "As a rule it is a bold venture indeed to recapture in words what music has achieved. But in the rare cases where the venture succeeds, as it does here, we are in the presence of sublime peaks of poetic language, and thus of verbal expression altogether. Here was one of the great passages

then, it is because it associates a movement of words with a movement of musical sounds. This association establishes a reciprocal relation in which the words make sense of the music and the music makes sense of the words. The storyteller's words value the music by responding to it; Mörike is, literally, moved by the music and passes that movement on to his readers, to Wittgenstein.

This, the most elusive of our examples, suggests that showing is itself a gesture or activity. When the sense of a significant sentence shows itself, what is shown is that the sentence stands in a certain relation to reality: if one places the sentence next to the pictured state of affairs, one sees that "they are ... in a certain sense one" (*TLP* 4.014). When we make sense of a gesture, life, or a nonsensical expression by prompting it to show what it cannot say, this showing reveals the ideas, thoughts, feelings, or movements we have associated with that expression: if one places Mörike's poetic expression next to Mozart's ominous chords, they do not stand in an internal relation to one another and yet, through their association, they are in a certain sense one. Wittgenstein provides another example of this in his "Remarks on Frazer's *Golden Bough*":

in literature touching on Wittgenstein's most central language problem: that of the border of the inexpressible in speech and yet somehow expressible." The ending of Mörike's story adopts Uhland's restraint when it subtly suggests how Mozart's life is surrounded by death:

> A little fir tree is springing up somewhere,
> who knows, in the forest,
> and a rosebush, who can say
> in which garden?
> They are already chosen,
> just imagine, oh soul,
> to take root upon your grave
> and grow there.
>
> Two black steed are pasturing
> in the meadow;
> they return home to their town
> at a cheerful trot.
> They will go at a walking pace
> with your corpse,
> perhaps, perhaps before
> from their hooves
> the shoes fall off
> that I see sparkling!

If one places that story of the priest-king of Nemi next to the words "the majesty of death" one sees that they are one. The life of the priest-king represents what is meant by these words. Someone who is gripped by the majesty of death can express this through this kind of life. – This, of course, is also no explanation, but merely substitutes one symbol for another. Or: one ceremony for another.[56]

In all these cases, showing consists in the placement of one thing next to another. It is a gesture which reveals that this can stand in for that, and it invites us to substitute one symbol, one ceremony for another.

This survey of the different ways in which expressions show what they do not say concludes with a nonsensical gesture that shows the correctness of an inference, that is, a gesture of showing that something is a tautology. In one of his discussions with members of the Vienna Circle, Wittgenstein elaborated, in effect, what he meant in *TLP* 5.132: "Laws of inference which – as in Frege and Russell – are to justify the inferences, are senseless, and would be redundant." Friedrich Waismann recorded the conversation, noting that "Frege, Peano and Russell believed that the 'if' plays a very special rôle in inference." Accordingly they therefore propose "$p \supset q$" as a law of inference: "if the premises are true, then the conclusion is true." An inference is supposed to be correct when this law is satisfied, and this in turn requires that we precisely understand its conditional character, that is, the "if" in this law.[57] But in the spirit of his "logic must take care of itself," Wittgenstein proceeds to dispute that the correctness of an inference has to be warranted in such a way. According to him, it simply shows itself and it does so through the performance of a simple gesture. Using his notation he creates a truth-table for "if the premises (p) are true, then the conclusion (q) is true":

p	q	$p \supset q$
T	T	T
T	F	F
F	T	T
F	F	T

[56] *PO*, p. 123; cf. Clack 1999, pp. 161–176.
[57] As usual with regard to technical matters of logic, I have simplified them for the purposes of this discussion.

This truth-table presents all four possibilities regarding the truth and falsity of premises and conclusion. The conclusion in the middle column is false (F) only in two of these possibilities (the second and fourth lines). In one of those two cases (line 4), we are not troubled by this: if the premises of an otherwise correct inference are false to begin with, why should its conclusion be true? That is why the fourth possibility agrees with the correctness of the inference as such, and we therefore call the inference true (T) in the fourth line of the third column. That leaves only one possibility to worry about, namely the second line where the premises are true but the conclusion is false. Under this possibility, the inference as a whole (third column) would be false. However, in a correct inference, this possibility simply does not exist! So, instead of contemplating the meaning of a law of inference, wondering how we can say that it is satisfied, Wittgenstein simply strikes the second possibility.

p	q	$p \supset q$
T	T	T
~~T~~	~~F~~	~~F~~
F	T	T
F	F	T

The correctness of an inference shows itself in that the second possibility does not exist. The law of inference thus proves to be redundant. With the stroke of a pen, Wittgenstein transforms the supposedly problematic law into a tautology that is always true: "Inference has really nothing at all to do with 'if.' In my notation the correctness of the inference *shows* itself in that '$p \supset q$' becomes a tautology."[58]

The correctness of the inference shows itself in that "$p \supset q$" becomes a tautology, and it becomes a tautology through the gesture

---

[58] See *WVC*, pp. 91f. – including the second of the two truth-tables, the one with the line crossed through. Wittgenstein elaborated his procedure in his 1929 paper "Some Remarks on Logical Form"; see *PO*, pp. 34f. It is characteristic of Wittgenstein's truth-table method that it exhibits or shows the sense of a significant sentence by way of a complete presentation of its truth-conditions. Rather than say something *about* the sentence, the truth-table gives us just another way of writing it down (*TLP* 4.31 and 4.442). Compare Black 1967, pp. 206–208, 369, and Glock 1996, pp. 368–371.

of striking out the case that simply does not arise for a correct inference. In all the remaining cases the third column shows that "p ⊃ q" comes out true (T).

The line that strikes out the second possibility is a mark on paper, but it is not part of our grammar and is thus ungrammatical or nonsensical. No part of the line stands for an object and the line as a whole pictures no state of affairs – it has no truth-conditions and thus no sense. And yet it makes sense because it shows how a correct inference becomes a tautology and that laws of inference are pointless or redundant (they make no sense).[59] Like the nonsensical gesture that produces the line, the line itself prompts the correct inference to show what it cannot say, namely that it says nothing, that it never leads from truth to falsity but preserves truth. And this is also, of course, what the nonsensical sentences regarding tautology and contradiction do (*TLP* 4.46ff.). They do so by way of a thought experiment of their own.[60] Reenacting it, we end up prompting the tautology to show that it says nothing. And just like the gesture that produced the line, the nonsensical sentences that produce the thought experiment therefore make sense. To call them nonsensical, as Wittgenstein does in *TLP* 6.54, does not preclude them from serving as steps on a ladder that ultimately leads not to knowledge of the world, but to an understanding of language and how, within its limits, it discloses the world.

FINDING THE WAY FROM CONTRADICTION TO CONCLUSION

One last step will conclude this reconstruction of Wittgenstein's critical argument. It must show how *reductio*-arguments – the thought experiment of the *Tractatus*, in particular – prompt gestures, actions, and other nonsensical expressions to show what they cannot say, for instance, that there is indeed the inexpressible in speech.

---

[59] The same can be said for Wittgenstein's truth-table method in general: any particular inference can be put into conditional form and if the inference is correct, the conditional shows itself to be a tautology. The possibility of all the premises being true and the conclusion false simply does not show up.

[60] This thought experiment consists in imagining the diagram, see p. 179, above.

Here is how far we have come in this chapter so far. There are two kinds of sense. Both can only be shown and not said. The sense of a significant sentence shows itself, it is internal to the common form of sentence and state of affairs. What is shown is how things stand in a possible state of affairs. What can be said is only that things do stand as the sentence shows they do. In other words, the significant sentence shows what it says, but it cannot say what it is that it shows. In contrast, we have to make sense of a nonsensical expression by prompting it to show what it does not, cannot say. Since these nonsensical expressions have no truth-conditions, they cannot be used to say anything true or false. Instead, the imaginative activity of making sense associates these expressions with gestures, actions, lives, performances, and through them with ideas, feelings, values, thoughts that are inexpressible in language and yet seek expression. Nonsensical expressions thus become meaningful. While they provide no knowledge of the world, we have seen that they can provide an experiential understanding of tautologies, of the difference between music and significant language, of documents produced by the desire to run against the limits of language, of miracles or the words of an apostle and how they would have to be conceived. As we will see now, they can help us understand the limits of language and that there is indeed the inexpressible in speech. (To be sure, in all these cases we can also not say or know what this understanding actually consists in or whether it refers to anything real. This continues to be the predicament of all our constructive efforts to create meaning and make sense of something that does not have sense.)

Wittgenstein goes beyond giving examples and providing an account of nonsensical expressions that make sense. By using the nonsensical stroke of a pen to show that correct inference becomes a tautology, he also appreciates the rôle of nonsensical expressions in the context of mathematical and philosophical argument, experiment, and proof. Indeed, he ended up writing and lecturing quite a bit about this matter,[61] and so it should serve us well to focus as closely as possible on the particular case of the

---

[61] Especially in his conversations with members of the Vienna Circle (1929–1932), in part II of the 1932–33 manuscripts published as *Philosophical Grammar* (*PG*), in his 1939 *Lectures on the Foundations of Mathematics* (*LFM*), and in the 1937–1942 *Remarks on the Foundations of Mathematics* (*RFM*).

reductio-argument in the *Tractatus*. As a reminder, here now a summary of that argument.

Let us assume, hypothetically, that any sense whatsoever is expressible in speech. This hypothesis has two immediate implications. First, as far as expressibility in speech is concerned, there is only one kind of sense. Second, if our assumption is true, we should definitely be able to express the sense of our hypothesis in speech.[62] Doing so requires that we say how the one and only kind of sense is expressed in speech. In pursuit of this task we discover that significant sentences are contingent configurations of words that stand in an internal relation to the world (which is made up of contingent configurations of things). The one and only sense is therefore in the world, that is, it is bound up with the worldly conditions that make significant sentences true or false. Since they are contingently bound up with the world, "all sentences are of equal value" (*TLP* 6.4). But if this is how sense is expressed in speech, what about "the sense of our hypothesis," "the sense of the world," and the idea that there is higher, or absolute value? If any sense whatsoever is expressible in speech, then these notions should surely be expressible, too. But on our explication of "the expression of sense in speech," they are not. This finding contradicts the hypothesis with its corollaries that there is only one kind of sense, that all sense is in the world, that the sense of our hypothesis is expressible in speech, and that any sense whatsoever is expressible in speech (*TLP* 6.41). We must therefore reject the hypothesis and conclude that there is indeed some sense that is inexpressible in speech. "This *shows* itself" (*TLP* 6.522).

The conclusion of the *reductio*-argument shows itself; or, the *reductio*-argument shows its conclusion. Along the lines of Wittgenstein's view of correct inference and his use of truth-tables, one can argue that all logical proofs show their conclusion. But as we saw above in chapter 2, the *reductio*-argument is a peculiar kind of proof, more appropriately designated a thought experiment. Those who refer to it as proof are careful to distinguish it from direct and demonstrative proof on the one hand, and inductive proof on the other. The "indirect" or "negative" proof provided by a *reductio*-argument does not establish its conclusion by calculation

---

[62] In chapter 2 I referred to this as the corollary of the hypothesis.

or extrapolation. It is indirect because it establishes only that the denial of the conclusion would produce a contradiction. Indeed, the later Wittgenstein might have preferred calling it an experiment rather than a proof.[63] Thus, in order to see how the *reductio*-argument shows its conclusion, we must consider the special conditions of a *reductio ad absurdum*, and those special conditions concern its hypothetical character. How can an indirect proof establish, for example, that the trisection of an angle is impossible?

It seems as if we first of all made an experiment which showed that Smith, Jones, etc. could not [trisect an angle] and then a mathematician shows that it can't be done. We get apparently an experimental result, and then prove that it could not have been otherwise at all.

But there is something queer about this: For how could the man try to do what could not be done?[64]

"How can one," Wittgenstein is asking here, "assume at all what is mathematically absurd?" Or, how could we assume that any sense whatsoever is expressible in speech – matters of feeling, value, belief *just like* matters of empirical fact? "That I can assume what is physically false and lead it to absurdity creates no difficulties for me. But how to think what is so-to-speak unthinkable?!"[65]

Since we cannot think anything unthinkable or contradictory (*TLP* 3.03 and 5.61), what appears absurd at the conclusion of the

---

[63] Due in part to his questioners, the *reductio*-argument is discussed as "indirect proof" in *WVC* and *LFM*. Both *LFM* and *RFM* struggle extensively with the relation between experiment and proof. On the one hand, proof is meant to provide more than an experiment. We mean something else by "repeating a proof" than by "repeating an experiment": "To repeat a proof does not mean: to reproduce the conditions under which a certain result was obtained, but to repeat every step *and the result*" (*RFM*, part III, 55). Also: "If one considers a proof as an experiment, the result of the experiment is at any rate not what one calls the result of a proof. The result of calculation is the sentence with which it concludes; the result of the experiment is: that I was led by these rules from these sentences to that one" (*RFM*, part I, 162). On the other hand, these distinctions are impossible to observe in practice (*LFM*, p. 121). A somewhat cryptic resolution of the difficulty is proposed in the following passage: "A proof, one could say, must originally have been a kind of experiment – but is then simply taken as a picture" (*RFM*, part III, 23). The picture offers the conclusion as a sentence in a formal relation to other sentences. It no longer captures the experimental activity that leads from some sentences to others. One might say that the *reductio*-argument is an experiment that, under certain contestable conditions, is taken as a picture (*WVC*, pp. 180f.).

[64] *LFM*, pp. 86f. (The example discussed in that passage concerns the impossibility of constructing a heptagon or 100-gon.)

[65] *RFM*, part III, 28. The remark began: "The difficulty which one senses in regard to *reductio ad absurdum* in mathematics is this: What goes on in this proof? Something mathematically absurd, and hence unmathematical?"

reductio-argument could not have seemed absurd beforehand. Initially we must have somehow been able to take nonsense for sense, to believe what under the special conditions of the thought experiment leads to a contradiction. Indeed, only in retrospect can we claim that the hypothesis of the *reductio*-argument is unthinkable – it has taken on that aspect because of a change of outlook that was effected by the *reductio*-argument itself. What plausibly suggested itself before the experience of the thought experiment is utterly absurd now. Indirect proof thus brings about a change in our conception of things.[66] It is not a mere discovery, it does not reveal an already implicit meaning, but is a critical intervention, an action. Wittgenstein uses the case of trisecting an angle to show that the importance of an impossibility proof is "that it changes our idea of trisection."

> The idea of trisection of an angle comes in this way: that we can bisect an angle, divide into four equal parts, and so on. And this leads to the problem of trisecting an angle. You are led on here by *sentences*. You have the sentence "I bisect this angle" and you form a similar expression: "trisecting". And so you ask, "What about the sentence, 'I trisect this angle'?"

Similarly, we are led on by sentences when we move from "I can express that this is the case" to "I can express that this has value." In both cases, "if we had learned from the beginning" how sectioning proceeds or how sense is expressed in language, "then nobody would ever have asked" whether trisection is possible: "The problem arose because our idea at first was a different idea . . . and then was *changed* by the proof."[67]

If we want to find out how this change came about, we need to understand what was proved – and vice versa. If we want to understand what was proved, we need to see how it brought about a change in our conceptions: "Let the *proof* tell you *what* was being proved."[68] In an indirect proof, for example, we take what seems plausible at first and associate it with a certain set way of using signs. In the case of trisection, we commit ourselves to the rules of sectioning, elaborate

---

[66] Compare *PI* remark 517: "many a mathematical proof leads us to say that we can*not* imagine what we believed we could imagine. (For example, the construction of the heptagon.) It leads us to revise what we considered the domain of the imaginable."

[67] *LFM*, pp. 88f.

[68] *PI*, part II, section xi; compare *PG*, part II, V, 24: "If you want to know *what* is proved, look at the proof."

them, and discover that they "leave out" the case of trisection – that case simply does not occur within our language of angle-sectioning.[69] In the case of the *Tractatus*, we commit ourselves to the rules of representation, elaborate them, and discover that they leave out the case of expressing value – that case simply does not occur within our language of determining what is true and false about the world. Like these *reductio*-arguments, "[e]very proof is as it were a commitment to a specific use of signs."[70]

I have previously discussed the conditions of the thought experiment in terms of its hypothetical character. The thought experiment, I have suggested, inhabits the subjunctive sphere of possibility, that is, a space in which our thoughts can roam playfully and explore in a noncommittal, perhaps unconstrained manner, how everything could be different, due to the contingency of the world. More needs to be said now about this sense of possibility in the light of Wittgenstein's suggestion that *reductio*-arguments involve a commitment to rules or to a specific use of signs, such that this commitment brings about a change in our initial conceptions. At least in the context of indirect proof, this hypothetical "what if" sense of possibility must be committed to action and change. In the *Philosophical Investigations*, Wittgenstein elaborates the hypothetical in just these terms. There he remarks that "the if-feeling is not a feeling that accompanies the word 'if'" but rather needs to be seen in the context of the "special circumstances in which it occurs." What appears to be the "atmosphere" of the word "if" proves to be no atmosphere at all. Instead, the if-feeling anticipates an imminent breakthrough, discovery, or change. It reflects the commitment to an action that is already latent when we explore a possibility in the subjunctive mood, when we attend to a musical gesture, or when we set up an indirect proof

---

[69] "The proof might be this: we go on [sectioning angles] and being very careful to observe certain rules. We should then find that [trisection] is left out. [If we want to section angles in that way, we proceed at the rate of 2^n sections, and so trisection is left out.] This would have the result of dissuading intelligent people from trying this game," *LFM*, p. 87 (again, I adapted this from the analogous case of proving the impossibility of constructing a 100-gon).

[70] *RFM*, part III, remark 41. It continues: "But to what does it commit? Only to *this* use of the rules of transition from one formula to another? Or also a commitment to the 'axioms' in some sense? . . . One could express the idea that proof creates a new concept roughly like this: The proof is not its foundation plus rules of inference, but a *new* house – even though an instance of this or that style. The proof is a *new* paradigm."

that will show its conclusion: "The if-feeling ought to be comparable to the 'feeling' which a musical phrase gives us. (One sometimes describes such a feeling by saying: 'Here it is, as if a conclusion were drawn', or 'I would like to say, "*thus* . . ."', or 'I always want to make a gesture here –' and then one makes it.)"[71]

Wittgenstein's characterization of the if-feeling thus adds a temporal dimension to the "space of possibility" or the "subjunctive sphere." A *reductio*-argument has the structure of a meaningful experience, it involves us in a self-contained movement from one state to another. In the case of the *Tractatus*, our initial state is a fundamental trust in the power of language to express any sense whatsoever. We experiment on ourselves by submitting this trust to the commitments implicit in the language with which we can truthfully describe the world. Our experiment prompts a contradiction which shows what it cannot say, but we make sense of "there is indeed the inexpressible" by taking action against our unqualified, fundamental trust. This action completes the experience or experiment; it provides a kind of closure and leaves us in a different state than the one we started in.

Accordingly, Wittgenstein's explicit reflections about *reductio*-arguments consider them in terms of practical commitments, actions, experience, experiment, movement, and change. Asking "What is indirect proof?" he answers: "An action performed with signs."[72] The action of the *reductio*-argument consists in showing something, and what is shown makes sense only within the particular context of that action. "There is a particular mathematical method, the method of *reductio ad absurdum*, which we might call 'avoid the contradiction.' In this method one shows a contradiction and then shows the way from it. But this doesn't mean that a contradiction is a sort of devil."[73] Instead of being a sort of devil, the contradiction is an integral, pivotal moment of a structured experience. The *reductio*-argument shows the

---

[71] *PI*, part II, section vi.   [72] *WVC*, p. 180.

[73] *LFM*, p. 209. Gödel's incompleteness theorem had mathematicians and logicians up in arms because it means that one cannot prove within a symbolic system that it is free of contradiction. Wittgenstein maintained against this that "a contradiction is no sort of devil." Instead of worrying that the mere possibility of a contradiction might "infect" all the valid inferences in the system, one should just stay away from contradiction or, as in the case of indirect proof, let the contradiction point the way away from it. Compare the continuation of this passage, also *RFM*, part VII, 11–15.

way from the contradiction to the conclusion, and what the conclusion shows is that it avoids the contradiction.

In order to find the way from the contradiction to the conclusion, the trajectory or movement of the *reductio*-argument has to start well before one arrives at the contradiction. We need to know just which conclusion must be reached in order to avoid the contradiction: "There now steps in a further rule that tells me what to do when an indirect proof has been given. (This rule may state, for example: if an indirect proof has been given, the assumptions from which the proof starts are to be deleted.) *Here nothing is self-evident. Everything must be said explicitly.*"[74] When we arrive, for example, at the contradiction in *TLP* 6.41 ("if there were value or something non-contingent in the world, it would be contingent and of no value"), all we know is that something is wrong, something must give.[75] Only by adopting the proposed rule that we should delete the starting assumptions that led to this contradiction (that is, the hypothesis and its corollary) do we arrive at *TLP* 6.522, "there is indeed the inexpressible in speech."

But why is this rule not self-evident, what else could Wittgenstein have done to avoid the contradiction? Instead of rejecting his faith in the power of language to express any thought whatsoever, he could have denied the power of language to express facts and state truths about the world. In other words, he could have maintained his hypotheses and rejected all or some of the background assumptions that led him to *TLP* 6.4: "All sentences are of equal value." By doing so, he would have joined Mauthner and Hofmannsthal with their global skepticism about language, with their sweeping doubt over whether it can convey any truth about the world, and at the same time with their conviction that what language does express are more or less free-floating, detached thoughts. Indeed, Wittgenstein had yet another option. Instead of rejecting the hypothesis outright, he could have narrowed the scope of "any sense whatsoever": if one rules out any thought of the "sense of the world" or of "absolute value," and if one limits "any sense whatsoever" to factual matters, then one would not arrive at *TLP* 6.41 and the contradiction of trying to express in

---

[74] *WVC*, p. 180.
[75] Compare the discussion of *reductio*-arguments in chapter 2, pp. 62f., above.

speech what is inexpressible in speech. Wittgenstein thus had a choice, and how he chose reveals his commitments: "The indirect proof says, however: 'If you want it like *that*, you may not assume *this*: for *with this* is compatible only the opposite of that which you want to hold on to.'"[76]

If you want to hold on to an idea of absolute value, and if you want to appreciate the power of language to state (scientific) truths about the world, you may not assume that any sense whatsoever can be expressed in speech, for with this assumption is compatible only the impossibility of value. Prompted by the contradiction in *TLP* 6.41, Wittgenstein's commitments show a particular way away from the contradiction. Once we are explicitly aware that the *reductio*-argument puts to the test only the hypothesis and not our other commitments, *TLP* 6.522 shows itself immediately upon our arrival at the contradiction. Fueled by our commitments, the contradiction consumes the starting assumptions of the thought experiment and "there is indeed the inexpressible in speech" appears as their negative afterimage. Or, yet in other words: like the line that is drawn through the truth-table for "correct inference," the contradiction of Wittgenstein's *reductio*-argument is a gesture that confers validity upon an undeniable recognition. The line underscores that a correct inference becomes a tautology, the contradiction presents the contrary of what we can evidently assume no longer.

THE SENSE AND NONSENSE OF THE CONCLUSION

The *Tractatus* concludes with a compelling gesture. It presents a definitive solution to the problems of philosophy, and "shows how little has been achieved when these problems are solved." Something, in other words, has been achieved. The *Tractatus* reminds us of the world as we find it, it discloses the world that is subject to our representations. By elucidating the intimate connection between sentences and states of affairs, it allows us to see how the world enters the sentences that we put together experimentally.[77]

---

[76] *RFM*, part III, 28.
[77] This "disclosure" of the world by the *Tractatus* is the subject of Friedlander 2001, pp. 16–25. He denies, however, that the disclosed world is limited to Schopenhauer's "world of representation"; see pp. 190–192.

This achievement does not count for much, however: "our problems of life have not yet been touched upon" (*TLP* 6.52). Among other things, this serves to underscore the fact that Wittgenstein's commitments, which took him from the contradiction to the conclusion, have not been justified. The thought experiment expresses them and the *Tractatus* as a whole is a document that testifies to them, reminds us of them. In the words of David Stern:

> A large part of what makes the *Tractatus* such a fascinating and elusive book is that it is the product of two opposed and unstable forces . . . On the one hand, its author had a metaphysical vision: the definitive solution to the leading problems of philosophy. On the other hand, he was gripped by an equally powerful anti-metaphysical drive, the aim of drawing a limit to language and to philosophy.[78]

By wishing not merely to appreciate the power of language to state (scientific) truths about the world but at the same time wanting to hold on to an idea of absolute value, Wittgenstein has a metaphysical vision that cannot be justified but that he nevertheless expresses through his critical thought experiment and the limits it sets. Paraphrasing what Wittgenstein says about the life of the apostle or the priest-king of Nemi, we can say: if one places the thought experiment of the *Tractatus* next to the pair of statements "There must be a way to state truths about the world" and "We must not surrender thoughts or feelings regarding absolute value and meaning," we can see that, in a certain sense, the experiment and the statements are one. Someone who is gripped by these ideas can express them through this kind of book – but not in significant sentences that are capable of being true or false. Incapable of justification, these commitments can make sense only within the context of our lives; and since they are inexpressible in speech, their expression is a problem of life.

While the two commitments are nonsensical statements that now make sense, the hypothesis that "any sense whatsoever is expressible in speech" is a nonsensical statement that no longer makes sense, except perhaps as a document of our tendency to run up against the wall of our cage. We have discovered in the course of the thought experiment that our prior commitments fail our best efforts to make sense of this implicit faith in the power of language.

---

[78] Stern 2003, pp. 125f.; cf. Horwich 2004, pp. 102f.

That leaves us finally to consider the rather curious status of the conclusion that "there is the inexpressible in speech." Once the hypothetical premise is abandoned, *reductio*-arguments typically return to the indicative mood: *were* we to assume this, we *would* arrive at a contradiction, and therefore the opposite of the assumption *is the case*.[79] Indeed, if any of the remarks in the *Tractatus* can claim to be a significant sentence in the indicative mood, *TLP* 6.522 would seem to be it. And yet, Wittgenstein makes no exception for it when he declares that his sentences are nonsensical. So, how are we to make sense of this conclusion?

As chapter 2 has shown, the conclusion is artfully ambiguous with regard to "existential import": one can make sense of it by taking it to deny that all sense is in the world and thus to establish "the higher" as a special sphere of being; one can also make sense of it by taking it to deny only that any feeling, value, thought can really be expressed in speech.[80] In order to decide, however, whether Wittgenstein's declarative verdict in the indicative mood is nevertheless nonsensical, that is, ungrammatical, one must consider it as the conclusion of a *reductio*-argument. As such, it expresses a particular experience: "I tried to make sense of the nonsensical hypothesis and failed." This sounds like a perfectly ordinary, purely descriptive statement about someone doing something in the world, and yet it is no significant sentence because I cannot know *what* I failed at. Before Wittgenstein's indirect proof changed my conception of things, "making sense of the nonsensical hypothesis" appeared to me no different than "making sense of an action" or "trying to lift 200 pounds": if I can specify for all three cases what success or failure consists in, the sentence "I tried to do this but failed" will be significant. However, the pivotal contradiction of the *reductio*-argument is a gesture that directed me from the hypothetical premise and its attendant commitments toward the conclusion with its changed conception of the hypothesis. Now, "I tried to make sense of the nonsensical hypothesis" is no different than "I tried to trisect an angle." It is pointless (makes no sense) to try the impossible. The expression lacks content (has no sense) because we

---

[79] Compare our previous examples. Hypotheses in the subjunctive mood were finally replaced by assertions in the indicative mood: "Wittgenstein did not die in World War I," "division by 0 is impossible," "one cannot trisect an angle."

[80] See pp. 53f., above.

can no longer specify under which conditions it is true or false.[81] All
this does not establish yet, however, that the conclusion is nonsensical
and that it is not a well-formed sentence in the grammar in which
the significant sentences of science as well as the senseless statements
of logic are formulated.[82]

"There is indeed the inexpressible in speech" is nonsensical because
it lacks the grammatical requirement of establishing a subject–
predicate relation. As such, it is no different than "there are 2 things"
or "there are unanalyzable subject–predicate sentences."[83] As opposed
to "there is a book in this drawer," these expressions use "there is"
not to specify a state of affairs but to make an existence claim.
TLP 6.522 employs "is" not as a copula that relates an object to
a specific location in space and time, but to express the existence
either of a limit to expression or of higher, inexpressible things
(cf. *TLP* 3.323).[84]

Thus, even though it is a denial in the indicative mood of a nonsensical as well as senseless statement in the subjunctive mood, *TLP*
6.522 is still nonsensical and lacks significance. As opposed to the
hypothesis that any sense whatsoever is expressible in speech, we can
make sense of its denial, however ("there is indeed the inexpressible in
speech"). And while the *Tractatus* demonstrated that the hypothesis is
not self-exemplifying (the sense of the hypothesis cannot be expressed
in speech), the conclusion is. That the words "there is indeed the

---

[81] Another attempt to construct truth-conditions might go as follows. The sentence stating the
conclusion is true if an attempt to express a thought, feeling, or value in a sentence results
in a string of words to which one cannot assign truth-conditions and which therefore has
no sense. However, one can never determine even the antecedent of this, namely whether a
string of words is one that attempts to express a thought, feeling, or value.

[82] One might argue, for example, that the conclusion of Wittgenstein's indirect proof has
thereby assumed the status of a logical truth, that like tautologies or contradictions it is
senseless but not nonsensical. This is not compatible, however, with the letter and spirit
of *TLP* 6.54: Wittgenstein's acknowledgment that his sentences are nonsensical would be
pointless if his solution to the problems of philosophy had consisted in the dissolution of
philosophical problems into logic and that which takes care of itself.

[83] Compare pp. 51f. and 55f., above. Logicians are familiar with a more generalized version of
the problem discussed here. Does the denial of a universally quantified statement (that is,
the denial of "all x are y") always have existential import ("there is an x that is not y")?

[84] Here we once again run up against our inability to assign meaning to a part of an expression.
What does "existence" mean either when we speak of the existence of a "limit of expression"
(not a feature of the world, not something one can talk *about*) or when one speaks of
the existence of some "ineffable being" (a higher entity *about* which one must remain
silent)?

inexpressible in speech" are nonsensical and have no sense makes the point that there is, indeed, the inexpressible in speech.

The curious status of *TLP* 6.522 shows that instead of being self-refuting, the *Tractatus* is self-exemplifying. Richard Brockhaus suggested that Wittgenstein's work "seems to be placed in the uneasy position of being nonsense if it is correct and correct if it is non-sense."[85] But this may not be an uneasy position at all. Along the lines of "this sentence consists of exactly seven words," Wittgenstein's "there is indeed the inexpressible in speech" or "my sentences are non-sensical" confirm themselves.[86] We recognize that they do so only after running up against the limits of language, against the contradiction in the *reductio*-argument. Our movement through the thought experiment brings forth bruises and the recognition that "there is indeed the inexpressible in speech." Our failure makes sense of *TLP* 6.522 and *TLP* 6.522 makes sense of our failure, but *what* sense we make of it is not contained in *TLP* 6.522 – it is a nonsensical expression that has no sense, specifying no condition that would decide its falsity or truth. Those who understand it, recognize it as nonsensical and without content. That it is nonsensical and lacks content validates it, but to understand it by making sense of it does not give us any kind of certifiable knowledge. Only for significant sentences can we know what they mean (*TLP* 4.021), but for expressions that we need to make sense of there is no sense to be known but only the product of our imaginative activity and of the associations we produce.

MOVING TOGETHER

We have already seen at the end of the previous chapter that the *Tractatus* is not self-refuting. Its finding that its own sentences are

85 Brockhaus 1991, p. 6.
86 As we saw in chapter 2, above (especially page 81 and note 47), Cora Diamond and James Conant read *TLP* 6.54 like this: "My sentences – but not all my sentences and certainly not this one – are nonsensical." But if any sentence is categorically different from the sentences of science and logic, this one would be it. According to the *Tractatus*, "p is a sentence" is nonsense (*TLP* 5.5351) and sentences can only show but not say what their sense is (*TLP* 3.13–3.142, 4.02f.). Moreover, Conant and Diamond consider *TLP* 5.5351, 3.13–3.142, and 4.02f. as among the sentences that Wittgenstein calls nonsensical in *TLP* 6.54. But if it is nonsense to say "'p is a sentence' is nonsense," and if it is nonsense to say "'this is the sense of p' is nonsense," why then should we exempt "'my sentences are nonsensical' is nonsense"? On the interpretation developed here, *TLP* 6.54 ("my sentences are nonsensical") is nonsense *par excellence* and therefore self-exemplifying.

nonsensical does not undermine the language in which it was composed. It is not written in the indicative mood in which one advances
knowledge claims, that is, it does not consist of true or false sentences
about how things are. We noted that statements in the subjunctive
mood are not *about* anything, that – just like music, actions, gestures,
lives – they are silent about the world in that they do not say anything.
Since "saying" is always an assertion that this or that *is* the case, subjunctive expressions of what under some condition would or might
be do not even attempt to say what they show or what we make them
show as we create meaningful associations for them. We have now
added to this that, aside from not being self-refuting, the *Tractatus* is
actually self-confirming. Its conclusion that there is indeed the inexpressible in speech cannot be expressed in speech; it is nonsensical and
lacks significance. But we can make sense of it as a self-confirming
statement in the larger context of the thought experiment in which it
occurs: we associate those words with our failure to express in speech
any sense whatsoever. The seven-word conclusion of Wittgenstein's
indirect proof does not say what was proved; instead, only the proof
as a particular action or movement of thought could tell us what was
proved.

This reconstruction of Wittgenstein's argument has attempted to
make sense of the *Tractatus* and of its conclusion, in particular, by
attending to the way in which its remarks are associated within the
context of a thought experiment. As such, it has traced out a movement of thought that is inaugurated by our first encounter with the
striking composition of the *Tractatus*. Immediately upon opening
this book, any reader will notice that the succession of isolated, yet
somehow related remarks resists the model of ordinary philosophical
argument. Each of the remarks is introduced by its own number, set
off from the ones that precede and follow it, thus literally surrounded
by a bit of space. This physical space on the page corresponds to
a space of thought of which the recorded remark is only an index
or vestige, perhaps an invitation to move into this larger space by
reenacting the conditions that may have produced the remark.[87] I
characterized these conditions as a thought experiment that is conducted in the subjunctive mood. Indeed, the space of thought that
surrounds each remark is the subjunctive sphere of possibility within

[87] See Nordmann 2001.

which thoughts occurred to Wittgenstein that were then recorded faithfully. Wittgenstein's aphoristic remarks do not obliterate or disguise the conditions under which they arose; he does not incorporate them into the seamless flow of a persuasive text. Instead, he intimates the continuity of an overarching train of thought by carefully preserving for each remark that it occurred in the larger context of a hypothetical exploration. We can understand Wittgenstein by reenacting his thought experiment, by going through some of the same motions.

Through this agreement of motions and associations we may also get bumps and bruises as we also run up against the limits of language. However, this kind of agreement is very different from a certifiable agreement on true (scientific) sentences about the world. While in the latter case we can agree on a shared sense, namely the known sense of the significant sentence, the readers of Wittgenstein's nonsensical sentences may be moving in parallel with him but all the while at an unbridgeable distance: we make sense of what he is doing by attempting to reenact what he is doing; we can thus understand him without knowing that we understand him. We cannot picture and then compare to some reality what Wittgenstein thought or meant to express.

Wittgenstein reflects on our parallel motions in the opening lines of the *Tractatus*: "This book will be understood perhaps only by those who themselves have thought at one time or another the thoughts that are expressed in it – or at least similar thoughts." An understanding of the book "depends upon the reader's actually undergoing a certain *experience* – the attainment of which is identified in 6.54 as the sign that the reader has understood the author of the work."[88] This certain experience of thinking the thoughts expressed in the book (not its sentences) must be the same or similar to Wittgenstein's own experience. The thinking of these thoughts concerning the power of language to express any sense whatsoever involves both author and reader in a contradiction and the recognition that there is indeed the inexpressible in speech.

Wittgenstein's opening sentence also reflects, however, that there is no criterion by which we could ascertain the sameness of thought other than the similarity, more or less, of our outward motions.

[88] Conant 2000, p. 197.

Wittgenstein makes himself understood by writing nonsensical sentences[89] and thereby cannot rely on what those sentences say or our ability to grasp their content. Instead, he must rely on our own imaginative activity, our ability to respond to his prompts, to mobilize sufficiently similar implicit commitments, and once his thought experiment is set up, to follow it through.

---

[89] It may appear that *TLP* 4.062 rules out subjunctive expressions. Wittgenstein here rejects the suggestion that one could make oneself understood by means of false sentences. But this remark criticizes merely the erroneous conception of "true" and "false" as attributes of sentences. If by saying "-p," I mean "p" and "p" is the case, then "-p" is true. All I have done is stipulate a different use for the sign "-." It is now no longer a sign for negation but one for assertion (and its absence now signals negation). What I have argued in this chapter is not that Wittgenstein makes himself understood by false sentences, but that he makes himself understood by demonstrating his failure to make sense of a nonsensical sentence that was introduced in the subjunctive mood.

Conclusion: a sense of familiarity

"The sense of the book is an ethical one," Wittgenstein wrote to Ludwig von Ficker, and suggested that because of this, the subject matter of the *Tractatus* "isn't foreign to you."[1] This book about the *Tractatus* began with a statement of "Wittgenstein's provocation" and has gradually revealed that his is not the kind of provocation that aims to shock and offend, but rather is one that literally provokes us to engage in a particular thought experiment. Indeed, an understanding of Wittgenstein depends on our willingness to support and sustain his movement of thought, to appreciate and endorse his commitments. Now, this dependency is familiar to every reader of the *Tractatus*. After ascending Wittgenstein's ladder, we no longer find it outlandish but very ordinary that Wittgenstein cannot rely on the sentences themselves to convey sense in virtue of their content, but that he must rely on the imaginative activity of his readers. By way of conclusion, I would like to emphasize just how familiar we are with Wittgenstein's predicament.

FEARFUL EXPECTATIONS

Wittgenstein's critics have been asking a question that appears to express bewilderment but that really is not a question at all in that it answers itself: if one writes nonsense, how can one hope to be understood?

This question answers itself by invoking a distinction that is fundamental to the critical philosophy of Kant and his various successors:

[1] Wittgenstein goes on to "recommend that you read the preface and the ending since these express its sense most immediately" (LvF, pp. 94f.). In this passage, the German "*Sinn*" has usually been translated "point."

if one writes nonsense, one can only *hope* and cannot expect to be understood. Wittgenstein has no right to be understood, no rational ground or metaphysical justification that would allow him to demand it. Thus, when he writes that "anyone who understands me eventually recognizes [my sentences] as nonsensical" (*TLP* 6.54), he does not thereby express the expectation that there actually are such persons. Indeed, in his preface he limits that group to those "who themselves have thought at one time or another the thoughts that are expressed in it – or at least similar thoughts," in other words he does not expect that the group of those who might understand him can be created by him or by his use of language. He must hope that this group exists, or perhaps, that he can bring it into existence by allowing us to participate in his thought experiment and thereby to experience the failure of language to express any sense whatsoever.[2]

If one has no right to expect that things will be as one wishes them to be, one's hope will always be accompanied by fear. Accordingly, Wittgenstein's hope to be understood was always shadowed by the fear of being misunderstood and, indeed, despair that he might never be understood by anyone. He wrote to Russell on June 12, 1919 that "the small remaining hope that my book might mean something to you has completely vanished." Two months later he added: "I also sent my MS to Frege. He wrote to me a week ago and I gather that he doesn't understand a word of it all. So my only hope is to see *you* soon and explain all to you, for it is VERY hard not to be understood by a single soul!" The most striking expression of Wittgenstein's anxiety appears in a letter dated March 13, 1919: "In fact you would not understand it [the *Tractatus*] without a previous explanation as it's written in quite short remarks. (This of course means that *nobody* will understand it; although I believe it's all as clear as crystal.)"[3]

What these expressions have in common is Wittgenstein's conviction that where his writing fails, further writing will not help the

---

[2] See the beginning of chapter 3, above (pp. 92f.).

[3] *CL*, pp. 115–117, 124–126, and 111; see also 131 and chapter 3, above, page 96. The first of these passages continues: "As you can imagine, I am incapable of writing a commentary on my book. I can only give you one orally. If you attach any importance whatsoever to understanding the thing and if you can manage to arrange a meeting with me, then please do so . . . It's galling to have to lug the completed work round in captivity and to see how nonsense has free play outside! And it's equally galling to think that no one will understand it even if it does get printed!"

situation but that an oral explanation might. Further writing will only compound the illusion that understanding the *Tractatus* is a matter of grasping the content of certain sentences. In contrast, a personal encounter is required by the "only strictly correct method" of philosophy (*TLP* 6.53). Oral explanation would allow Russell to directly experience the struggle for and ultimate failure of expression, face to face with the stuttering intensity of Wittgenstein's often unfinished sentences.

Hoping to be understood in philosophical matters is a rather special matter, but situations beyond the limits of language are commonplace. We often speak with fear of not being understood, and just as often we refrain from speaking out of the same fear. What is more touching, for example, more desperate and fragile than a declaration of love? When I say that I love you, Angela, I am reaching across an unbridgeable abyss. You have no means to compare the content of this statement to the real state of affairs in my head and heart, nor can I be sure that what you understood me to say is just what I meant by it. In fact, I cannot control the meaning of this phrase even for myself. I may be uttering it, not for knowing what it says about me, but out of a vague yearning for you to reciprocate by saying that you love me, too. We would then have an agreement between strings of words, but what would this agreement signify? We find comfort and delight in such an agreement, of course, and we trust that surely it means something, that perhaps it signifies a shared commitment upon which we can build the rest of our lives together. But for as long as we live, we find ourselves wondering, sometimes doubting what these words refer to in ourselves and in the other, whether, for instance, they could be a conventional reflex that does not necessarily correspond to an authentic feeling.[4] And since we cannot secure any clear content or substantial basis for what we are saying, we offer each

---

[4] Compare the following dialogue from the film *Run Lola Run* in which Lola queries her boyfriend Manni. "Do you love me?" – "Sure, I do." – "How can you be so sure?" – "I don't know. I just am." – "I could be some other girl." – "No." – "Why not?" – Because, you're the best." – "The best what? The best girl of all the girls in the world?" – "Sure." – "How do you know?" – "I just do." – "You think so." – "Okay, I think so." – "You see?" – "What?" – "You aren't sure." – "Are you nuts or what." – "What if you never met me?" – "What do you mean?" – "You would be telling the same thing to someone else." – "Okay, if you want to hear it." – "I don't want to hear anything, I want to know how you feel." – "Okay, my feelings say . . . that you are the best." – "Who is 'your feelings,' anyway?" – "It's me. My heart." – "Your heart says 'Hey Manni, she's the one'?" – "Exactly." – "And you say 'Thanks for

other affirmations, signs, or "proofs" for the rest of our lives, reassuring each other that whatever we mean by "I love you," it is still there. Or, as the later Wittgenstein might say, the meaning of the sentence "I love you" lies in the mode of its verification, in our life together.[5] Indeed, our continued attempts to give meaning to this phrase is just what love and marriage are. When such attempts break off, many of us move beyond a crisis simply of a relationship into a fundamental crisis of faith regarding our power to know one another's minds and meanings.

Wittgenstein's later philosophy develops just such a conception of how we adopt a common form of life in order to secure meaning where we cannot judge what is said by peeking into someone's mind or by otherwise simply comparing the sentence to a state of affairs.[6] Love does not serve as Wittgenstein's example in the *Philosophical Investigations*.[7] Instead, he shows that we have no right to expect assent when we express pain. No matter how certain we are of our physical or mental pain, we must hope or trust that the communicative situation is such that we can actually receive the customary dose of sympathy and understanding.

MATTERS OF HOPE

Love and respect rather than pain serve Kant as examples when he distinguishes between what we have a right to and what we must hope for.[8] The *Critique of Pure Reason* establishes that we have a

---

the information. See you around.'" – "Exactly." – "And you do what your heart says?" – "Well, it really doesn't say anything. I do know. It just feels." – "So what does it feel now?" – "That someone is asking rather stupid questions." – "Man, you aren't taking me seriously." – "Lola, what is wrong? Do you want to leave me?" – "I don't know. I think I have to make a decision" (Tykwer 1999).

[5] MT, diary pp. 73f.

[6] Each in his own idiom, Saul Kripke (1982) and Stanley Cavell (1979) brought out this skeptical dimension of Wittgenstein's philosophy – a skepticism not about our ability to know the world but about our ability to express ourselves and to understand others.

[7] But see *PI* remarks 583–585.

[8] See Kant 2000, pp. 177f. and 271 of the Akademie edition: "[T]here are desires in human beings through which they place themselves into contradiction with themselves . . . While we are in certain fanciful desires quite conscious that our representations are insufficient (or even unfit) to serve as *cause* of their objects, it is nevertheless the case that every *wish* contains within it that causal relation, thus the representation of its *causality*. This becomes visible especially when this wish is an affect, namely *longing*." – "[T]he intellectual (moral) goodness

right to expect agreement between mind and experience. This is due to the manner in which the mind contributes to the formation of experience. Since it serves as lawgiver to nature, we can know that every event in experience is caused by a preceding one. This does not imply, however, that only a few causal laws will hold for a vast and diverse array of experiences, as is the case in mechanics, for example. There is nothing in the nature of reason and rationality, nothing in the necessary conditions of any experience whatsoever that should lead us to expect such simplicity. Even a world full of causal processes could resist all our efforts to formulate very general theories of motion. While our powers of reason might create a sort of obligation to look for such generalities, we can only hope to be successful. Indeed, whenever we formulate general hypotheses we speak as if nature was somehow created for us, hoping that it may conform beyond our expectation to the capacities and capabilities of human comprehension and will. A remark of Wittgenstein's echoes this: "Even if everything we wished for would happen, still this would only be as it were by the grace of fate, for there is no *logical* connection between the will and the world, which would vouchsafe it, and the supposed physical connection itself is not something that we could will" (*TLP* 6.374).

Accordingly, Kant treats the search for a generalized understanding of nature in the *Critique of the Power of Judgment* alongside the question of beauty and under the general heading of what we cannot know but must hope for.[9]

("SELF"-)EXPRESSIVENESS

Kant's critical philosophy sought a middle road between skepticism and dogmatism, and so does Wittgenstein's. As we have seen, Wittgenstein rejects the skepticism of Mauthner and Hofmannsthal. While

---

which is purposeful in itself must not be considered beautiful from the aesthetic point of view but rather as sublime, thus awakening rather the feeling of respect (which resists impulse) than the feeling of love and confidential affection. For human nature harmonizes not by itself with the good but only through the force which reason inflicts upon sensibility."

[9] Again, compare various passages in Kant 2000, pp. 180, 183–185, 217f., 228 of the Akademie edition, as well as the following from 188: "Thus, if one were to tell us that any deeper or more comprehensive inquiry into nature would finally reach a manifold of laws which no human understanding can reduce to a principle, we shall be content with it, though we much prefer to hear it when others give us hope."

we cannot express the essence of things in speech and while language is not in Mauthner's sense *true to* the world, we can express facts in speech and the descriptive sentences of the natural sciences can be *true of* the world (*TLP* 3.221). Wittgenstein also rejects the dogmatism which insists that just because we say "I love you" to one another and just because a good strong feeling accompanies this exchange of phrases, we have already agreed on some*thing*. This dogmatic illusion tempts us to believe that we know the nature of our commitment, we have described or compared our feelings and have found them to be equal. However, the very conditions that make language capable of stating (scientific) truths about the world set the limits to what we can express in speech. We can state truths because we can express facts and compare them to the facts of the world, and we can express facts because sentences are facts, that is, because names can stand in for objects, because sentences are objective, composite, externalized structures, because they can be negated (are contingent). We cannot express values, feelings, objects, and so on for the very same reasons – because sentences can be negated (are contingent rather than absolute), because sentences are objective, composite, externalized structures rather than inner states, and because names can stand in for objects but are materially different from them.

This seemingly straightforward conception of Wittgenstein's critical philosophy is at odds with other interpretations. The recent discovery of a "new Wittgenstein" by Cora Diamond, James Conant, and others adds a dialectical twist to Wittgenstein's critical philosophy. It sees him as a critic of critical philosophy who ends up making room for the dogmatic position.[10] Instead of setting limits to what we can express in speech, they argue, Wittgenstein denies that philosophy can set such limits. Diamond urges that "[w]e need to trust Wittgenstein more than we do. There is – if we read the *Tractatus* right – no fact-value distinction in it" and, in particular, no taxonomic

---

[10] The restoration of the dogmatic position is most evident in Friedlander 2001. It marries Diamond's "realistic spirit" to an "ineffability interpretation," with its "recognition of life or will beyond the perspective of representation" (pp. 192f): "There is no piecemeal nonsense in the *Tractatus*. This or that sentence taken by itself is not nonsensical. The work shows itself to be nonsense only when it tries to express or elucidate the world as a whole. It then proves that it elucidates nothing" (p. 205). Since Diamond and Conant reject the ineffability interpretation, they may also be rejecting Friedlander's approach.

scheme by which some sentences are classified as meaningful, others as meaningless.[11] Juliet Floyd argues "that the *Tractatus* dialectically portrays the whole notion of drawing limits to thought and to experience as thoroughly nonsensical."[12] On this account, Wittgenstein sets his readers a far more sophisticated trap than the thought experiment described here. The trap is not simply that the *Tractatus* invites us to take nonsense for sense and then reveals our mistake through a *reductio*-argument. Instead, the *Tractatus* tempts us to take one particular kind of nonsense for sense, namely the illusion that we have learned something when something is shown to be nonsensical. Nonsensical is not what lies beyond some limit, but rather the very idea of critical philosophy that limits are to be drawn.[13]

Conant, Diamond, Floyd, Gunnarsson, and others arrive at this dialectical understanding because they find the notion that one might be trying to say something that cannot be said to be deeply confused. If it cannot be said, how can one be trying to say *it*? For them, to entertain this possibility is tantamount to adopting the mystical "ineffability interpretation" of the *Tractatus*.[14] But this notion is confused only if one assumes that the something to be expressed is always some, perhaps ineffable *thing* and thereby something *about* which one cannot say anything. However, our more or less common experience of trying to express something that cannot be expressed in speech does not concern things, ineffable or otherwise, but the very different problem of "self"-expression and the expression of attitudes, values, feelings, beliefs, including an expression of the limits of language or of an aesthetic or religious sense of the world as a whole, the world in flux. These "unsayables" are ineffable, but ineffable precisely because they might not refer to objects or states of affairs at all. Indeed, they might not even admit a relation of "aboutness" (to say something

---

[11] Diamond 2000, p. 164.   [12] Floyd 1998, p. 79.

[13] I agree with Floyd that the *Tractatus* does not draw limits to thought and experience. Indeed, it says in the preface that this cannot be done. I disagree that the *Tractatus* is primarily concerned with the nonsensicality of drawing limits. On the contrary, that sentences about such limits are themselves nonsensical makes the point that there are limits to the expression of thought in speech. Similarly, I agree with Diamond that, ultimately, there is no fact–value distinction in the *Tractatus*: once one admits that only facts and not values can be expressed in speech, the enormous difficulty of expression takes on an ethical flavor in its entirety.

[14] Conant 2002, p. 389.

about myself is rather different from trying to express myself). For these "unsayables," it is very unclear even whether or in what sense they "are."[15]

Conversely, just as familiar as our struggle to say what cannot be said ("I love you") is our confidence that lives, actions, and gestures are more expressive than the constative or descriptive sentences that express facts only – even though gestures or actions provide no logical connection to vouchsafe understanding, agreement, or successful communication.

NEW PHILOSOPHY IN THE LANGUAGE OF THE OLD ONE

Not just the author of the *Philosophical Investigations* but already the author of the *Tractatus* conceived of philosophy as practice or activity. Instead of offering a fixed taxonomy of sentences, the *Tractatus* explores the limits of language and world, runs up against the walls of our cage as it attempts to make sense of the world. The thought experiment conducted in the *Tractatus* is just such an activity. This exploration can issue in sentences that have sense. But when we fail to give meaning to all the signs in our sentences (*TLP* 6.53), what we are producing is perhaps no more than a document of this tendency of ours to run up against the limits of language. If we do so unwittingly, if we simply take nonsense for sense, and speak, say, of aesthetic or ethical matters as if these were states of affairs, we produce pointless nonsense, meaningless gibberish. Once we become aware that we have taken nonsense for sense and are aware also of our failure to express such matters in speech, this failure may yet serve as a meaningful (though contentless) gesture which shows that there is indeed the inexpressible in speech. It thus depends on our activity of assigning meaning to signs and of making sense, whether we can overcome or surpass nonsense, including the nonsensical sentences of the *Tractatus*.

By throwing away the ladder, Wittgenstein wrote, we "must overcome these sentences and then see the world right" (*TLP* 6.54). Heinrich Hertz has shown what this might mean. Already as a young man,

---

[15] Compare chapter 2, above, pp. 50ff. regarding the artfully ambiguous construction and interpretation of "there is indeed the inexpressible in speech"; see also pp. 86ff.

in January 1878, Hertz pondered the principles of mechanics and espe-cially the words "force," "time," "space," and "motion." At the very end of his short life he presented in 1894 the result of his intense and arduous reflections – with a "somewhat anxious feeling to come out with something that I have never talked or consulted over with any human being."[16] His *Principles of Mechanics* mathematically develop an account as complete as that of Newton, but one that does not treat "force" as a basic concept. What Newton and his various successors constructed from four fundamental terms (time, space, mass, force or energy), Hertz managed to get with three. The term "force" appears in his presentation, too, but pretty far down the road as a derivative and, as such, well-defined notion. Hertz was by no means modest about his accomplishment. He thought that his picture of mechanics was the only one that did not give rise to conceptual confusion. And yet, he never imagined that his account would be adopted by his peers. Why, then, did he bother at all?[17]

Hertz's development of his picture of mechanics served as a ladder that allowed us to see the world right and which could then be thrown away. Its very existence proved that force is a nonessential term in the construction of theories of motion. Hertz has shown that "force" is a convenient but dispensable shorthand expression, a term of art that helps us to represent motion, not a name that stands in for some entity. Now, does this insight force us to abandon the old represen-tations of mechanics and to embrace Hertz's more rigorous and also more complicated account? Not at all. Instead, it allows us to speak Newtonian nonsense knowingly, that is, aware that the term "force" is eliminable from mechanics and plays no essential, no referring rôle in it. Even as we continue to speak nonsensically, we now see the world right and will be careful not to take "force" for anything more than an arbitrary building block of a particularly simple and as such, somewhat naïve presentation of mechanics.

Go ahead, talk all the nonsense you like, Wittgenstein was to have said.[18] As long as you know that it is nonsense there is no harm in

[16] Johanna Hertz 1977, pp. 77 and 343.
[17] Hertz writes that in "reference to practical applications or the needs of humankind . . . it is scarcely possible that the usual representation of mechanics, which has been devised expressly for them, can ever be replaced by a more appropriate system" (Hertz 1956, p. 40).
[18] See chapter 4, note 56, above.

it: "What I want to teach is: the transition from unacknowledged nonsense to an acknowledged one."[19] Accordingly, as we reach the end of Wittgenstein's thought experiment in the *Tractatus*, we will be seeing the world right by undergoing a *Gestalt*-switch of sorts. Looking at the same jumble of lines as before, we no longer see a bearded old man but now a scarfed young woman. In the course of our thought experiment, all those numbered sentences of the *Tractatus* were supported by an "as if," by the notion that the relation of language and world might be factual subject matter like any other, and that our thoughts regarding the agreement of mind and world can be expressed in speech. Now, all those sentences appear as mere vestiges of the thought experiment – we can appreciate how each advanced it, how each provides testimony to Wittgenstein's commitment and the conflicting desire to express any sense whatsoever in speech.[20] And by appreciating this, we do not just abandon Wittgenstein's sentences but learn to read them differently. On one reading they appear to do what sentences do, they try (and fail) to put together a state of affairs out of words that refer to something. On another reading they withdraw from the economy of picturing and do not even pretend to say anything *about* anything and thus remain silent about the world.

"There is indeed the inexpressible in speech. This *shows* itself, it is the mystical" (*TLP* 6.522). We tend to read this remark backwards: there is the mystical and it shows itself because we cannot express it in speech (we thus create a picture of the mystical as a layer of reality that somehow lurks beneath or behind language). Read forwards, the "it" no longer relates to a something, to a feature of the world. When we find that we have run against the limits of language and cannot express the feeling, value, belief that we are trying to express, this shows itself through our experience of failure, and to such an experience of limits Wittgenstein associates the term "mystical."

"In the sentence a situation is as it were put together experimentally" (*TLP* 4.031). If sentences put situations together, this sentence is a nonsense.[21] In contrast to sentences, this nonsense fails

[19] *PI* remarks 464 and 524; cf. *PPO*, p. 365. On this aspect of the relation between Hertz and Wittgenstein, see also Hamilton 2002.

[20] See chapter 5, especially pp. 192f.

[21] See my previous extended discussion of this remark in chapter 3, especially on p. 110.

to put a situation together thought-experimentally. It has no sense and is nonsensical because it does not clearly determine a state of affairs that can decide its truth or falsity. But by failing to have sense it thought-experimentally makes sense: it lacks content but as an experiment itself invites the discovery of its nonsensicality and thus advances the investigation whether all sense whatsoever is expressible in speech. And in this way, quoting Lichtenberg, "we always teach true philosophy with the language of the old one."[22]

THE LANGUAGE OF MODERN PHILOSOPHY

At first, the *Tractatus* speaks authoritatively on the assumption that one can speak sensibly about mind and world, language and logic. Once this assumption breaks down, we must begin to make sense of sentences that have no sense. From this effort arise books like the one in front of you.

This, then, might be the history of philosophy in brief, and the place of the *Tractatus* in that history: philosophers write unacknowledged nonsense. Their critics and, later on, the teachers of philosophy turn what they wrote into acknowledged nonsense. What they say is that Plato's or Descartes's or Schopenhauer's doctrine fails as a doctrine, but that we can appreciate what Plato, Descartes, or Schopenhauer were trying to do. They thereby make sense of a body of work that – considered as doctrine or theory – is metaphysical nonsense.

When Wittgenstein writes the *Tractatus*, the critique of metaphysical nonsense has become so pervasive that one can no longer write brazenly unacknowledged nonsense. In the twentieth century most philosophers do not take their language for granted or trust that they will be understood. We carefully develop a communal bond with our readers, trying to draw them into a common use of terms where agreement on those terms may or may not signal the presence of a

---

[22] Lichtenberg 1968/71, H 146 (p. 53 in Lichtenberg 1969). Compare *PI* 120: "When I speak about language (word, sentence, etc.) I must use colloquial language . . . That I need to apply to my explanations regarding language the fullness of language (and not some preparatory or tentative language) shows already that I can produce only superficial statements about language." Also *CV*, p. 47: "The language of philosophers is already deformed, as though by shoes that are too tight."

more pervasively shared understanding. We write tentatively, hypothetically, in a barely suppressed subjunctive mood: "if this makes sense to you, I suggest that you should also agree with this," "on this conception of the problem, the right thing to do would appear to be this," "let x be y," and even, "this book will be understood perhaps only by those who themselves have thought at one time or another the thoughts that are expressed in it."

Like Wittgenstein, I can only hope to be understood. Just as I try to find my way through the *Tractatus*, trying to retrace its steps by reenacting what I take to be its thought-experimental strategy, I conjure up all of the means at my disposal to foster a conspiracy of understanding between myself and my readers. Far less rigorous than Wittgenstein, I do not rely on you to make meaning but try to lure you into a rather hermetic world in which certain concepts and notions are so frequently repeated that they become familiar and begin referring to one another even though they fail to have sense and concern no matters of fact. I try even harder after looking over old notes and drafts, realizing that I cannot even understand myself anymore unless I frame my thoughts very carefully. Indeed, if I want to make sense of them again, I need to remind myself, recreate and preserve the context in which these thoughts arose (as I tried to do for Wittgenstein's thought experiment).

So, whether they mean to engender a critical attitude or not, philosophical books tend to initiate their readers into a small sect that affords its members the feeling that they actually understand one another. And thus the history of post-Wittgensteinian philosophy does not show that the *Tractatus* is wrong just because here we are agreeing and disagreeing about philosophical matters, "proving" that one can speak of such things and need not be silent about them. Quite the contrary, this history proves the *Tractatus* right, because philosophy has now become a permanent inhabitant of the subjunctive mood. It is self-consciously predicated upon an assumed shared understanding, an artificially induced linguistic community, and a conspiracy of those who are working hard to foster the illusion that the agreement on words may signal a common understanding about some ineffable subject matter (metaphysics, ontology, ethics, aesthetics). All the while, this subjunctive philosophy is actually a form of silence about the world. People who speak tentatively and carefully are not invited to deliver sound bites on political talk shows, they do not provide slogans for action, they do not praise the good, condemn the evil, or read the writing on the wall.

One might view this as a crisis of a philosophy that is doomed to irrelevance. In contrast, I see in this restraint of philosophy an example for a more general "critique of language" – though not in the sense of Mauthner but rather in the sense of Georg Christoph Lichtenberg or Karl Kraus.

CAREFUL LIVING

According to Friedrich Schleiermacher, "we are permanently probing whether the others construct what we take to be our shared world as we do."[23] One way of sounding out the extent to which we live in a shared world with shared meanings is by sending out sentences and seeing how they come back. On one's wedding anniversary or in the intimate setting of a congregation, one can feel rather safe transmitting "I love you" or "I believe in Jesus Christ our Lord and Savior." The world lacks this kind of robustness and stability on a first date or during a business luncheon. The safe surroundings of a shared form of life can make us forget that we are uttering nonsense and depend entirely on the generosity of others to make sense of what we say.

You are on a first date with the *Tractatus* while I have been claiming the vantage point of a deceptive familiarity. But roughly since the time of Wittgenstein, no philosopher can take shared meanings for granted and every philosopher lives in constant fear of being interrupted by a thunderous "What do you mean?" or by someone who follows the only strictly correct method of philosophy, says nothing but keeps pointing out that I failed to give meaning to certain signs in my sentences (*TLP* 6.53).

In the *Philosophical Investigations* Wittgenstein suggested that shared forms of life can sustain language games that appear to depend on shared meanings. The *Tractatus* laid the groundwork for this. It showed that clearly we can make things out of words, namely sentences that are facts which can represent other facts. It thereby exposed

---

[23] See Schleiermacher 1977, pp. 459f.

as a superstition that we can somehow put things into words, as if words were containers in which we can stuff what is inside us and thereby somehow convey it to others. Whatever its source, the feeling that I know what Wittgenstein means is a far cry from the communicative success that results from the adoption of shared norms of representation and the subsequent scientific comparison of representations among one another and with the world.

It is easy to lose sight of the categorical distinction between making things out of words and putting things into words, between agreement on the truth and falsity of a descriptive sentence and a feeling of mutual understanding. And far from being a harmless philosophical misunderstanding, the confusion of these things can actually be dangerous. If we start believing that our co-ordinated use of words (she says: "I love you," he says: "I love you, too") somehow contains real understanding, shared values or common truths, we may take the fact of communal co-ordination as evidence for a grounding in meaning, values, cultural norms. We might thus allow the sheer pervasiveness of a nonsensical phrase to make us forget that it is nonsensical: "Saddam Hussein was evil," "I know exactly what you are going through," "We need to restore the credibility of corporate America," "All religions posit a Supreme Being," "These are the results from our unscientific poll," "They died as heroes." To avoid linguistic totalitarianism we need to be reminded of the categorical difference between sentences that have sense and the many ways in which we make sense of nonsense.[24] We probably live more safely in a society that does not take the possibility of mutual understanding for granted. This would be a society where we have to be careful with one another and listen attentively to the nonsense each of us produces. We would have to make an effort to reach out and make ourselves understood, to somehow express what really matters to us. We must therefore live and speak carefully, tentatively, hypothetically. In this we can learn from those who have been most thoroughly disabused from taking shared meanings for granted, those who shy back from saying anything

---

[24] There is also intellectual, even spiritual danger involved – for example, the intellectual dishonesty of believing that we can express ourselves rather than remaining opaque behind our linguistic constructions. The spiritual danger would consist in considering religious and ethical questions matters of opinion as if we were choosing a best theory rather than struggle against the imposing demands of tradition.

but are permanent residents of the subjunctive mood, namely philosophers.

We have seen how Wittgenstein's language has been transformed through his thought experiment. Hypothetically introduced candidates for significant sentences turned out to be irredeemably nonsensical, and what first appeared to be a series of apodictic proclamations turned out to be careful probings of the limits of language. This breakdown of a seemingly authoritative language, I suggested, is of continued importance, as we need to remind ourselves that many of the sentences that testify to our communal bonds are nonsensical. (Rather than somehow grounding these bonds, they derive their apparent meaningfulness only from them).

How did this transformation of Wittgenstein's language come about? Like many interpreters before me (Cora Diamond, James Conant, and Matthew Ostrow certainly among them), I have attempted to read his writing as it was meant to be read: "Sometimes a sentence can only be understood if it is read at the *right tempo*. My sentences are all to be read *slowly*." And following the example especially of Karl Kraus, this is, of course, how we should be reading the sound bites that surround us – we must allow for their nonsensicality to sink in: "Where others keep on walking, I remain standing." And thus my roundabout praise for philosophy even as it always appears to lag behind the times, ends with Wittgenstein's cheerful injunction. This is how philosophers should salute each other: "Take your time!"[25]

---

[25] *CV*, pp. 65, 75, and 91 (dating from 1947 to 1949).

References

WORKS BY WITTGENSTEIN

Bemerkungen zur Philosophie. Bemerkungen zur philosophischen Grammatik. Ed. Michael Nedo. Vol. IV of *Ludwig Wittgenstein, Wiener Ausgabe.* Vienna: Springer, 1995.

The Big Typescript. Ed. Michael Nedo. Vol. XI of *Ludwig Wittgenstein, Wiener Ausgabe.* Vienna: Springer, 2000.

Briefe an Ludwig von Ficker. Salzburg: Otto Müller, 1969; English translation "Letters to Ludwig von Ficker," in C. Grant Luckhardt (ed.), *Wittgenstein: Sources and Perspectives.* Ithaca: Cornell University Press, 1979, pp. 82–98.

Cambridge Letters: Correspondence with Russell, Keynes, Moore, Ramsey and Sraffa. Ed. Brian McGuinness and G. H. von Wright. Oxford: Blackwell, 1995.

Culture and Value. Revised edition, ed. G. H. von Wright and Heikki Nyman. Oxford: Blackwell, 1998.

Geheime Tagebücher. Ed. Wilhelm Baum. Vienna: Turia und Kant, 1991.

Last Writings on the Philosophy of Psychology. Oxford: Basil Blackwell, 1982.

"Lecture on Ethics," in *PO*, pp. 37–44.

Lectures and Conversations on Aesthetics, Psychology and Religious Belief. Ed. Cyril Barrett. Berkeley: University of California Press, 1967.

Letters to C. K. Ogden. Oxford: Basil Blackwell, 1973.

"Movements of Thought: Diaries 1930–1932, 1936/1937," in *PPO*, pp. 1–255 (cited according to the original page numbers of the diaries); first published in German in Ilse Somavilla (ed.), *Denkbewegungen.* Innsbruck: Haymon, 1997.

Notebooks 1914–1916. Ed. Elizabeth Anscombe. Oxford: Basil Blackwell, second edition, 1979 (cited according to date of entry).

On Certainty. Oxford: Basil Blackwell, 1969.

Philosophical Grammar. Ed. Rush Rhees. Berkeley: University of California Press, 1974.

Philosophical Investigations. Second edition. Oxford: Basil Blackwell, 1958. Compare Joachim Schulte (ed.), *Ludwig Wittgenstein: Philosophische Untersuchungen – Kritisch-genetische Edition.* Frankfurt-on-Main: Suhrkamp, 2001.

Philosophical Occasions. Ed. James C. Klagge and Alfred Nordmann. Indianapolis: Hackett, 1993.

Philosophical Remarks. Ed. Rush Rhees. Oxford: Basil Blackwell, 1975.

Philosophische Betrachtungen. Philosophische Bemerkungen. Ed. Michael Nedo. Vol. II of *Ludwig Wittgenstein, Wiener Ausgabe.* Vienna: Springer, 1994.

Prototractatus. Ed. Brian McGuinness *et al.* Ithaca: Cornell University Press, 1971.

Public and Private Occasions. Ed. James C. Klagge and Alfred Nordmann. Lanham: Rowman and Littlefield, 2003.

Remarks on the Foundations of Mathematics. Third edition. Oxford: Basil Blackwell, 1978.

Tractatus Logico-Philosophicus. Trans. C. K. Ogden. London: Routledge and Kegan Paul, 1922. Compare *Tractatus Logico-Philosophicus*, trans. D. F. Pears and B. F. McGuinness. London: Routledge and Kegan Paul, 1961; *Wittgenstein's Tractatus*, trans. Daniel Kolak. Mountain View: Mayfield, 1998. Critical editions: Brian McGuinness and Joachim Schulte (eds.), *Logisch-philosophische Abhandlung / Tractatus logico-philosophicus: Kritische Edition.* Frankfurt-on-Main: Suhrkamp, 1998; Gerd Graßhoff and Timm Lampert (eds.), *Logisch-philosophische Ahandlung: Entstehungsgeschichte und Herausgabe der Typoskripte und Korrekturexemplare.* Vienna: Springer, 2004.

Wittgenstein and the Vienna Circle: Conversations Recorded by Friedrich Waismann. New York: Barnes and Noble, 1979.

Wittgenstein's Lectures: Cambridge 1930–1932. Ed. Desmond Lee. Totowa: Rowman and Littlefield, 1980.

Wittgenstein's Lectures: Cambridge 1932–1935. Ed. Alice Ambrose. Totowa: Rowman and Littlefield, 1979.

Wittgenstein's Lectures on the Foundations of Mathematics Cambridge, 1939. Ed. Cora Diamond. Ithaca: Cornell University Press, 1976.

Zettel. Oxford: Basil Blackwell, 1981.

OTHER SOURCES

Albers, Martin 2000. "Jetzt brach ein ander Licht heran: Über Aspekte des Musikalischen in Biographie und Werk Ludwig Wittgensteins," in Martin Albers (ed.), *Wittgenstein und die Musik: Briefwechsel Ludwig Wittgenstein – Rudolf Koder.* Innsbruck: Haymon, pp. 138–193.

Ambrose, Alice 1959. "Proof and the Theorem Proved," *Mind* 68: 435–445.

Anscombe, G. E. M. 1965. "Aristotle and the Sea Battle," *Mind* 65: 1–15.
  1971. *An Introduction to Wittgenstein's Tractatus*. London: Hutchinson University Library.
Arens, Katherine 1984. *Functionalism and Fin de Siècle: Fritz Mauthner's Critique of Language*. New York: Peter Lang.
Augustine 1991. *The Confessions of Saint Augustine*. New York: Quality Paperback Club.
Ayer, A. J. 1959. "Introduction," in A. J. Ayer (ed.), *Logical Positivism*. New York: Free Press, pp. 3–28.
Bell, Julian 1966. "An Epistle on the Subject of the Ethical and Aesthetic Beliefs of Herr Ludwig Wittgenstein," in Copi and Beard (eds.), 1966, pp. 67–73.
Bernhard, Thomas 1982. "Goethe stirbt," *Die Zeit*, no. 12, March 19, p. 41.
  1989. *Wittgenstein's Nephew*. New York: Knopf.
Bernstein, Richard J. 1966. "Wittgenstein's Three Languages," in Copi and Beard (eds.), 1966, pp. 231–247.
Biletzki, Anat 2003. *(Over)interpreting Wittgenstein*. Dordrecht: Kluwer.
Black, Max 1964. *A Companion to Wittgenstein's "Tractatus."* Ithaca: Cornell University Press.
Bogen, James 1996. "Wittgenstein's Tractatus," in Stuart Shanker (ed.), *Philosophy of Science, Logic and Mathematics in the Twentieth Century*. London: Routledge, pp. 157–192.
Brockhaus, Richard 1991. *Pulling up the Ladder*. La Salle: Open Court.
Carnap, Rudolf 1959. "The Elimination of Metaphysics through the Logical Analysis of Language," in A. J. Ayer (ed.), *Logical Positivism*. New York: Macmillan, pp. 59–81.
Carroll, Lewis 1936. *Complete Works*. New York: Modern Library.
Carruthers, Peter 1989. *Tractarian Semantics*. Oxford: Basil Blackwell.
  1990. *The Metaphysics of the Tractatus*. Cambridge: Cambridge University Press.
Cavell, Stanley 1979. *The Claim of Reason: Wittgenstein, Skepticism, Morality and Tragedy*. Oxford: Oxford University Press.
Conant, James 1989. "Must We Show what We Cannot Say," in R. Fleming and M. Payne (eds.), *The Senses of Stanley Cavell*. Lewisburg: Bucknell University Press.
  1992. "Wittgenstein, Kierkegaard and Nonsense," in T. Cohen, P. Guyer, and H. Putnam (eds.), *Pursuits of Reason*. Lubbock: Texas Tech University Press.
  2000. "Elucidation and Nonsense in Frege and Early Wittgenstein," in Crary and Read (eds.), 2000, pp. 174–217.
  2001. "Two Conceptions of *Die Überwindung der Metaphysik*: Carnap and Early Wittgenstein," in McCarthy and Stidd (eds.), 2001, pp. 13–61.

2002. "The Method of the Tractatus," in Erich Reck (ed.), *From Frege to Wittgenstein: Perspectives on Early Analytic Philosophy*. Oxford: Oxford University Press, pp. 374–462.

Conant, James and Diamond, Cora 2004. "On Reading the *Tractatus* Resolutely: Reply to Meredith Williams and Peter Sullivan," in Kölbel and Weiss (eds.), 2004, pp. 46–99.

Copi, Irving and Beard, Robert (eds.) 1966. *Essays on Wittgenstein's Tractatus*. London: Routledge and Kegan Paul.

Crary, Alice and Read, Rupert (eds.) 2000. *The New Wittgenstein*. London: Routledge.

Deubzer, Franz 1980. *Methoden der Sprachkritik*. Munich: Wilhelm Fink.

Diamond, Cora 1988. "Throwing Away the Ladder," *Philosophy*, 63: 5–27.

1991. "Throwing Away the Ladder: How to Read the *Tractatus*," in Cora Diamond, *The Realistic Spirit: Wittgenstein, Philosophy and the Mind*. Cambridge, MA: MIT Press, pp. 179–204.

2000. "Ethics, Imagination and the Method of Wittgenstein's *Tractatus*," in Crary and Read (eds.), 2000, pp. 149–173.

Döring, Sabine 1999. *Ästhetische Erfahrung als Erkenntnis des Ethischen: Die Kunsttheorie Robert Musils und die analytische Philosophie*. Paderborn: Mentis.

Duffy, Bruce 1987. *The World as I Found It*. New York: Ticknor and Fields.

Eagleton, Terry and Jarman, Derek 1993. *Wittgenstein: The Terry Eagleton Script, the Derek Jarman Film*. London: British Film Institute.

Engelmann, Paul 1967. *Letters from Ludwig Wittgenstein, with a Memoir*. Oxford: Basil Blackwell.

Fann, K. T. 1969. *Wittgenstein's Conception of Philosophy*. Berkeley: University of California Press.

Favrholdt, David 1964. *An Interpretation and Critique of Wittgenstein's Tractatus*. Copenhagen: Munksgaard.

Floyd, Juliet 1998. "The Uncaptive Eye: Solipsism in Wittgenstein's *Tractatus*," in Leroy S. Louner (ed.), *Loneliness*. Notre Dame: University of Notre Dame Press, pp. 79–108.

Fölsing, Albrecht 1997. *Heinrich Hertz*. Hamburg: Hoffmann und Campe.

Forgásc, Péter 1992. *Wittgenstein Tractatus* (film). Films by Forgásc can be found in numerous museum collections such as the Centre Pompidou, Museum of Modern Art, Berkeley Film Archive, or the Getty Institute.

1997. *Maelstrom* (film).

Frank, Manfred 1992. *Stil in der Philosophie*. Stuttgart: Reclam.

Frege, Gottlob 1989. "Briefe an Ludwig Wittgenstein," in Brian McGuinness and Rudolf Haller (eds.), *Wittgenstein in Focus – Im Brennpunkt: Wittgenstein*. Amsterdam: Rodopi, pp. 3–33.

Friedlander, Eli 2001. *Signs of Sense: Reading Wittgenstein's Tractatus*. Cambridge, MA: Harvard University Press.

Friedman, Michael 1992. *Kant and the Exact Sciences*. Cambridge, MA: Harvard University Press.

Gabriel, Gottfried 1991. *Zwischen Logik und Literatur: Erkenntnisformen von Dichtung, Philosophie und Wissenschaft*. Stuttgart: Metzler.

Garver, Newton and Seung-Chung Lee 1994. *Derrida and Wittgenstein*. Philadelphia: Temple University Press.

Geschkowski, A. 2001. *Die Entstehung von Wittgensteins Prototractatus*. Berne: Berne Studies in the History and Philosophy of Science.

Glock, Hans-Johann 1996. *The Wittgenstein Dictionary*. Oxford: Blackwell.

Gockel, Heinz 1973 *Individualisiertes Sprechen: Lichtenbergs Bemerkungen im Zusammenhang von Erkenntnistheorie und Sprachkritik*. Berlin: de Gruyter.

Goff, Robert 1969. "Aphorism as *Lebensform* in Wittgenstein's *Philosophical Investigations*," in James Edie (ed.), *New Essays in Phenomenology*. Chicago: Quadrangle, pp. 58–71.

Goldstein, Laurence 2004. "Wittgenstein as Soil," in Kölbel and Weiss (eds.), 2004, pp. 418–178.

Graßhoff, Gerd 1997. "Hertzian Objects in Wittgenstein's *Tractatus*," *British Journal for the History of Philosophy* 5: 87–120.

  1998. "Hertz's Philosophy of Nature in Wittgenstein's *Tractatus*," in Davis Baird, R. I. G. Hughes, and Alfred Nordmann (eds.), *Heinrich Hertz: Classical Physicist, Modern Philosopher*. Dordrecht: Kluwer, pp. 243–268.

Gray, Richard 1986. "Aphorism and *Sprachkrise* in Turn-of-the-Century Austria," *Orbis Litterarum* 41: 332–354.

  1987. "From Impressionism to Epiphany: The Aphorism in the Austrian *Jahrhundertwende*," *Modern Austrian Literature* 20, no. 2: 81–95.

Grenzmann, Wilhelm 1976. "Probleme des Aphorismus," in Gerhard Neumann (ed.), *Der Aphorismus*. Darmstadt: Wissenschaftliche Buchgesellschaft, pp. 177–208.

Griffin, James 1964. *Wittgenstein's Logical Atomism*. Oxford: Clarendon Press.

Gunnarsson, Logi 2000. *Wittgensteins Leiter: Betrachtungen zum Tractatus*. Berlin: Philo.

Hacker, P. M. S. 1996. *Wittgenstein's Place in Twentieth-Century Analytic Philosophy*. Oxford: Blackwell.

  2000. "Was he Trying to Whistle it?," in Crary and Read (eds.), 2000, pp. 353–388; also in Hacker 2001, pp. 98–140.

  2001. *Wittgenstein: Connections and Controversies*. Oxford: Clarendon Press.

Hadot, P. 1959. "Réflexions sur les limites du langages prospos du 'Tractatus logico-philosophicus' de Wittgenstein," *Revue de Metaphysique et de Morale*: 469–484.

Haller, Rudolf 1990. *Questions on Wittgenstein*. Lincoln: University of Nebraska Press.

Hamilton, Kelly 2002. "*Darstellungen* in the *Principles of Mechanics* and the *Tractatus*," *Perspectives on Science* 10: 28–68.

Hampshire, Stuart 1991. "'A Wonderful Life,'" *New York Review of Books* 38, January 31: 3–6.

Hertz, Heinrich 1956. *The Principles of Mechanics*. New York: Dover Publications.

　　1962. *Electric Waves*. New York: Dover Publications.

　　1999. *Über die Constitution der Materie*. Ed. Albrecht Fölsing. Berlin: Springer.

Hertz, Johanna (ed.) 1977. *Heinrich Hertz: Erinnerungen, Briefe, Tagebücher/Memoirs, Letters, Diaries*. Second enlarged edition. Weinheim: Physik Verlag/San Francisco: San Francisco Press.

Hintikka, Merrill B. and Hintikka, Jaakko 1986. *Investigating Wittgenstein*. Oxford: Basil Blackwell.

Hofmannsthal, Hugo von 1952. "The Letter of Lord Chandos," in Hugo von Hofmannsthal, *Selected Prose*. New York: Pantheon, pp. 129–141.

Horwich, Paul 2004. "Wittgenstein's Metaphilosophical Development," in Kölbel and Weiss (eds.), 2004, pp. 100–109.

Hutto, Daniel 2003. *Wittgenstein and the End of Philosophy: Neither Theory nor Therapy*. New York: Palgrave Macmillan.

Ishiguro, Hide 1981. "Thought and Will in Wittgenstein's *Tractatus*," in *Ethics: Proceedings of the 5th International Wittgenstein Symposium* 7: 455–463.

Janik, Allan 1966. "Schopenhauer and the Early Wittgenstein," *Philosophical Studies* 15: 76–95.

　　1989. "Between Enlightenment and Counter-Enlightenment: The Self-Critical Rationalism of G. C. Lichtenberg," in Allan Janik, *Style, Politics and the Future of Philosophy*. Dordrecht: Kluwer, pp. 197–210.

Janik, Allan and Toulmin, Stephen 1973. *Wittgenstein's Vienna*. New York: Simon and Schuster.

John, Peter C. 1988. "Wittgenstein's 'Wonderful Life,'" *Journal of the History of Ideas* 49: 495–510.

Kant, Immanuel 1997. *Critique of Pure Reason*. Ed. and trans. Paul Guyer and Allen Wood. Cambridge: Cambridge University Press.

　　2000. *Critique of the Power of Judgment*. Ed. and trans. Paul Guyer. Cambridge: Cambridge University Press.

Kerr, Philip 1993. *A Philosophical Investigation*. New York: Farrar, Straus and Giroux.

Kölbel, Max and Weiss, Bernhard (eds.) 2004. *Wittgenstein's Lasting Significance*. London: Routledge.

Kosuth, Joseph 1989. *Wittgenstein: The Play of the Unsayable*. Vienna: Wiener Secession.

Kraus, Karl 1955. *Beim Wort genommen*. Munich: Kösel Verlag.

Kremer, Michael 2001. "The Purpose of Tractarian Nonsense," *Nous* 35: 39–73.

Kripke, Saul 1982. *Wittgenstein on Rules and Private Language*. Oxford: Basil Blackwell.

Lampert, Timm 2000. *Wittgensteins Physikalismus: Die Sinnesdatenanalyse des Tractatus Logico-Philosophicus in ihrem historischen Kontext*. Paderborn: Mentis.

 2003. "Psychophysical and Tractarian Analysis," *Perspectives on Science* 11: 285–317.

Lichtenberg, Georg Christoph 1968/71. *Sudelbücher*. 2 vols. Munich: Hanser.

 1969. *Aphorisms and Letters*. Ed. Franz Mautner and Henry Hatfield. London: Jonathan Cape.

 1972. *Aufsätze, Entwürfe, Gedichte, Erklärung der Hogarthischen Kupferstiche*. Munich: Hanser.

 1990. *Aphorisms*. Ed. R. J. Hollingdale. Harmondsworth: Penguin.

Mach, Ernst 1914. *The Analysis of Sensations and the Relation of the Physical to the Psychical*. Chicago: Open Court.

Magin, E. P. H. 1913. *Über G. C. Lichtenberg und seine noch unveröffentlichten Handschriften*. Hamburg.

Malcolm, Norman 1984. *Ludwig Wittgenstein: A Memoir*. Oxford: Oxford University Press.

Markson, David 1990. *Wittgenstein's Mistress*. Elmwood Park: Dalkey Archive Press.

Maslow, Alexander 1961. *A Study in Wittgenstein's Tractatus*. Berkeley: University of California Press.

Mauthner, Fritz 1901/02. *Beiträge zu einer Kritik der Sprache*. 3 vols. Stuttgart: Cotta.

 1923. *Wörterbuch der Philosophie. Neue Beiträge zu einer Kritik der Sprache*. Second expanded edition, 3 vols. in 2. Leipzig. First edition, 1910.

Mautner, Franz H. 1968. *Lichtenberg: Geschichte seines Geistes*. Berlin: de Gruyter.

 1976. "Der Aphorismus als literarische Gattung" and "Maxim(e)s, Sentences, Fragmente, Aphorismen," in Gerhard Neumann (ed.), *Der Aphorismus*. Darmstadt: Wissenschaftliche Buchgesellschaft, pp. 19–74 and 399–412.

McCarthy, Timothy and Stidd, Sean C. (eds.) 2001. *Wittgenstein in America.* Oxford: Clarendon Press.

McGinn, Marie 1999. "Between Metaphysics and Nonsense: Elucidation in Wittgenstein's *Tractatus*," *Philosophical Quarterly* 49: 491–513.

McGuinness, Brian 1966. "Pictures and Form in Wittgenstein's 'Tractatus,'" in Copi and Beard (eds.), 1966, pp. 137–156.

    1974. "The *Grundgedanke* of the *Tractatus*," in G. Vesey (ed.), *Understanding Wittgenstein.* London: Macmillan, pp. 49–61; also in McGuinness 2002, pp. 103–115.

    1988. *Wittgenstein: A Life. Young Ludwig, 1889–1921.* London: Duckworth.

    2002. *Approaches to Wittgenstein: Collected Papers.* London: Routledge.

Merkel, Reinhard 1988. "'Denk nicht, sondern schau!' Lichtenberg und Wittgenstein," *Merkur* 42, no. 1: 27–43.

Monk, Ray 1990. *Ludwig Wittgenstein: The Duty of Genius.* New York: Free Press.

Mörike, Eduard 1976. *Sämtliche Werke.* Munich: Hanser.

Murdoch, Iris 1954. *Under the Net.* New York: Viking.

Musil, Robert 1980. *The Man Without Qualities.* New York: Putnam.

Neumann, Gerhard 1976a. *Ideenparadiese: Untersuchungen zur Aphoristik von Lichtenberg, Novalis, Friedrich Schlegel und Nietzsche.* Munich: Wilhelm Fink.

    1976b. "Einleitung," in Gerhard Neumann (ed.), *Der Aphorismus.* Darmstadt: Wissenschaftliche Buchgesellschaft, pp. 1–18.

Nieli, Russell 1987. *Wittgenstein: From Mysticism to Ordinary Language.* Albany: State University of New York Press.

Nietzsche, Friedrich 1998. *On the Genealogy of Morality.* Indianapolis: Hackett.

Nordheim, Arne 1986. *Tractatus.* Musical score published by Wilhelm Hansen, recorded by Aurora.

Nordmann, Alfred 1986. "Ernsthafter Zweifel und gründliche Skepsis: Lichtenbergs Konjunktive, Wahrheit und Wissenschaft," *Photorin* 10: 47–56.

    1988. "'. . . denke immer du bist ein Mitglied des Rates': Lichtenbergs Imperativ und die französische Revolution in der Chemie," in Jörg Zimmermann (ed.), *Lichtenberg: Streifzüge der Phantasie.* Hamburg: Dölling und Galitz, pp. 115–128.

    1998. "'Everything could be Different': The Principles of Mechanics and the Limits of Physics," in Davis Baird, R. I. G. Hughes, and Alfred Nordmann (eds.), *Heinrich Hertz: Classical Physicist, Modern Philosopher.* Dordrecht: Kluwer, pp. 155–171.

    2001. "The Sleepy Philosopher: How to Read Wittgenstein's Diaries," in James C. Klagge (ed.), *Wittgenstein: Biography and Philosophy.* Cambridge: Cambridge University Press, pp. 156–175.

2002a. "Another New Wittgenstein: The Scientific and Engineering Background of the *Tractatus*," *Perspectives on Science* 10: 356–383.

2002b. "Noch einmal zu Lichtenberg und Wittgenstein – die gegenwärtige Quellenlage," in *Lichtenberg Jahrbuch 2001*. Saarbrücken: SDV, pp. 163–170.

2003. "'I have Changed his Way of Seeing': Goethe, Lichtenberg, and Wittgenstein," in Richard Raatzsch, Fritz Breithaupt and Bettina Kremberg (eds.), *Goethe and Wittgenstein – Seeing the World's Unity in its Variety (Wittgenstein Studien)*. Bonn: Peter Lang, pp. 91–110.

Numminen, M. A. 1989. *The Tractatus Suite*. Musical recording published in 2003, Frankfurt-on-Main: Blue Angel/Zweitausendeins.

Ostrow, Matthew B. 2002. *Wittgenstein's Tractatus: A Dialectical Interpretation*. Cambridge: Cambridge University Press.

Pears, David 1987. *The False Prison: A Study of the Development of Wittgenstein's Philosophy*, vol. 1. Oxford: Clarendon Press.

Proops, Ian 2000. *Logic and Language in Wittgenstein's Tractatus*. New York: Garland.

Putnam, Hilary 1998. "Floyd, Wittgenstein, and Loneliness," in Leroy S. Louner (ed.), *Loneliness*. Notre Dame: University of Notre Dame Press, pp. 109–114.

Rapic, Smail 1999. "Subjektivtität und Öffentlichkeit bei Lichtenberg und Wittgenstein," *Lichtenberg Jahrbuch 1998*. Saarbrücken: SDV, pp. 92–114.

Rhees, Rush (ed.) 1984. *Recollections of Wittgenstein*. Oxford: Oxford University Press, with a "Postscript" by Rhees, pp. 172–209.

Ricketts, Thomas 1996. "Pictures, Logic, and the Limits of Sense in Wittgenstein's *Tractatus*," in Sluga and Stern (eds.), 1996, pp. 59–99.

Russell, Bertrand 1959. *My Philosophical Development*. London: Allen and Unwin.

Schleiermacher, Friedrich 1977. *Hermeneutik und Kritik*. Ed. Manfred Frank. Frankfurt-on-Main: Suhrkamp.

Schmidt-Dengler, Wendelin, Huber, Martin, and Huter, Michael (eds.) 1990. *Wittgenstein und: Philosophie Literatur*. Vienna: Verlag der Österreichischen Staatsdruckerei.

Schöne, Albrecht 1982. *Aufklärung aus dem Geist der Experimentalphysik. Lichtenbergsche Konjunktive*. Munich: Beck.

Schopenhauer, Arthur 1966. *The World as Will and Representation*. 2 vols. New York: Dover Publications.

Sluga, Hans and Stern, David (eds.) 1996. *The Cambridge Companion to Wittgenstein*. Cambridge: Cambridge University Press.

Spicker, Friedemann 1997. *Der Aphorismus: Begriff und Gattung von der Mitte des 18. Jahrhunderts bis 1912*. Berlin: de Gruyter.

Stegmüller, Wolfgang 1970. *Main Currents in Contemporary German, British, and American Philosophy*. Bloomington: Indiana University Press.

Stekeler, Pirmin 2004. "A Second Wave of Enlightenment: Kant, Wittgenstein and the Continental Tradition," in Kölbel and Weiss (eds.), 2004, pp. 282–300.

Stenius, Erik 1960. *Wittgenstein's Tractatus*. Oxford: Basil Blackwell.

Stern, David 1995. *Wittgenstein on Mind and Language*. Oxford: Oxford University Press.

  2003. "The Methods of the Tractatus: Beyond Positivism and Metaphysics?," in Paolo Parrini, Wes Salmon, and Merrilee Salmon (eds.), *Logical Empiricism: Historical and Contemporary Perspectives*. Pittsburgh: Pittsburgh University Press, pp. 125–156.

Stern, J. P. 1959. *Lichtenberg: A Doctrine of Scattered Occasions*. Bloomington: Indiana University Press.

  1990. "Literarische Aspekte der Schriften Ludwig Wittgensteins," in Schmidt-Dengler, Huber, and Huter (eds.), 1990, pp. 23–36.

Sterne, Laurence 1940. *Tristram Shandy*. Indianapolis: Odyssey Press.

Sullivan, Peter M. 2004. "What is the *Tractatus* about?," in Kölbel and Weiss (eds.), 2004, pp. 32–45.

Szemzo, Tibor 1992. *Tractatus*. Musical score to Forgásc's 1992 film, separately released by Leo Feigin on the Leo label.

Tykwer, Tom 1999. *Run Lola Run*. Movie released by Sony Pictures Classics.

Uhland, Ludwig 1910. *Uhlands Gedichte*. Berlin: Oestergaard.

Weiler, Gershon 1970. *Mauthner's Critique of Language*. Cambridge: Cambridge University Press.

Williams, Meredith 2004. "Nonsense and Cosmic Exile: The Austere Reading of the *Tractatus*," in Kölbel and Weiss (eds.), 2004, pp. 6–31.

Wright, Georg Henrik von 1942. "Georg Lichtenberg als Philosoph," *Theoria* 8: 201–217.

  1955. "Ludwig Wittgenstein: A Biographical Sketch," *Philosophical Review* 64: 527–544.

  1967. "Lichtenberg, Georg Christoph," in Paul Edwards (ed.), *The Encyclopedia of Philosophy*, vol. IV. New York: Macmillan, pp. 461–465.

  1982. *Wittgenstein*. Oxford: Basil Blackwell.

Zimmermann, Jörg 1986. "Metaphysik als Zweig der phantastischen Literatur," *Zeitschrift für Didaktik der Philosophie* 8: 202–212.

Index of names and subjects

Index of passages